In My Defense

Leigh Ann Bryant

Authentic

Published by Authentic Publishers
188 Front Street, Suite 116-44
Franklin, TN 37064

Authentic Publishers is a division of
Authentic Media, Inc.

Library of Congress Cataloging-in-Publication Data

Bryant, Leigh Ann

    In My Defense: An unlikely romance, a deadly gunshot, and a young woman's road to redemption / Leigh Ann Bryant
p. cm.

ISBN 978-1-78078-106-8
    978-1-78078-206-5 (e-book)

Printed in the United States of America

21 20 19 18 17 16 15 14 13   12 11 10 9 8 7 6 5 4 3 2 1

To my Lord and Savior, Jesus Christ.
Thank you for your love, peace, joy, and forgiveness.
But mostly, thank you for your grace—giving me things
I don't deserve—and Your mercy—and for not giving me
what I do deserve.

To my son, Vincent. Love for you taught me about fighting
with all that's in me for someone I love with all that I am.
Your love made me a survivor. I love you "more than
tongue-can-tell," and am so proud of the man you have become.

To my sweet Joseph. Loving you has been the easiest thing
I've ever done. Thank you for all your understanding when
I had to write instead of spending time with you.

And last, but certainly not least, to my kindhearted, patient,
and understanding husband, Lonnie. Thank you for loving me,
comforting me, and being my safe port as I relived the storms
of traumatic and overwhelming emotions.

[A C K N O W L E D G E M E N T S]

Thank you to my family, especially my sister, mother, and father for all your love, support, and help, even when I didn't realize it, and particularly when I brought you through sufferings no one should have to experience.

To my agent, Greg Johnson, and publishing director, Kyle Duncan, for seeing the potential of my story and believing in the impact it can bring to so many hurting and lost people.

To Lissa Halls-Johnson, who put so much into making this story better. Thank you for your wisdom, advice, encouragement and compassion as you helped me continue on my healing journey. And to Katy McKenna, who helped me cut words and tighten it up.

To Authentic Publishers, for all you did to get this book published and into the hands of those needing to find freedom.

Thank you to North Texas Christian Writers, where I first learned and continue to learn about writing under the leadership of Frank and Linda—through conferences, seminars, mentoring clinics, and writers' groups. Thank you to all my critique buddies, but most especially Lori, Lisa, Janet, Henry, Tamara, Sandy, Christina, John, Jan, Scott, Pam, Nancy, LaWanda, Olivia, Emily, and Melinda. Thank you for your invaluable input.

To Doug Mulder, for your masterful defense of me, your continued friendship, and your help with bringing truth to my book. Thank you to Curtis Glover and John Hagler for your input during my trial, and thank you to Judge Wilson, for being fair and impartial as you presided over my trial and for reading my manuscript to help keep the courtroom scenes accurate.

Thanks to my jurors, for your time and attention during my trial and for believing in me.

And finally, thank you to my multitude of friends and extended family, for lifting me up and praying for me as I endured the arduous task of writing this book.

[CONTENTS]

Introduction

While recounting these events and writing this book, I continually cringed, cried, and begged for forgiveness over the state of my life and the choices I made. Blinded by love and manipulated by the man of my dreams, hundreds of red flags escaped my attention.

I looked to my husband for love, acceptance, and worth. With deep needs and a co-dependent personality, I accepted increasing levels of abuse in order to receive his continued affection, which always came on strong as soon as his anger diminished.

This transparent account of my life has many details you may find hard to read, but I believe specifics are necessary for a number of reasons. One is my desire for the reader to see, feel, and understand the power of the love of God by contrasting Leigh Ann, follower of Christ, with Leigh Ann, a person lost without God. Another is my hope of demonstrating the serious consequences that can result from remaining in an abusive relationship.

Hopefully every reader who picks up a memoir understands they're reading a biased account of events. The author's account. This author would have liked to re-create every event and dialogue exchange precisely the way they happened, but this is impossible. Obviously, I don't have transcripts of either happy conversations or arguments I had with Vincent—or with anyone else for that matter—although I do have transcripts from much of my trial. Every word I attributed to someone in my recreated dialogue was done so with the best of my memory.

I have done as much as I can to preserve truth. I have questioned others who lived this with me. I have read pages and pages of actual transcripts from my trial, as well as police reports, statements, court documents, and extensive notes my attorney and I both took during the trial. I've poured over evidence and talked with my trial attorney at great length. Both he and the trial judge have read the manuscript for accuracy.

Every book needs to take shape and form by including pertinent events while eliminating ones that do not contribute to the story's progression and would simply make it ponderous. Thus, I have left out many things, including some events that paint me in a less-than-positive light. I was no saint and do not claim to be. I did much that I'm not proud of. I'm sure there are many people in my past who would like to point to poor choices I made in all areas of life. I do not deny them, but did not feel they were pertinent to this particular story I wish to tell of grace and freedom through Jesus Christ.

I invite you to stick with me to the end of my story—and I pray that along the way, God speaks to your heart about the hope that is found in Him.

Prologue

I couldn't think. Couldn't breathe. My mind a tangle of chaotic confusion. Like threads of a nightmare woven together.

My heart begged me to wake up, to return to a world where all was right, but the blood streaming down my thigh, over my knee, between my toes, told me I wasn't sleeping.

Gripping the cordless phone, a lifeline in my hand, I peered out the peephole. My husband lay crumpled on the lawn, the ten feet between us inches and miles at the same time. I cracked the door, bracing my foot behind the hollow aluminum barrier.

Shock injected itself like anesthesia into each beat of my runaway heart.

"Help. Me. Leigh Ann... *heeeelp.*" Vincent's voice, a low, wheezy whisper, strained across the porch.

Instinct took over. I staggered outside. Dropped the phone. Pulled on his arm. Tried to make him stand.

Why was he so heavy?

His breathing was wrong. His skin was pale. His lips were blue.

"Vincent?" I fell to my knees, fumbling in the dim light of the waning moon, my hands frantic, racing across his body. Seeking. Searching for something. Anything.

Wet. His shirt was wet. I ripped it open.

My fingers settled on a perfectly round hole in his stomach surrounded by... blood.

Dear God. A gunshot wound.

"Vincent, no!" The stabbing pain of nerves coming to life shook me. My mind blurred.

"Vincent?

Stay with me.

I'm getting help..."

CHAPTER ONE

Meeting

My insides tumbled awkwardly, like a gymnast learning a new skill. I pulled into the parking lot, shut off the engine, and tried to dry my sweaty palms. The psychiatric hospital had no barbed wire fences, tall gates, or guard towers to keep the crazies in. In fact, it looked no different than any other small hospital.

I exited my 1986 Buick—although five years old, it was brand new to me—and drew in as much of the crisp air as my lungs could hold, huddling in my jacket to keep the early January chill at bay. My legs carried me to the door as quickly as my hesitant nerves would allow.

Oh, to be anywhere but here.

Relief trickled through me when I saw Pam. She reminded me of my Gran with her deeply lined face and thin, fuchsia lips. Her hair, the same stark white as her lab coat, was held in twirls and loops high on her head. Greeting me with a smile, she pointed me in the direction of the meeting room.

Nausea surged, making me detour into a restroom. I didn't want to be here wearing this silly, white uniform with ruffles and pleats, but a psychiatric clinical was required for my nursing degree, so I swallowed my fear and did what had to be done. Sure, I'd dealt with loonies in my job as a paramedic, but this would be entirely different. I wouldn't be able to practice the "rule of thumb" my paramedic instructor once told our class to use with bipolar patients. He'd held his thumb high, squinted one eye shut, and said, "With manic depressants, always use the rule of thumb. Put your thumb in the air between you and the patient, and if you can still see the patient, you're too close."

Such a funny guy.

I opened the restroom door and a familiar face greeted me. Relief pushed the anxiety aside. If I had to do this, at least Kerri would be with me. My forced smile became almost genuine.

After nervous chatter about the required clinical, we walked down the hall and entered the meeting room. Several classmates looked up, distressed expressions covering their faces. I took a calming breath, sat down, and worked to keep my leg from bouncing while waiting for our instructor.

Pam ushered in the last of the students. She moved with the grace and authority of an experienced professional, commanding our silence with her teacherly look. "You have each been assigned a patient. You will shadow your patient and attend their group sessions. You will sit with them during non-group times."

She handed out several sheets of paper. "Here are questions to ask. Get to know your patient. Do a full assessment and care plan. At the end of the day, meet back here."

Pam turned, indicating the meeting was over. We followed her down the barren hallway and into a tiny elevator. On the second floor, she led us through a series of doors, unlocking them with a key attached to a bracelet on her wrist. As each door slammed behind us, the immense sound of locks clicking back into place made me want to run. My lungs burned and my heart raced. An antiseptic odor wrinkled my nose.

I'd never felt so trapped.

Pam led us to the chemical dependency nurses' station, leaving four students with their instructions. She turned to the rest of us. "This way."

We followed her through yet another locked door, ending at another nurses' station where Pam handed each of us a chart. "Get busy. You have only a few minutes to find out as much as you can about your patient."

I sat down at the table, rubbed my forehead, and opened my patient's chart.

DIAGNOSES:

    1.) Bipolar Disorder

    2.) Antisocial Personality Disorder

3.) Major Depression

4.) Chemical Dependency

Alarming words popped out at me:

>> Just released from two weeks in jail.

>> Pled guilty to robbery and criminal mischief.

>> Voluntary admission the day after accepting probation.

The information made me want to escape. Antisocial Personality Disorder. Better known as psychopath. Sociopath. Terrifying visions came to mind of the man who would be my patient. Would I be safe? What would it be like to get to know and talk one-on-one with a mentally ill, drug-addicted criminal? The bipolar diagnosis brought back the words of my paramedic instructor.

So much for the rule of thumb. Not that it would help with a psychopath anyway.

A man walked down the hallway, stealing my attention from the chart. My breath caught and my heart skipped a beat. His designer jeans and forest-green dress shirt flattered his strong body. My gaze lingered on him as I watched the way he moved. Mesmerized, I took in every detail, down to his tasseled black shoes.

As if sensing me, he turned. When our eyes met, a smile spread across his face. Heat rose in my cheeks, and I averted my eyes. After a moment, I couldn't help myself and glanced his way again. His smile flooded me with warmth, like being wrapped in a blanket fresh from the dryer. As he vanished from sight, I wondered who he was. One of the nurses? A mental health tech? I'd never seen anyone so handsome in my life, and the thought of working near him sent tingles of anticipation through me.

Pam returned. "Okay, students, everyone is gathered in the dayroom. It's time to meet your patients and see how they start their day."

I stood, smoothing wrinkles from my pants and fluffing my bangs. When I entered the dayroom, there he was. The guy from the hallway. A tickle rose in my tummy. He batted his eyes and flashed a pouty half-smile that showed off his perfect teeth. His sultry eyes, the color of a Christmas tree trimmed with gold, pierced me to the bone. It felt as though he could see inside me.

"Hello? Leigh Ann? Are you listening?"

Blinking, I turned to my instructor. She stood stiffly, arms folded across her chest.

"I'm sorry. Yes?"

"What is your patient's name?"

"Oh, um . . ." I searched for the name on my paper. "Vincent Bayshore." Scanning the room, I nearly fell over when the same good-looking guy I'd been exchanging glances with waved. His smile shone even brighter.

Speechless, I stared at my paper again. How could he be a patient? I never expected my mentally ill, drug-addicted, criminal patient to appear so innocent. So handsome. He pulled up a chair and motioned for me to have a seat.

And a gentleman, too. Unbelievable.

Dumbfounded, I walked to the chair and sat.

"Vincent." He held out his hand. "Nice to meet you."

His crooked smile turned my legs to jelly. I shook his hand, my wrist as limp as my knees. "Leigh Ann."

As my instructor paired the other students and patients, I sensed Vincent staring. Even though I knew it shouldn't, his gaze sent shivers of excitement through me.

After introductions, each patient stated their daily goal. For his turn, Vincent looked me up and down and grinned mischievously. "My goal? For me and Leigh Ann to get to know each other very well."

[C H A P T E R T W O]

Captivated

Like a Siren's song, Vincent's eyes hypnotized me. His soothing voice calmed my frantic nerves and drowned out any remembrance of the lore—a deadly lethargy that, if heeded, would lead to a disastrous result.

Pushing aside thoughts of the wonderful way his mouth moved as he talked and smiled, I told myself to focus. Be professional. "Tell me about your parents."

"Which ones?" He picked at his fingernails. "I'm adopted."

"Do you know your biological parents?"

"Not really. Mostly only what others have told me."

Vincent's eyes moistened as he spoke, painting a desolate picture of a mother who chose drugs over her family, abandoning them when he was a toddler, and a father who led his children into homelessness and starvation. According to others, his father fled the country after shooting an undercover police officer in a drug bust gone bad, dumping Vincent, his older sister, and baby brother with their grandmother.

Sympathy welled deep inside, churning my stomach. "So your grandmother raised you?"

With a pained expression, he said that his grandmother didn't want them, either—at least not the boys. She kept his sister, but ditched Vincent and his younger brother, Matt, with an aunt. Vincent's words grieved me. The circumstances of his life broke my heart. I thought I'd known emotional pain growing up, but at least my parents never physically deserted me. "So, your aunt raised you?"

"Wrong again." He dropped his head and shook it, telling how his aunt took the brothers to church and asked if anyone would take them. "Guess she figured strangers could give us a better home."

My mouth fell open. In an effort to hide my disbelief, I pressed my lips together. "Did she find you a home?"

"Yeah." He sighed. "That's when Mara and Stan got us."

Not wanting to hurt his feelings or make things worse, I paused to think of the right thing to say. "At least you and your brother got to stay together."

Vincent tore at his cuticles. "If only. Mara and Stan adopted me, but another family adopted Matt, and that family wouldn't let us see each other."

Wanting to comfort him, I began to move my hand toward him, but something stopped it. I searched for words. "I'm sorry. That's. . . awful. Do you ever get to see your brother?"

"No." He gave a strained smile. "But that's gonna change. Soon as I'm outta here, we'll spend lots of time together."

A nurse interrupted us, calling everyone to group. We entered a room with twenty chairs in a circle. Vincent held one for me and sat in the one next to it. For an hour, we learned about coping skills.

At lunchtime, I sat across from Vincent in the cafeteria. I took a bite of food, but had trouble getting it down. *Why is he staring?* Unable to eat, I pushed my plate away.

"No wonder you're so thin. You should eat more."

"We're supposed to be talking about you."

"So, I don't get to know about you? That's not fair. It's my turn to ask questions."

I grimaced, wondering what I could share and still be professional. "Well, since it's lunchtime. . . what do you want to know?"

"Hmm. How old are you?"

Without thinking, I gave my pat answer. "Old enough to know better and young enough to not care."

He grinned wide enough to show off his molars. "What is it you do that you shouldn't be doing?"

I gave a half-breath and flipped my long braid. "It's just a silly saying. I'm twenty-two."

"You don't ever do anything you shouldn't do?"

"I didn't say that."

He bit his lower lip, dimpling it with his teeth. "What kinds of naughty things do you do?"

Heat flooded my cheeks. I opened my mouth to speak, but decided against it. Why did he have to be so gorgeous?

"Is the question that hard?" His voice deepened. "Are you a *bad* girl?"

My heart fluttered. Was he flirting? "We're supposed to be talking about you."

"If I'm gonna spill my guts, it's only fair for you to share, too. Come on, let me ask one more question."

He was right. Building rapport required some sacrifices. "Okay, one question."

He blinked slowly. "Are you married?"

He *was* flirting. "What does that have to do with anything?"

"Just answer the question."

Why *would* he flirt with me? "Actually, I'm divorced."

He leaned back in his chair, his eyes lingering. "What kind of stupid fool would divorce you? And what made you get married so young?"

"Let's just say my dad was difficult. He wasn't very loving or accepting. Keith—my ex—rescued me from living at home. I moved in with him when I was seventeen, the summer before my senior year of high school."

"Wow. That was bold. When did you get married?"

"As soon as I turned eighteen and graduated."

"What happened?" He cocked his head. "You weren't deliriously happy?"

I laughed. "At first. Very happy. But he was a jealous man with anger issues. The happiness drained out of our marriage as his temper grew."

Vincent's jaw muscles twitched. "He didn't treat you right?"

"Not when he was angry."

I took a sip of my tea and set the glass down. The color reminded me of my Long Island Iced Tea from my last night with Keith.

Painful memories flew at me like vultures diving toward a carcass. . .

❀ ❀ ❀

Keith and I were at a club with a bunch of paramedics and firefighters I worked with, when he accused me of sleeping with one of them—simply because we said more than hello to each other. He made a scene, calling me names and pushing me to the floor. Humiliated, I left with my friend Diana and stayed the night with her. I went home the next day and told Keith I wanted a divorce.

Hysterical, he put a half-loaded gun to his head and threatened to kill himself.

My blood drained to my feet. I begged him to put the gun down and moved closer to try to stop him. Ignoring me, Keith kept the weapon to his head. His finger twitched on the trigger.

I squeezed my eyes shut.

Click.

My legs trembled, threatening to collapse.

No loud bang. I opened my eyes. No blood. No bits of brain scattered on the wall.

My heart beat in my ears like a metronome at its fastest tempo. I rushed to get the gun before he could try again. As we wrestled over it, the realization of what I was doing turned my blood cold. My five-foot-five, size zero frame wouldn't be enough to stop his six-foot, two-hundred pound body. If he intended to kill himself, it wasn't worth me being shot in the process.

I ran. With him chasing close behind, I managed to get inside my car and lock it. He cracked my window and kicked a dent in the door as I started the car and drove away.

Sobs came out in gulps. Not knowing where to go, I ended up at my dad's. Through weeping and spasmodic breathing, I told him what happened.

Refusing to have a divorced failure of a daughter, he told me to go back, explaining no one would want someone else's leftovers.

Stunned, I gasped for air.

Dad's implication—that if I were a better wife, Keith wouldn't have to act that way—crushed me.

"Leigh Ann?"

Startled, I returned my attention to Vincent's gentle face. "Yes?"

"You looked like you were somewhere else."

I pushed the distressing thoughts away. "Enough about me. Back to you."

His gaze pierced me. "You know, you deserve better. You should be treated like the special person you are."

An electric buzz hummed through me. *Special?* "What makes you say that?"

He frowned. "You don't know you're special?"

My chest hammered as I scanned his convincing eyes. "It's not something I hear very often." *Or ever.*

"Well you are." His voice had a sultry edge. "You definitely are."

I pretended to examine the floor. It didn't matter how flattering his attention was, it had to stop. Gathering my professionalism, I sat up straight. "Back to you."

His lower lip drooped in a pout and he sighed. "What else do you want to know?"

"What's it like living in a psychiatric hospital?"

"Not too bad. In fact, it's pretty good. They serve three squares a day and keep the fridge filled with snacks. And everyone likes me. Besides, I have nowhere to live once I'm released."

"What about your parents?"

Vincent lowered his face into his hands and shook his head, as if his response was too painful to contemplate. After a moment, he let loose with words of pain and rejection, telling a story about a fake funeral his family held for him, saying he was dead to them. According to him, only his mother and oldest sister, Mary, still loved him.

His story sounded too harsh to be true, but the emotion he displayed persuaded me to believe him. When I suggested he turn to his mother or sister, he told me his mother worked and lived in a tiny bed and breakfast and couldn't afford to help him. Mary lived overseas and wasn't available.

Vincent leaned back in his chair, his eyes and face drooping. Stan—his dad—had room, but didn't trust him or want him, Vincent claimed.

I contemplated Vincent's grim situation. Even though I'd felt unloved and unwanted in my life, it was impossible to imagine either of my parents turning their back on me when I needed them most.

A touch on my shoulder made me jump, as if I'd been caught doing something I shouldn't. "Hey, Leigh Ann, how's it going?"

I turned to Kerri's voice. "Great. How 'bout you?"

"Wonderful." She grinned and motioned to the woman standing next to her. "Cindy's quite interesting." She looked at Vincent. "What's your name again?"

He smiled warmly and took her hand. "Vincent."

Pink flushed Kerri's face as she removed her hand. "Y'all ready to go to group?"

Did he fluster her too? I checked my watch. "Hard to believe. Seems we just got here."

Vincent eyed me and smiled his crooked smile. "You know what they say—time flies when you're having fun."

Pam asked questions and gave us homework assignments, including a full nursing care plan on at least two diagnoses. She then dismissed us, reminding us to be back in the morning at 7:30 sharp.

The events and resulting emotions of the day replayed in my mind while driving home. Deep in thought, I took a wrong turn and ended up lost. The unfamiliar streets matched how I felt—disoriented and perplexed. I pushed past my confusion, focusing on the road while thinking about my assignment. Which diagnoses would I work on? Certainly not Antisocial Personality Disorder, an obvious misdiagnosis. No way could such a nice guy be a sociopath. But major depression? Who wouldn't be depressed after a lifetime of rejection? His emotional pain had to be real and deep.

Compassion rose within me. Vincent's feelings were familiar. I'd been there—alone, unloved, and unworthy. All he needed was love and acceptance.

With the sight of a familiar street, a sense of responsibility overtook me. I could help Vincent find his way home, too.

Fixing Vincent and restoring him to his family became my new objective. I longed to be a better, more worthy person, and if I could fulfill my purpose by helping him, I'd finally have done something right.

I just had to figure out how.

[CHAPTER THREE]

Significant

Sleep eluded me. I tossed the covers off, flipped over yet again, and punched my pillow. Vincent's crisis occupied my mind. He needed help. He wanted to go home, but had no idea where home was.

A deep ache permeated my chest. Vincent's confessions of abandonment, rejection, and loneliness stirred feelings of empathy.

I wanted to help. *Needed* to help. And he wanted help so desperately—after all, he voluntarily checked himself in to a psychiatric hospital. Who would do that if they didn't truly want to get better? There had to be a way to make things right between him and his father. Then Vincent would feel, if not loved, at least accepted.

The lack of sleep was worth it. I drove to the hospital with a lighter heart. Solutions floated through my head and bolstered my spirit, giving me a renewed sense of hope.

During lunch, I shared with Vincent the ideas I'd come up. "You can tell your dad this is the first time you've really wanted to change. That you finally understand the importance of taking your medications every day and you'll always—"

"Wait. Stop." He touched my shoulder. His earnest expression told me he'd do anything to make things right. "Do you have a pen and paper?"

When I passed them to him, his fingers lingered on mine, sparks thrumming up my arm. I took a long drink of water in an effort to quench the fireworks within.

Vincent wrote furiously. "You're amazing. And so smart. These ideas are great." He reached over and touched my arm. "I'm gonna talk to Stan tonight. Surely he'll believe this stuff."

I drained my glass of water, but the fire inside raged on. The flirting should cease, but I wasn't sure how to stop it. Besides, his beaming smiles and light touches couldn't mean anything—he was too gorgeous to be interested in someone like me. "You know, when you talk to Stan, you should call him Dad."

His eyebrows furrowed for a beat, then relaxed. Vincent agreed, but admitted it was hard to call him Dad when he didn't really act like one. "Besides, it's not like he's my real dad."

"Maybe he isn't your biological father, but he adopted you and committed to raising you. That counts for something."

He acquiesced, but my efforts to take my eyes away failed. "Also, you need to be sincere. I'm sure he can tell if you're being manipulative."

"Oh, I know how to sound sincere." He winked. "Don't you worry."

Sound sincere? Surely he meant *be* sincere.

"Too bad it's Friday," I said, finally able to break eye contact. "I hate having to wait until next Thursday to find out what happens with your father."

"You know, beautiful, I'd love to call you and tell you all about it."

Beautiful? I wanted to soak it in, but it wasn't professional. He was definitely flirting, but I couldn't believe it meant anything. He was probably like that with all the women.

Vincent's desire to share the conversation with his father seemed innocent enough, and really, part of his treatment plan. There wasn't one reason he'd be interested in anything more than a nurse-patient relationship. Besides, I did want to hear about it. But giving him my number would be inappropriate. "How about if I call you on the patient phone?"

"You call me?" His face tightened, but quickly relaxed into a smile. "Sure, that'd be great. I'm supposed to call Stan at 7:00, so call me at 8:00."

"Eight's good." I tapped the notepad. "What's the number?"

He wrote it down and handed it to me. Once again, his fingers lingered longer than necessary. "I'll be waiting by the phone."

At 8:00 o'clock, my fingers trembled as I dialed the number. I reassured myself that because it didn't mean anything, I didn't need to be nervous.

Vincent's alluring voice answered on the first ring.

"How'd it go?" I tried to sound professional.

"Hello, beautiful." His tone indicated a broad smile. "It went much better than expected, thanks to how wonderful you are."

Wonderful? Beautiful?

Joy filled my heart as the rest of what he said sank in. "That's awesome! Tell me what he said."

He recounted their conversation and how his father didn't want to give in until he told him the stuff he learned from me. According to Vincent, his father was impressed by his change in attitude and was willing to give him another chance.

"Now you don't have to worry about where you're going to live."

Our easy conversation continued until I realized we'd been talking for an hour. "Oh dear. It's getting late. I have to get some studying done."

"Are you sure?" Disappointment laced his voice. "Can't you talk for just a few more minutes?"

"I have a test coming up."

"That sucks. When can we talk again?"

"Next Thursday, when I'm back at the hospital."

He whimpered. "That's six days away."

An image of his lower lip sticking out formed in my mind, melting my resolve.

"I don't want to wait that long. *P-l-e-a-s-e?*" He stretched the word out like a toddler asking for a toy. "I *love* talking to you. This place is so boring, and your voice brightens my day. Can't you spare a few measly minutes for me tomorrow?"

Guilt flooded me, and I didn't have it in me to resist him. How could I say no to someone who needed me so badly? "Okay. But only for a few minutes."

"You're the best." His delight came through the phone and penetrated me.

Although I didn't understand why his need gratified me so much, that night I went to bed comforted by the foreign feelings of importance and significance.

CHAPTER FOUR

Foundations

The university's food court reminded me of meals in the hospital's cafeteria. The cashier wore the same cologne as Vincent. Lost in the scent, I floated to an empty table and allowed my thoughts to flow freely. I imagined Vincent's smile, heard his flirtatious voice, felt the warmth that pulsated through me with his touch, and wished he was sitting with me. Then I chastised myself for thinking of him again.

Why did his presence bring such peace and comfort?

He was charming and enchanting and made me feel good about myself, that's why. My brain knew the feelings were wrong, but I couldn't help it. Knowing I'd helped ease the rift between Vincent and his father boosted my self-esteem. Nothing before had ever felt so good.

Ever since I could remember, I craved acceptance and approval. My needs began in grade school when I was the ugly girl with red hair and freckles, the one the kids made fun of. It hurt when all the other girls were invited to a birthday party or sleepover, but even worse were the boys with their thoughtless words and playground taunts.

Maybe I could have ignored the teasing if I'd felt more love at home, but I was never able to live up to my father's expectations. Even with straight A-plus report cards, my dad yelled at me for a "needs improvement" in conduct. Every week I dusted, polished, vacuumed, scrubbed bathrooms, did laundry, and cooked. Often, I did extra chores in search of recognition and appreciation. But instead of hearing "I'm proud of you," or "thanks for doing a great job," my father's controlling perfectionism came out in belittling insults for overcooking the green beans or accidentally breaking something while cleaning.

When I broke a rule, my mother expressed disappointment. My father put me in my place with harsh words, making me feel like a failure. Before long, I believed myself to be a worthless loser who would never find love.

In sixth grade, I found a best friend—Jennifer. We did everything together, including swimming and all-day trips to Six Flags amusement park. Her older brother Danny became a benefit of our friendship. Finally, a boy who didn't make fun of me. And not just any boy, but a cute boy in ninth grade. Each time he smiled, giddiness flooded my insides.

Then one day as I snuggled under a blanket watching a movie with Jennifer's family, Danny sat beside me. He winked before slipping his hand under my blanket, intertwining his fingers with mine. My heart pounded. Curious tingles swept through me. I hoped he'd never let go.

After that, he held my hand every chance he got. For the first time in my life, a boy made me feel special. One night on a sleepover with Jennifer, Danny woke me with light caresses to my face, then led me from Jennifer's room to his. He kissed me, a wet, sloppy kiss that sent shivers of delight down my spine, across my chest, and down my belly. Heat pulsated throughout my body, and my insides melted with his touch.

The intensity of it frightened me, causing me to push away. "Danny, this is too much." I ran from him, back to the safety of Jennifer's room, but lay awake the rest of the night reliving the marvelous feeling of his lips and fingers.

Danny and I continued to kiss and touch as often as we could, until Jennifer and I drifted apart. Maybe it was guilt over the secrets. Maybe I wasn't ready for what Danny wanted. Whatever the reasons, Jennifer and I found new friends—and, although I continued to think of Danny often, we no longer saw each other.

As I walked home from school one day nine months later, a blue 1966 Mustang stopped beside me. Danny rolled down his window and winked. "Wanna ride?"

Within seconds of joining him, Danny held my hand, stirring up familiar feelings. He drove to a secluded spot, then kissed me long and hard. As he fumbled with buttons, an electric hum surged through my body, heating me up in places that seemed to belong only to him.

"Do you want this?"

Danny knew I did.

The windows steamed up as I relinquished my most precious gift—a gift I didn't think was worth anything. Then he held me as I shook for reasons I couldn't comprehend.

Back at home, my mind told me things would never be the same.

I wanted more. Danny, however, never came around again. I tried to understand—after all, he was in high school and I was only in eighth grade—but I wanted a boyfriend. Even though guys began noticing my blossomed body, makeup, and tight jeans, none showed interest in me as a girlfriend. Envious of my friends who received phone calls, love notes, and gifts for special occasions, I searched for ways to prove I was worthy of love and affection.

The search led me to my friend Joy's youth group at church. Several cute boys attended, and every Wednesday night the students got together to play games and have fun. When the youth pastor announced an upcoming trip, I whispered to Joy, "Let's do it."

Fundraising included a car wash and several weeks of work on a haunted house for Halloween. During one long night of creating and painting props, Ron held my hand and kissed me. Once again, the attention of a boy made me feel special.

On the bus ride to our destination, Joy sat next to her boyfriend, Steve, and Ron sat next to me. We talked, held hands, kissed, and napped on each other. Everyone accepted me on that trip—students and adults. I'd never had so much fun.

On our last night, Joy had a plan. "We're gonna sneak over to the boys' lodge. I'll give the secret knock, and Steve will let us in."

At midnight, we silently crept from our cabin. We stepped into the night, the wind slapping me in the face, seeming to want to push me back to where I belonged.

Five minutes later, Steve opened the door to Joy's knock. He took her into the darkness, leaving me alone with Ron. We began kissing, but two other boys barged in. When they talked about their plan, dread paralyzed me. Ignoring my pleas, the three overpowered me.

In a full state of alarm, every muscle began to quake. I begged them to stop. Told them I didn't want it. Pleaded to be left alone.

"Shhh." One of the boys said. "You don't want to get caught. Just think how much trouble you girls'll get in if the adults hear you."

I tried to push them off, tried to stop them, but they were too strong.

After they finished and left me alone, shame and guilt shrouded me. Deciding to say nothing, I waited for Joy. As my friend, I didn't want to make her feel bad or get us into trouble for sneaking out.

On the bus ride home, I couldn't get what happened out of my head. Humiliation covered me like a fog. Defiled and degraded, I wanted to tell someone—anyone—about the violation, but how could I? The boys weren't the ones who broke curfew. I'd put myself in that situation, and if I hadn't, this never would have happened. The burden became my secret.

Before the lunch bell rang on the first day back at school, everyone knew I'd had sex with three boys. I'd earned a reputation that got me a whole new level of attention—just not the kind that led to being a girlfriend.

A couple weeks later, Joy sat across from me at lunch as we discussed our weekend plans. The vice principal interrupted us and, without explanation, took Joy to the office.

I never saw her again.

Joy's cousin later told me that the news of our sexual escapade reached her parents, and they'd decided to enroll her in a new school to get her as far away from me as possible.

Not long after that, my older brother, Mike, my idol and hero, got an apartment with a friend. My sister, Michelle, and younger brother, Chris, somehow knew ways to avoid Dad's suspicions, so I became his new scapegoat for whatever went wrong in the house.

An inexplicable void saturated me. I'd lost my brother and my best friend, and once again became the subject of teasing and taunting at school. Desperate to find happiness and to feel I mattered, I did anything to impress others, including alcohol, cigarettes, and pot. I believed the lies the boys doled out—that I was special, the one they wanted as their girlfriend. But once they got what they really wanted, they pretended I didn't exist.

With each failed act in search of acceptance, I felt less deserving of love. Emptiness pushed me to thoughts of suicide. I decided to jump off an overpass. Not wanting to hurt anyone else, I avoided the road below and aimed for the embankment. Instead of dying, all I managed to do was injure my ankle, knee, and elbow. The next time death enticed me, I jumped out the back of a pickup truck traveling thirty-five miles an hour. Once again, I escaped with minor harm.

Even a failure at suicide, my sense of inadequacy deepened. I yearned for the emptiness to be filled, but feelings of significance only came when I eased someone else's pain or played peacemaker. I took advantage of every opportunity to end a fight between others, fix their problems, or bring comfort—even to strangers. When no one needed my help, I escaped meaninglessness through the same avenues I used to impress—drugs, alcohol, and sex.

My new best friend, Diana, amplified my rebellious behavior. With divorced parents and a dad who spent weekends at his girlfriend's, Diana and I used his house for parties. Although fourteen and unlicensed, we used his spare car to drive around in search of beer and boys.

The emptiness within grew and deepened. Guilt and shame smothered me. On the one hand, I believed Mom loved me—on the other, I was convinced her love would stop if she knew all the reprehensible things I did. Worse still, I believed the hurtful things Dad said about me. My actions proved I was what he said—a despicable failure no one could ever love.

With my sixteenth birthday, a new chance to earn worth opened up in the form of a waitress job at Pizza Hut. There I met twenty-year-old Keith—tall, blond, and handsome, he was thoughtful and funny. Plus, he didn't abandon me after sex.

Keith's jealousy and anger sometimes got out of control, but I assumed his behavior was normal. After all, his anger wasn't any worse than what I'd observed between my parents. Most of the time, he was caring and kind. He gave me gifts for no other reason than to see me smile.

Although seventeen and still in high school, I jumped on his offer to save me from my miserable home life. We moved in together, and less than a year later, we married.

After three years of enduring his escalating abuse, I realized Keith wasn't the answer to my unhappiness and ended our marriage.

Why couldn't I find a guy who put me first and treated me with love? A guy who saw me as special and beautiful?

I thought again about Vincent. His baggage, which would overburden an elephant, was a result of abandonment and rejection by those who should have loved him. Not his fault. He just needed love, affection, and affirmation.

Same as me.

[CHAPTER FIVE]

Released

Each time I called Vincent at the hospital, he somehow persuaded me to call again. Before long, we were on the phone every day.

When it came time for my group to switch to the chemical dependency ward, I expected to be assigned a new patient. But since Vincent had "dual patient" status and attended groups on both the psychiatric and chemical dependency wards, he remained my patient.

As the weeks went by, I found it harder to deny Vincent wanted more than a professional relationship. He looked at me in a way no other man had, seeming to drink in every detail. Helpless to resist his magnetism, he consumed my thoughts and monopolized my time. If we weren't together at the hospital or talking on the phone, my piles of homework revolved around him as my patient.

On the last day of my psychiatric clinical, I drove to the hospital with a heavy heart. Only one more day with Vincent. I tried to convince myself it didn't matter. Sure, I'd miss his gorgeous face, enticing smile, and flirtations, but I'd known since the beginning we couldn't be anything more than nurse and patient. Besides, once released, he wouldn't need me anymore.

Vincent approached me, his entire body burdened with sorrow. "Don't let this be the end of us. I need you to help me stay on the straight and narrow. I can't do it without you." His doe-like expression broke my resolve. "Please say you'll still call me."

He knew so well how to pull my heartstrings. I resisted the urge to hug him. "You're about to get released."

"You can call me at my dad's once I go home."

I shook my head. "I don't think so. We've both known this day would come."

Pouting, he looked at the ground and kicked imaginary dirt. "Please don't abandon me like everyone else." He fixed his gaze on me, locked in like a guided missile. "I *need* you."

He needs me. I couldn't deny how good it felt to be needed, and I didn't want to let him down—I knew how much that hurt. He deserved to succeed and be happy.

Even though I knew better, I agreed to call. He embraced me, lifting me off my feet and twirling me around. The professional in me knew his behavior was inappropriate, but the woman in me suppressed the urge to stop him. For a fleeting moment, I gave in and didn't worry about what people thought. It felt wonderful having someone so gorgeous not only notice me, but be so overjoyed with my attention. It was what I'd always wanted.

Vincent's release day arrived. Thrilled about the opportunities that lay ahead of him, I didn't stop to think when he caught me off guard with a question.

"Wanna go to a movie?" His voice cracked like an adolescent going through the change. "It's been so long since I've gone to the movies, and it'd mean so much if you'd go with me."

I didn't even realize words had come out of my mouth until he expressed his delight. What had I just agreed to?

"Do you like thrillers?"

"Oh, um. . .whatever you like," I said. "It's your celebration of freedom. You choose."

"You're amazing." His voice purred like a kitten. "You're the most wonderful girl I've ever known. So kind and giving and caring. I can't wait to see your beautiful face outside this dreary hospital. When can we go?"

Fearing he misunderstood my intentions, I felt the need to clarify. "You know this isn't a date, right? We can't be anything more than friends. I was your nurse. It wouldn't be right."

"You're not my nurse anymore."

Although I wanted to help him get his life in order and see him happy, I'd already decided he had more baggage than I was willing to take on. "Still, it's not right."

"Whatever you want. Just friends. When can we go?"

"How about Saturday?"

"Saturday? That's so far away."

Was that disappointment in his voice, or anger? "It's the soonest I can go. You may have lots of time on your hands, but I have school."

"But we can talk on the phone between now and then, right?"

I hesitated. "I guess that's okay."

"Then I can wait, even though I don't want to."

Three days later, I searched my closet for something to wear. Denim? Too casual. Mini-skirt? Too provocative. Yellow dress? Too plain. Rejecting outfit after outfit, I finally settled on my green jeans, a beige blouse, and a green-and-beige embroidered sweater. *Perfect.*

When I arrived at his dad's house, Vincent was waiting on the porch. He strode to the car and slid into the passenger seat. Taking notice of my jeans, he smiled. "You look great in green."

I meant to giggle, but it came out more like a sigh of pleasure. "Thanks."

At the theater, Vincent asked for two tickets to *The Silence of the Lambs.*

That was unexpected. I didn't usually watch horror movies, but I'd told him he could choose. Knowing he didn't have a job or money, I paid for the tickets.

The movie had several intense moments, and during those scenes, my body reflexively cowered toward the nearness of his capable body. The fourth time I leaned in, he put a reassuring arm around my shoulder and held me. It felt as though his body was designed for holding me. His fingers caressed my arm, sending irresistible warmth through my veins. He placed his hand on mine. Tendrils of fire heated my skin, melting my hand into his.

He leaned over and brushed my cheek with a kiss as light as a butterfly's wings. The fact I'd crossed a line of no return settled deep inside.

Once outside, he pulled me toward him and leaned me against the wall. Cupping my face with his hands, he stared into my eyes, letting his fingers flutter down my neck. His hot breath warmed my ear. "Baby, we were made for each other." His velvet kisses evolved to hard and passionate, and my body dissolved into his.

As we spent more time together, Vincent drew me deeper into his heart and life, showing me he was a good man trapped in bad circumstances. His past difficulties, which were not his fault, were clearly the reason for his troubles.

He promised to stay away from alcohol, drugs, and his old gang of friends, assuring me the love of a good woman would make him a happy, normal person.

I believed him.

Vincent's never-ending attentiveness intoxicated me. He said words I'd longed to hear all of my life—words that cancelled out the past insults and humiliations. He showed me I was special. Important. Worthy. His overwhelming love and ability to satisfy my longings completed me.

My heart told me if I could help him move into a productive life, fix his problems, make his family accept him again, I'd finally deserve love. All I had to do was figure out how to make everyone see him the way I did.

[CHAPTER SIX]
Addicted

Vincent's cologne lingered on my shirt. I breathed him in, thinking about his eyes, his hands, his breath on my face.

Our song came on the radio and I turned it up, longing for him. No, craving him.

The light was red.

I slammed on my brakes and skidded a foot into the intersection, glancing into the rear view mirror just in time to see the guy behind me barely miss my bumper.

I'd almost caused an accident.

What was wrong with me? Why couldn't I get him out of my head? And how had I fallen for him so fast? Simple, really. Being with Vincent made the emptiness inside me disappear. He needed me. And I desperately needed to be needed.

It was more than need though—he wanted me. Showered me with love.

A deep ache consumed me when we were apart. With his absence, two things dominated my thoughts—memories of our last date, and anticipation of our next. I'd learned the traits of an addict in my chemical dependency class: Unable to concentrate or think of anything else, cravings and urges, obsessed with the next fix, preoccupied with how to get more.

I was addicted. My drug of choice? Vincent.

My pager beeped with Vincent's special message—07734—"hELLO" upside down.

Satisfaction came out in a sigh.

Arriving at school a few minutes before my first class, I detoured to the pay phone. His sleepy voice answered, sending shivers of delight down my spine. "Good morning, sunshine."

"When do I get to see you?"

"Class ends at 2:30."

"So, 2:45?"

Pleasure burst forth in a giggle. "You're so cute when you first wake up."

"I miss you. It's been nine hours and forty-three minutes."

A smile crept across my face. "You're even cuter when you're desperate."

"Part of me is missing when you're not around."

He was addicted too. I twirled the phone cord around my finger. "Same here, but class is about to start."

"See you in six hours and fifty minutes." *Mwah.*

The sound of his kiss tickled my ear.

Throughout the day, my thoughts remained on Vincent. I closed my eyes and imagined his kisses. I wrapped my hand around my waist and thought of being lost in his arms. As soon as class ended, I jumped out of my seat and rushed to the door.

"Hey, girl, wait up." Kerri jogged to me. "You and Vincent wanna come to my uncle's wedding on Friday? There'll be food. And dancing."

"Sounds fun. I'll ask him."

Vincent had told me he could dance, but we hadn't had the chance yet. My heart hummed as I imagined him moving to music.

I pulled up to Vincent's house and found him pacing on the lawn.

He furrowed his eyebrows, pointing to his watch. "You're late. You were supposed to be here five minutes ago."

I chuckled. "Aren't you Mr. Punctual? Kerri stopped me."

"What did she want?"

"To invite us to a wedding. Wanna go?"

His arms slid around me, pulled me close. "I'll go anywhere with you, babe."

I gave him my biggest grin. "Will you dance with me?"

He swayed his hips, moving mine with his. "I'd love to dance with you."

We danced, the chemistry between us undeniable. At my apartment, we'd barely shut the door before he leaned in for a passionate kiss. He looked at me, his eyes pools of pleasure, then turned on the cassette player. The soulful sounds of Color Me Badd added to the mood.

"They're playing our song." His strong hands ran down my back and pulled me close as we danced to the sensuous music.

All evening he overwhelmed me with his affection. Candles flickered while we fed each other strawberries dipped into creamy chocolate.

His lips touched my throat, my shoulder, the back of my neck. "I love your hair. It's so beautiful."

"So, it's my hair you love?"

"I love the way you smile." He kissed me on the lips. "The way you look at me." Kisses on my eyes. "The way you touch me." Kisses for each finger. "I love your gorgeous eyes, your beautiful red hair, your cute freckles." Kisses all over my face. "I love your beauty mark, and—"

I pulled away from him and crinkled my forehead. *Beauty mark?* It's an ugly mole."

He kissed the brown spot on my chin. "It's your mark of beauty and I love it."

I laughed. "You're crazy."

His breath in my ear. "Crazy for you."

"Crazy when we're apart."

He rested his forehead on mine. "You're right, and it's time we do something about it."

"What do you mean?"

"I want to move in with you. So we can be together all the time."

Live together? I pushed away. "But we've only been dating two months."

He pulled my body back to his. "Our love is stronger and deeper than people who've been married for years. Besides, I miss you so much at night, I can't stand it. Don't tell me you like spending your nights alone."

"No, but. . . that's so serious."

He released me and sat back, his eyes narrow and angry, a gritty bite in his voice. "Don't you love me?"

"Of course I do."

"Don't be like everyone else. Don't say you love me if you can't show it. Prove it. Let me move in, or I won't believe you."

A pain in my chest felt like an ice pick. "If I won't let you move in, you'll think I don't love you?"

"You planning on dumping me?"

"No. It just seems. . . fast."

He pulled me to him. "If we hate to be apart, then why shouldn't we be together all the time?"

I couldn't come up with a reason. "I. . . don't know."

He put his mouth to my ear. "I love you, baby. I don't ever want to lose you. Please say yes. It'll be perfect."

His enchanting eyes and irresistible words drew me in. Weakened me. *Perfect.* How could it not be? My doubts dissolved like cotton candy in a child's mouth.

With one word, I knew my life would change forever.

"Yes."

[CHAPTER SEVEN]

Europe

Vincent slammed his fist on the table, his eyes impenetrable stones. "You're not going. Not without me."

We'd been living together a month, and his distrust was a punch in the stomach. I reached out to touch him, but he yanked his hand away.

"You can't run off to Europe and leave me all alone."

"This trip has been planned for months. I promised my sister. And Diana—we haven't done anything together for years."

"The girl you used to troll for guys with? No way. She's single. She'll just get you into trouble."

I sighed, tiring of his insecurity. "But I'm not single. You're the only man for me. Besides, the trip is paid for."

"And just where did you get the money?"

It occurred to me he hadn't asked where my money came from when I bought him the Mustang he wanted. Sure, he needed a car, but we could've gotten something cheaper. "You know I'd give you whatever I could to make you happy."

"If you want to make me happy, don't leave me."

"I'm not leaving you. It's ten days."

He pouted. "But I can't be apart from you for so long."

I pulled his face to mine and kissed him. "I'll make it up to you. Promise."

The moment we landed in Switzerland, I found a pay phone and called Vincent.

No answer.

Standing outside, I drew in crisp, fragrant air. Flowers bloomed, reminding me of the bouquet Vincent gave me the first time he professed his love. Everything was beautiful. If only he could experience it with me.

The next day, we took a train to Lucerne. Mesmerized by the mountains, I knew Vincent would love to paint a landscape of them. At the station, I again searched for a phone. Twice more that day I dialed our number. Each time the machine answered, my emptiness grew.

We hopped off and on trains, visiting cities in Switzerland, Italy, and France. All attempts to reach Vincent failed. I tried to convince myself it was good he wasn't at home brooding. Still, I worried something was wrong.

In Nice, France, I finally got an answer.

"Hello?" Even through the bad connection, I could tell the voice wasn't Vincent's.

Why is a girl answering our phone?

[C H A P T E R   E I G H T]

Jailed

She sounded familiar, but with the poor connection, I couldn't be sure. "Who is this?"

"It's me, Haley."

Relief sighed through me. Of Course. My brother Chris's girlfriend. She must be picking up the stuff she left when she moved out. "Where's Vincent?"

She paused before answering. "I don't know how to tell you this."

Fingers of dread laced around my throat. "What is it?"

"It's Vincent. He... he was—"

The phone went dead, buzzing with the harsh tone of a lost call.

I slammed down the receiver. What happened to Vincent? Was he hurt? In trouble? Heart racing and hands trembling, I redialed four times before getting the number right.

Haley again answered and accepted the charges. "Leigh Ann? Vincent was arrested."

Something heavy coiled in my stomach. I readjusted the phone and pressed it to my ear. I must have heard her wrong. "What did you say?"

"Arrested. Last night."

Cold sweat formed on my neck. I shook my head, as if denial could make everything better. "For... for what?"

She hesitated. "Not sure. All I know... he had a gun."

"A *gun*?"

A black hole of despair pulled my numb mind into oblivion. I fought to regain control. "Where is he?"

"Everman jail."

Hanging up, I dropped my purse with a crash. My belongings littered the floor. The mirror in my compact shattered.

What do I do? This couldn't be right. Everman? The town where he grew up and couldn't wait to leave? The city I worked in as a paramedic and quit because I couldn't stand it there?

"Earth to Leigh Ann?" Diana stood inches away, waving her hands in front of my face. "What's wrong? You look like someone pulled your pants down in the middle of a parade."

"Nothing. Everything." I related my conversation through hiccupping sobs, while Diana rocked me in her arms and let me cry. "I have to talk to him. Find out what happened."

"We'll figure it out. But right now, everyone's waiting." She handed me a tissue. "Clean your face."

She wrapped her arm around my waist and held me up as we joined our group. At the bed and breakfast, I found the concierge and explained my need to make an overseas call using a credit card. He nodded and led me to a phone.

My mind didn't remember the number. My fingers did.

Three rings. "Everman Police, this is Sam."

"Sam?" Remembering the detective, I pictured him sitting at the desk tugging his bushy eyebrows. "It's Leigh Ann. Paramedic from two years ago."

"Oh yeah. How's it goin', girl?"

"This is going to sound crazy, but I'm in France—" I tried to pace, but the cord wasn't long enough—"on vacation. Listen, I need some information."

"What kinda information?"

"Do you have a Vincent Bayshore in the jail?"

"Whyyyy?" he drawled. He'd never been good at hiding his distaste for the inmates.

My stomach somersaulted. "I know him. Heard he was arrested last night."

"Yep. Caused quite a stir, too."

"What do you mean?"

"He went craaazy." His voice rose to emphasize his words. "Smashed his head into the bars. We had to take him to emergency for stitches." He whistled. "Man-o-man, I never seen so much blood."

Shock raced through me. "Is he okay?"

"Oh, he's fine now. Suicide watch. Said he was tryin' to kill hisself."

Bile rose in my throat. I massaged my forehead, trying to erase the images popping into my brain, and braced myself. "Sam, what was he arrested for?"

"Let's see"—papers rustled—"here it is." He made a clucking noise. "Oh dear. Aggravated robbery with a deadly weapon."

"Did he. . . did he hurt anyone?"

"Nah. Just shook the lady up. She was real scared when she saw the gun, but he didn't hurt her none."

Mustering courage, I wiped my face. "You suppose I could talk to him? Please?"

"You know we're not s'pposed to." He hesitated. "But what the heck. Since it's you. Hang on."

Several minutes later, I heard Vincent crying. "Oh, baby, I'm sorry. I'm so, so sorry. Please—"

"Don't." My voice came harsh and loud. "What were you—"

"Baby, I love—"

"Stop it." My hand went up like a traffic cop. "I don't want to hear all your 'baby' nonsense. Tell me what happened."

He sniffed. "I have no idea."

"What do you mean, you have no idea?"

"Can't remember anything. I was with my friends, and the next thing, I woke up in jail with a pounding head and blood all over me." Sobs interrupted his words. "They told me I was drunk. Please don't leave me. . ."

Enraged, I wanted to yank him through the phone and shake him. Hot, angry tears streamed down my face.

"Don't abandon me like everyone else. Tell me you still love me."

I trembled. "No. . . you don't. . . the only thing. . . good-bye." I slammed the phone down so hard it bounced out of the cradle. Picking it up, I slammed it down again, then held my head and wept.

Loser.

Emotions collided within. Anger. Sadness. Disappointment. Fear. And love.

How do I turn off the love?

[C H A P T E R N I N E]

Fault

My mind was a prisoner of war.

Why did he go out drinking? Was this my fault?

He promised never to hang out with his old friends again.

He was alone because of me.

I really am a failure.

If only I'd stayed home, this wouldn't have happened.

He's the one who chose to drink.

But if it's his fault, why am I wracked with guilt?

A strange smell swirled into my nose and an acrid taste bit at my tongue. Holding up the cigarette I'd just lit, I realized the wrong end was burning. I crushed it out and lit another, inhaling deeply. Like the dissipating rings of smoke, my frail heart weakened.

Exhaustion pulled at me, but sleep was as plausible as fishing without a hook. I punched the pillow and turned to my left. What was he doing with those "friends"? Unable to get comfortable, I rolled to my right. "Where did he get a gun?"

My chest tightened and I gasped, jerking upright. "Oh no! Please. Not *my* gun." The gun an ex-boyfriend—a cop—had given me for protection.

Vincent wouldn't have. . . would he?

Fingers of sunlight reached around the corners of the curtains and dimly lit the room. Morning, and I hadn't slept. Somewhere in the middle of the night, I'd accepted the disturbing fact that he'd probably used my gun.

It really is my fault.

An unfamiliar thought struck me. *Pray.* Odd. Although I never prayed, I'd heard it could help. A memory from years ago came to mind: My mother lighting a candle in church and kneeling on a bench. The candle, she said, makes the prayers more effective.

As our group wandered around Monte Carlo that day, I came across the perfect church—cozy and ornate with candles lining the walls. Their soft, amber glow warmed my vacant soul. A massive crucifix hung behind the elevated altar. The life-sized Jesus loomed from the cross above, making my problems feel smaller.

My tentative steps echoed on the marble floor. What degree of reverence was called for? I lit a candle and gingerly knelt on the red padded board in front of it, then bowed my head and searched for words. "Please. . . please, God. Help me."

Emotions churned inside like a whirlpool, exaggerating the sensation of drowning.

"I don't know how to pray, but surely You know what's needed." Tears poured down my cheeks as I beseeched an unknown entity. "What do I do? How should I feel?"

I remained on my knees for what seemed like ages. When an answer didn't come, I wiped my face and stood, then walked out of the church somehow feeling lighter.

On the train to Austria, I tried to sort through my thoughts by writing them down. Questions filled every piece of paper I found, yet answers continued to evade me.

How could he do this to me? To us?

He'd promised.

Nothing made sense.

A cloud of despair overshadowed the rest of my trip—the trip I'd planned and looked forward to for so long. Now the only thing I cared about was getting home. Unable to appreciate the beauty of the Alps, images of Vincent flooded my mind. His gorgeous face behind bars. Covered in his blood. Robbing a woman at gunpoint.

I didn't want to face Vincent again, but talking with him might help. There had to be a way to end things without him killing himself. His suicide would be more than I could handle.

With each church we came upon, I stopped to light a candle and pray. Every candle lifted the burden a little more.

Finally at my apartment after the long plane ride home, I collapsed on our bed and let out the feelings I'd held at bay. Didn't our love mean more to him than drinking with his friends? Would he accept the end of our relationship without hurting himself?

I went to the bathroom and washed my face. The towel smelled like Vincent. His toothbrush and deodorant sat on the counter. This had been his home. Could I really abandon him like everyone else?

His favorite shirt lay on the floor. I held it to my nose. Inhaled his scent. Stumbled to the gun's hiding place.

Empty.

My legs folded and I crashed to the floor.

A flashing light caught my eye. I pulled myself up and went to my answering machine. A red 22 taunted me. *Twenty-two messages?*

I pushed the play button, and a mechanical voice sounded off. "You have a collect call from the Tarrant County Jail from—"

Vincent's voice blurted out, "Baby, I love you!"

The mechanical voice returned. "Press one to accept the charges."

Message after message greeted me with the same mechanical voice, but the two seconds allotted to Vincent changed each time: "Love me!" and "Don't give up!" and "Please, baby!"

The impossibility of what I needed most—Vincent's comforting arms—made me weep even harder. Images of his loving eyes and perfect smile behind iron bars tormented me.

A ringing jolted me out of my reverie. I reached for the phone.

"You have a collect call from the Tarrant County Jail from—"

"Please, baby, pick up."

"Press *one* to accept the charges."

I reached for the button, then pulled back. Did I want to talk to him? Could I? Conflicting thoughts swirled through me. Something inside me needed to hear what he had to say. I pushed one.

"Baby? You there?" Vincent's voice pleaded for an answer.

My grip on the phone loosened. "Yes."

"Thank you for picking up. For accepting my call. I love you. I'm sorry." He spoke at warp speed, as if knowing a pause would allow me to hang up. "Please forgive me. Don't be mad. I need you. . . ." Moans came through the phone with the sound of his weeping. "Say something. Please talk to me."

The lump in my throat prevented words.

"You're all I have. Don't give up on me. On us."

I blotted my eyes and blew my nose. "What. . . what am I supposed to say?"

"Say you still love me."

"How could you do this?"

"I missed you so much it hurt. If only you hadn't left me."

Needing the calming effect of nicotine, I lit a cigarette and inhaled deeply. "So, it's my fault?"

"I need you. I'll die without—"

"No! You won't die."

Would he really kill himself? His death would be my fault, and there'd be no returning from that degree of failure.

He groaned. "I *can't* live without you."

"And I *can't* do this."

"Give me one more chance. I won't ever let you down again. Don't leave me alone."

My mind sorted through emotions. Would it hurt to just visit?

The mechanical voice interrupted my thoughts. "Two minutes remaining."

"Please, baby, I *need* to see you."

And I needed to end things without his suicide. Unable to listen to his crying any longer, I gave in. "When?"

"Saturday morning?"

I took a deep, smoke-filled breath and crushed out my cigarette. "I guess so."

"Thank you. I can't wait to see you. Don't you miss me?"

Miss him? With all of my being. But I couldn't get past the way he slaughtered our future. How could I reconcile the ache of not being with him over the agony of being with him?

He sighed. "Okay baby. I get it. You're mad. See you Saturday."

I hung up and lay back on the bed. There was no way I could just dump him. Love still lived inside me, whether I wanted it or not, and my conscience couldn't take his death. I had to figure out a way to end the relationship in a safe way.

But how?

[CHAPTER TEN]

Visit

Rejecting outfits as I tore through my closet, my mind recalled the jail's rules: no open-toed shoes, shorts, sandals, or tank tops. Not that I'd have worn those anyway. Deciding to show Vincent I didn't care what he thought, I chose jeans, sneakers, and a souvenir T-shirt from my trip.

Parking in downtown Fort Worth presented the next challenge. Finally secure in a spot five blocks from the jail, I began the long walk, driver's license in hand. As the building came into view, I saw a line of visitors spilling out the door. My stomach flip-flopped.

A thorough questionnaire, a walk through a metal detector, a verification of my ID, and three hours later, it was finally my turn. Beads of cold sweat dotted my neck.

A sheriff's deputy escorted four of us to the elevator. He took our information cards, wrote on his form, handed the cards back. "Seventh floor. Exit to the right."

The door opened and we piled in. A strong locker-room odor saturated the tight space, making me dizzy. On the seventh floor, the guard took our cards and gestured toward metal stools bolted to the floor. "Have a seat."

Glaring fluorescent lights amplified the vandalism and filth littering the room. Five different conversations, all spoken in loud voices, bounced off the walls. Eight metal stools faced the ceiling-high glass separating visitors from inmates. Metal walls partitioned the sections, each with a phone receiver. I found a vacant stool and sat on the cold seat facing the bulletproof glass.

"What are you talking about?" An angry woman at the end of the room shouted. "You don't know anything." She slammed the phone down and stood.

"You're the one who doesn't know anything, b#@*&." The raging voice of the tattoo-infested inmate on the other side wasn't diminished by the two-inch thick glass.

The woman wagged her finger. "I'm never coming here again. You can rot in prison for all I care." She turned to yell at the guard. "Boss, get me out of here."

A slender guard came to her rescue. A thick guard rushed to the inmate, who continued to rant and rave. "Smitty," the guard yelled, "settle down, or it's lock up."

The inmate invaded the guard's space. "This is messed up. I didn't do—"

The guard slammed the inmate against the wall and handcuffed him.

My throat tightened and my stomach pulled into a knot.

A tapping sound caught my attention. Vincent smiled his crooked smile, and my anxieties vanished.

He picked up his phone and pointed to mine. The phone looked grimy and covered with germs, but I put it to my ear.

"You're beautiful." He leaned toward me. "I've missed you so much."

A tingle ran to my toes. I glanced at his forehead, a two-inch, inflamed scar bearing evidence of his torment twelve days earlier. "How are you?"

"Much better now." He jerked his head toward the shouting. "Sorry 'bout Smitty. You shouldn't have to see stuff like that. Dude's always causing trouble."

"You know him?"

"He's in my tank. Doesn't get along with anyone."

In his tank? Worry slithered through me. "Are you safe? Have you been hurt?" I didn't want to love him, but my concern told me I did.

"No one in here can hurt me." He tilted his head, his face filled with sadness. "The only person who can hurt me is you."

His words stabbed my heart. "I don't want to hurt you."

Tears pooled in his eyes. "Then don't. Tell me you won't abandon me. You're all I have. I love you and need you."

I wiped my hands on my jeans in an effort to dry them. "This is too hard."

His eyes pleaded. "You promised. Before you left for Europe, when I begged you to not leave me, you promised you'd make it up to me."

Haunted by my own words, I rubbed my forehead. "Didn't expect to make it up to you while you were locked up for trying to rob someone."

Gathered tears spilled down his cheeks. "I'm sorry. When my friends called and wanted to hang out, I figured it'd take my mind off the pain of missing you. I didn't plan to rob someone. I don't even remember it."

"Just because you don't remember doesn't mean it didn't happen."

He wiped his face on his shirt and gave me his puppy dog eyes. "Will you let me call you?"

I tried to push the guilt down, but it wouldn't surrender. This *was* partly my fault. How could I completely abandon him? And what if he hurt himself again? "You can call."

Covering his heart with his hand, he closed his eyes and smiled. "Could you write me? And visit?"

Why does he have to be so irresistible? He played me like an addict needing a fix. The enabler side of my heart melted with his intensity. I could at least be a friend. "We can write. And I can probably visit you too."

Face beaming, he blew me a kiss. "If only we could kiss for real."

A jolt of electricity raced through my veins. *How does he do this to me?*

His smile faded. "You're not gonna date anyone else, are you?"

I shifted on the stool. Even after what he did, I couldn't imagine being with another man. "There's no one else."

Grinning, he clasped his hands to his heart. "Wish I could hold you. Feel you."

"But you can't, can you? You could go to prison for a long time." Hot tears stung. "How could you do this to us?"

"I don't know what came over me. I couldn't stop myself."

"Weren't you taking your medication?"

His face went slack. "You weren't there to remind me. After forgetting for a couple of days, I felt so good." He hung his head. "Thought I didn't need it anymore."

"You *need* your medication."

"They're giving it to me here, and I promise I won't ever stop—"

"Bayshore." A harsh voice broke into our conversation. "Visit's over."

Desire for more time with Vincent eclipsed my urge to be out of this place. Why did the visit have to be so short? Twenty minutes wasn't enough.

Vincent put his hand on the glass. "Love you, baby. Can I call you tonight?"

My brain was numb. "Sure. I . . . um . . . stay safe."

Walking away from the jail, feelings warred within. I could walk into a new life and leave Vincent and all his troubles behind, but could I stop loving him? Would my life be better without him? Without his love?

Could I ever overcome such a massive failure?

How could I not at least be his friend when I was also to blame? Even though he begged me not to go on my trip, I left him alone. Wasn't there to remind him to take his meds. If he'd been on his meds, this never would have happened.

And it was my gun.

[C H A P T E R   E L E V E N]

Convinced

Vincent's tears flowed into puddles on the rusty metal ledge in front of him. His left hand pressed against the grimy glass separating us, his right one clung to the phone as if it were a life raft.

My heart wept with him. Instinct to make things better kicked in. "What happened?"

He wiped his face on his shirtsleeve. "They offered me twenty-agg." His voice whined, the scissors-on-chalkboard sound grating my spine.

"What's agg?"

"Agg—aggravated. As in an aggravated charge. Twenty-agg means prison with no possibility for parole for ten years."

Icy fingers clenched my throat. "Ten years?"

"With an aggravated charge, you serve half before coming up for parole."

Could he handle ten years in prison? Would being locked up for ten years be a tragedy, or a blessing? "You don't have to take it, do you?"

"I don't know what to do." He scowled at the guard as though it was his fault. "Apparently, I've also received a charge of aggravated assault."

"What? Why?"

"Some guy says I pointed a gun at him. He got my license and called the cops."

I rubbed my face. "Why would you do that?"

"I don't even remember it, but they charged me anyway. And my dumb appointed attorney doesn't care. He's a jerk. Said I should take the deal."

"Can't he do better?"

"He won't even try. The only way I'm gonna get a better deal is with an attorney who cares and knows his head from his butt."

We both sat in silence while the world stood still. Finally, I shifted on the unforgiving stool. "How do we find an attorney who cares?"

"Really?" A glint of hope shone on his face. "A buddy in here gave me a name. But he won't work for free, and I don't have any money."

A lump grew in my throat. "How much would it cost?"

"I don't know." He chewed his lip. "How much do you have?"

A headache formed at the back of my neck. Things were going better between us, but even though I had no interest in dating anyone else, I couldn't imagine ever offering him anything more than friendship again.

My brain argued with itself, making me feel like the one with bipolar disorder. The left side of my brain scolded: he's the one who messed up. The consequences are his to deal with. Not my problem. I'm better off without him. The right side tugged at heartstrings, reminding me I still loved him. Without me, he'd be all alone.

In my mind, it boiled down to simple math. Forgetting his medications amounted to mania. Mania multiplied by boredom caused him to reach out to old friends. Being in mania while hanging with his old friends equaled disaster. Subtract my leaving him, and none of this would've happened. He wouldn't have forgotten his medications or gone into mania, he wouldn't have gotten bored, and he wouldn't have gone out with his friends.

My leaving him was a large part of the equation, and that put blame on me. In addition, the fact that he used my gun haunted me. My relentless guilt won. I had to do anything within my power to help him.

"Leigh Ann, did you hear me?"

My head snapped up. "I'm. . . thinking."

"Ten years, baby. *Ten.* You don't want that for me. For us. How much money do you have?"

I massaged my temples. It was only money. It wasn't like I was making a marriage vow. Hiring an attorney wouldn't mean a life sentence for me.

"Can I call you with the attorney's information?"

A weak smile formed. "Okay. I'll see how much, but no guarantees."

His face softened. "I'll pay you back soon as I'm free. Promise."

Pay me back? Was it more ridiculous to expect we'd still be speaking when he was free, or to believe he'd actually keep a promise?

"Bayshore," the deep voice broke into our conversation. "Time's up."

He kissed his hand and placed it on the glass. "This has to work. I can't live without you for ten years."

Rising from the cold stool, legs wobbling and mind spinning, I grabbed the ledge to keep from toppling. Emotions whirled within: love and anger, mercy and resentment, compassion and exasperation. Like a game of tug-of-war, I experienced all of them at once.

The metal door opened to the free world, but I felt more locked up than ever.

CHAPTER TWELVE

Persuasion

I parked the car and stared at the high rise. As much as I hated driving in downtown Fort Worth, it had become a habit. Balancing an armload of books, I entered the law office.

A middle-aged woman with platinum hair and dangly earrings sat behind a glossy desk. "May I help you?"

Intimidation crept through me. "I have an appointment with Mr. Warren."

She handed me a clipboard with papers to fill out and pointed to a couch. "Would you like something to drink? Soda? Coffee?"

Worried my shaking hands would cause a spill on something I couldn't afford to replace, I politely declined and walked to the velvet couch.

The paperwork included an invoice. It would take over four hundred hours of work to cover the bill, but it was the right thing to do. And it was only money. I turned in the papers and a check, then followed the receptionist down a long hallway to the attorney's office.

A stylish man with dark hair and a welcoming smile greeted me, shaking my hand. "Tom Warren. Call me Tom. Please, come in." Taking my books and papers, he placed them on his desk. "What I can do for you?"

I took a steadying breath. "Where do I start?"

He pointed at the books. "Tell me what these are for."

My nursing mode kicked in. I opened the top book to my marker. "Vincent has Bipolar Disorder. The highlighted symptoms are ones he has displayed."

Tom took the book and studied it. When he set it aside, I picked up another. "This one explains how people in mania behave. Vincent was manic because he'd stopped taking his medication, and this caused him to do things he wouldn't have done otherwise. Things he'll never do again. Mania distorts a person's perception of reality." I paused to slow my own manic monologue. "Vincent was confused and never meant to hurt anyone."

"So, you assert that he went into mania because he stopped his medications?" Tom examined the book. "Why did he do that?"

I cleared my throat. "He wasn't used to taking these new meds. I left town for over a week and, without me to remind him, he forgot."

He stood and walked to a large window overlooking the city. "I see. What makes you so sure he won't stop taking them again?"

"Before this happened, he believed medication was a short-term thing. He thought he could stop after he got better. Now he understands he has to take his medications every day for the rest of his life."

Tom returned to his desk. "That all sounds good, and I can probably do better than the twenty-agg Vincent was offered. But I don't think the prosecutor will be satisfied. He's going to insist on quite a while in prison."

The weight of responsibility for Vincent in prison settled on my shoulders. "What if I talk to the prosecutor? Maybe I could show him another point of view."

Tom considered me. "Would you want to?"

Could I really do that? "It can't hurt to try."

He hesitated, then nodded and picked up his phone and dialed. "Let me see what I can do." After a moment, he spoke with the ease of familiarity, asking for an appointment. Smiling at the other person's response, he gave me a thumbs-up and scribbled on a piece of paper. "Yes, yes. That would be perfect. You're the best."

Tom hung up and handed me the paper. "Here's the date, time, and address. You have a fifteen-minute appointment. Hope it works for you."

I swallowed hard as the realization of speaking with a prosecutor sank in, then grinned ear to ear. "Oh, I'll make it work. Thanks so much."

Tom walked me out of the office, stopping at the door. "Good luck. Let me know how it goes."

I once again prepared for battle. Using the allotted fifteen minutes, I tried everything possible to convince the prosecutor Vincent wasn't in his right mind on the night in question, he didn't mean to hurt anyone, and he wouldn't break the law again.

"What do you expect from me?" he asked.

"Is there any way Vincent could get probation?"

He laughed. "Absolutely not. We tried that already. He was on probation when he was arrested."

"Okay. But does the time have to be aggravated?"

He picked up some papers and scanned them. "It's obvious he has someone who cares about him, and that means a lot. A support system is important. I imagine you'll be there for him through all of this and after he gets out?"

Caught off guard, I hesitated before answering. "Yes." I could tell he wanted more. "I'll support him through everything. And when he gets out, too."

"Maybe we can work something out. What do you say to him pleading guilty to a reduced charge of robbery by threat? I can reduce the aggravated assault charge to assault by threat as well, and have them served concurrently. That would take the aggravated off his sentence. I'll give him eight years non-agg, which means he'll be eligible for parole after serving eight months."

I mentally calculated the dates. Since he'd already spent three months locked up, he'd only have to do another five. "He'll definitely go for that."

The prosecutor made some notes and then stood. "I'll get the paperwork done and see you in court."

Suppressing the urge to hug him, I shook his hand. "Thank you so much."

His gaze penetrated me. "Be sure he doesn't mess up again."

Would it really be up to me? "I will."

Euphoria surged as the realization hit me—I accomplished something others said couldn't be done. I did this.

Elation over the offer buoyed me, but hesitation weighed me down. Would Vincent be as excited as I was? I tried to push my worries aside, but instead they escalated. What did I just agree to? Would his getting out in five months be a good thing?

How would I make sure he never messed up again?

[C H A P T E R   T H I R T E E N]

Pled

A sea of people filled the courtroom, but the face I searched for was nowhere in sight. I glanced at my watch. Twenty-three minutes before court would be called to order. I sank onto a bench near the entrance, my foot beating a rapid rhythm in the air. The squeaking door, the jangling of coins in pockets, the rustling of papers—I jumped at every noise.

The door opened again, and for the hundredth time I looked up. Tom Warren strode in. *Finally.* I stood and walked toward him.

Tom greeted me with a firm handshake. "You really did it. I can't believe you managed to get Mr. Green to drop the agg and reduce the sentence to eight years. Very impressive." He winked. "Have a seat while I go find Vincent."

My fingers moved to my throat and absently played with a gold chain. "Will I get to see him?"

"Sure. He'll come out and stand in front of the judge for sentencing."

"Can I"—I cleared my throat—"is there any way I can see him face to face?"

He cocked his head and smiled. "Let me see what can be done." He disappeared through a large metal door at the back of the courtroom guarded by a short, stocky bailiff.

A thin bailiff with the height of a basketball player stood and announced, "All rise for the Honorable Greg Scott."

The judge stepped up to the high platform and sat in an overstuffed leather chair. Dipping his head, he said, "Be seated."

A seemingly endless stream of people faced the judge one by one.

Finally, basketball bailiff walked to stocky bailiff and spoke in his ear. Stocky bailiff unlatched a thick set of keys from his overburdened belt. Using a brass key at least four inches long with notches as big as my pinky, he opened the metal door behind him and lumbered through it. He returned with a line of men, their hands cuffed in front. Vincent stood number five out of twelve, dressed in a navy blue scrub-like outfit. Three of them wore bright orange jumpsuits. I wondered what they'd done to warrant the different uniform, then shuddered at the thought of hard-core criminals being so close to Vincent.

He found me and smiled his crooked smile. My heart fluttered. With no glass between us, I wanted to hop the rail, run the twenty feet to his side, and hug him.

For Vincent's turn, basketball bailiff escorted him to stand next to Tom in front of the judge. I strained to hear what they said, but couldn't make anything out. The judge focused on Vincent and spoke directly to him. Vincent nodded several times in response. The bailiff took him to a desk for signatures before escorting him back to the line with the others.

Tom approached stocky bailiff and spoke into his ear, pointing at me.

I swallowed hard. My leg bounced faster. Would he let me see Vincent up close? Would I be able to touch him? I didn't want it to mean so much, but couldn't help myself.

The judge finished with the inmates and the bailiff again used his massive keys to open the door. He led the prisoners out, but left Vincent standing with Tom. My heart skipped a beat. Tom turned and waved me forward. Aching to feel Vincent's strong arms around me, I bolted toward him.

With tears in his eyes, Vincent whispered, "Oh, baby. It's so good to see you."

My heart told me to take him in my arms and kiss him, but my head cautioned to show restraint. "It's good to see you, too, sunshine."

Vincent raised an eyebrow at Tom. "Can I hold her?"

The bailiff approached. "You can, but if you'll give me a second. . ." He reached into a pocket and pulled out a small key. Holding it up, he said, "Let's get those cuffs off you."

A smile stretched across Vincent's face as he lifted his hands. "Yes sir, boss."

The bailiff removed the cuffs and gave a warning. "Two minutes. Got it?"

Vincent wrapped his arms around me and kissed me, jumpstarting my heart. Lost in his embrace, I melted against his chest. I'd missed his touch, but hadn't realized how much. Love swelled up and overwhelmed me, silencing my brain's logical objections.

His hands ran through my hair, sending tingles from my scalp to my toes, crushing my attempts to push the passion down. I returned his kisses with an intensity I hadn't felt since the morning I left for Switzerland.

"I love you so much." His breath warmed my face, dissolving every shred of hesitation.

My world shifted. I held him tight, not wanting the moment to end. "I love you too." The words came out without my knowledge or consent. I wished I could take them back, but knew I couldn't.

And I wasn't sure I really wanted to.

His grip tightened as he kissed me harder.

A hand touched my shoulder. "Okay, lovebirds. Enough."

My lips instantly missed his. Blinking back tears, I looked at the bailiff. "Thank you." It didn't seem enough, but no other words came.

"You're welcome." He held the handcuffs toward Vincent. "Back to reality."

Just like that, Vincent was again cuffed and off-limits. "I can't wait to do that again." He gave his crooked smile. "Five months. You'll wait for me, right baby?"

Feeling like clay spinning on a potter's wheel, I steadied myself. "I'll be waiting."

The bailiff took my love by the arm and walked him to the heavy metal door. Vincent turned and called out, "This is the happiest day of my life!"

Bewildered by conflicting sensations of contentment and emptiness, I sighed.

Back to my own reality and alone with my emotions, I walked out of the courtroom. Two minutes of affection had left me undone. I'd gone over the edge. The truth could no longer be denied.

God help me, I love him.

CHAPTER FOURTEEN

Catching Chain

Vincent's biological brother stood at my front door, head down, shoulders hunched. "Matt? You okay?"

He ran his hand through his chestnut hair. "Had a fight with my parents."

It didn't take long to figure out what he needed—a place to stay. Would it make Vincent jealous, or would he want me to help his brother? After the brothers talked, Vincent begged me to let Matt move in. Fear dampened my desire to help. This could turn out badly. Brother or not, Matt was a guy. Could Vincent ignore his out-of-control jealousy, which had quadrupled since being locked up?

My hesitation angered him. "Of course I trust him. This is best for everyone. It's my way of helping my brother, it gives him a place to live, and he'll be there for you."

I wasn't sure which hurt more—his insinuation he trusted Matt but not me, or my growing suspicion that Vincent wanted Matt to act as a spy. Vincent's love for his brother, however, came through loud and clear when he told me to let Matt use his precious Mustang. He didn't even allow me to drive it—and I bought it.

It didn't take long to appreciate Matt moving in. His presence and his love for Vincent brought me comfort, and he quickly felt more like a brother than a roommate.

Then, the phone rang with Vincent's daily call, but the voice on the other end wasn't his.

"Hi dere ma'am," a deep voice said. "Dis here's Tyrone. Vince's cellie."

Fear rose in my chest. "Is he all right?"

"Oh, yes ma'am. Everthing's good. He axed me to call, cuz he can't call no mo. He caught de chain."

"Catching the chain" meant being moved from the jail to prison. It was the day we most dreaded—and looked forward to. As much as I worried about Vincent going to prison—hated the idea of him being there—I reminded myself serving his time in prison moved us one step closer to being together.

I tried to imagine how Vincent felt when he heard. Prison. Hard time. Shuddering, I asked, "Was he okay?"

"Yeah. He tried to hide how scart—"

"Scared?" My heart pounded. "He was scared?"

"Oh, no ma'am. Not scart. Excited and nervous bowf. Smilin' and cryin'. Kep sayin' he was one step closer to de love of 'is life."

I breathed a sigh of relief.

"Said he loves ya mo' dan toncan tell. Is dat right?"

I smiled. *More than tongue can tell.* "Yes."

"Also, said he'd write you taday, an he specs you ta write all de time."

"Of course."

"Okay den. I letcha go. Anoder thing—I wanna say you's picked a good un. He's a good man."

A tear escaped and slid down my cheek. "Thank you."

I hung up and sank onto the sofa, picturing Vincent pacing back and forth, rubbing his hands together over and over. My stomach flip-flopped as I thought of him getting ready to board the bus that would take him to prison.

One moment, happiness reigned; the next, terror took over.

Thanks to Vincent's description of the transfer process, I had an idea of what was happening. He'd be on a long bus ride as part of a line of prisoners chained together, shackled at the ankles to a stranger, wrists handcuffed to a chain around his waist. An image of Marley's ghost from *A Christmas Carol* came to mind. Would he be chained to a hardened criminal? My Vincent didn't deserve that.

I longed to comfort him, but knew it'd be at least three weeks before I would see him again. His first stop would be the diagnostics unit of the prison system, where visitation wasn't allowed. There, they'd perform a battery of tests and physicals to decide which unit would be called his home until release on parole.

With over forty prisons for male inmates throughout Texas, I hoped he'd be classified at one of the closest. A one hundred mile drive for visits sounded better than a four hundred mile drive each way. But more than that, I wanted him assigned to a safe unit.

My stomach tumbled with thoughts of Vincent in prison. Would he be beaten up? Would the guards be too harsh? And, God forbid, what if another man. . . I couldn't even think it.

"What's up, sis?"

Matt settled on the sofa near me, concern on his face.

"Vincent's on his way to prison." I pulled a throw pillow to my stomach and hugged it, trying not to cry.

He put a comforting arm around me. "Look at the bright side. Time goes faster in prison. He gets to go outside, right?"

I leaned into him and nodded. "He'll get a job. And go to the cafeteria for meals and be able to shop in an actual store (called the commissary). But we won't—" Unable to hold the tears back any longer, I buried my face in my hands—"he's only allowed one phone call every three months."

"But y'all can write."

"I'll write to him every day. And visit him each week."

"There you go then. His time'll be up before you know it."

Matt held me as I cried. Comforted me like no one else but Vincent could.

My first letter from prison arrived five days later:

> *My sweetie, angel, precious, gorgeous baby,*
>
> *I was so happy when they pulled me out for the chain. I'm that much closer to holding you again. I was nervous too, but mostly happy. I miss hearing your voice. I wish we could talk. How am I going to make it through each day without hearing your voice? How am I going to make it through the next few weeks without seeing your beautiful face? It's too long. It pisses me off we can't have visits at diagnostics. It's so stupid.*
>
> *The bus ride took forever. I couldn't get comfortable. They chained me to some nappy-headed dude with terrible breath.*

He breathed and coughed all over me. I thought I was going to throw up. He'd been down before, so he just slept the whole way, but I was wide awake and couldn't sleep at all. I was wiped out when we got here.

Check-in was ridiculous. The officers yelled and cussed and put us down. They said we're the scum and they're the bosses, and they wanted to make sure we got that right. They cut off all my hair. I hate it. I hope it grows out before I get to see you because I want to look good for my baby. I can't wait to see you!

After haircuts, they stood us in a long line and made us strip. We had to stand there butt-naked. We had to turn around one at a time and spread our butt cheeks and then squat and cough to make sure we didn't bring in any contraband. It was so embarrassing.

When I finally got to my bunk, I wrapped myself in my blanket and collapsed. I slept until they woke me for chow, then I went back to my bunk. But now I have to go. I have a lay-in (that's what they call an appointment) for blood tests.

I love you baby and miss you so much! I can't wait until we can be together! I'm so happy you're waiting for me! Just another four-and-a-half months. Don't forget to write to me every day. It makes me so happy to hear my name at mail call. I don't know what I'd do if I didn't get a letter from you every day.

I'll write you again later, before I go back to bed.

All my love,
Your Sunshine

Tears streamed down my cheeks and landed on the paper, smearing the ink. My poor baby. How could they treat him that way? So inhumane. So humiliating.

Forcing myself not to think about the bad stuff, I focused on the good: more freedom, fresh air, a job. And once assigned to the prison where he'd stay until released, the paperwork could start making its way to the parole board.

Step by step, my love was making his long way home.

CHAPTER FIFTEEN

Prison

I tried to ignore the dance in my stomach as I day-dreamed of seeing my love in five short hours. Would he look different? Would his handsome face be even more striking framed by his prison haircut? Would the paleness of jail be replaced with the tan of outdoors? Tingles pulsed through my body at the thought of his gorgeous eyes and smile.

Not wanting to forget anything, I again went through my mental checklist. Driver's license, check. Map, check. Cassette tapes, check. Coffee, water, snacks, check.

Vincent had been assigned to a prison over two hundred miles away. Staying within the 55 mph speed limit, I arrived in less than five hours.

The sight of guard towers and razor-wire fences sent icicles down my spine. I took a calming breath before pulling up to the uniformed officer at the entrance gate and rolled down my window.

The guard sauntered over, pulled his sunglasses off, and visually searched every inch of my car. "Convict's name and TDC number?"

It took a moment to find my voice. I swallowed hard and told him.

He wrote on a clipboard, then spoke out of the side of his mouth not occupied with chewing tobacco. "Pop your trunk and hood."

I pulled the latches and watched him walk around the car. He lifted the trunk, and I heard him rummaging through my belongings. Something about the whole thing made me feel violated. Like I had done something wrong and deserved to be caught. He closed the trunk, walked to the front, and inspected my engine. Next, he walked to his guard booth and returned with a long-handled mirror, using it to check out the underside of my car.

Finally, he returned to my window. "Drive forward to the parking lot on the right. After you park"—he pointed to one of the towers in the distance—"enter the building to the left of that guard tower."

Must have passed the "not a terrorist" test. I looked at the top of the guard tower and gulped at the sight of a man pacing back and forth with a large gun.

Gravel crunched beneath my tires as I traveled the posted speed limit of ten miles an hour. Large black letters on a white sign caught my attention:

"NO HOSTAGE SHALL PASS THROUGH THIS GATE"

No hostages. The meaning of the sign brought reality into focus. I choked down fear as a shudder passed through me.

After walking through the first gate, a loud clang jolted my nerves. Hands trembling, I pushed on the second gate. Locked. The sun beat down as a cold sweat broke out on my neck and palms. Was something wrong? I waited, locked in limbo, for the second gate to open. A loud buzzing sounded and a guard yelled down at me to push it open.

Another loud clank announced my new status—locked in a Texas prison. My feet, which wanted to run in the opposite direction, moved as though they wore concrete shoes. The hairs on my neck stood on edge with the feeling of eyes on me. A drum beat inside my chest.

Passing through the heavy metal door was like entering a tunnel. Voices sounded funny. Faces looked odd. My shoes made squeaky noises on the floor, and the odor filling my nostrils had the same dirty-gym smell the jail had. I blinked, trying to focus. People of all colors, shapes, and sizes stood or sat everywhere. Some waited in lines, others just waited. My mind searched for clues as to where I should go.

A voice broke through the confusion. "Honey, are you lost?"

I turned.

A gray-haired lady with a crooked nose and friendly face said, "You here for a contact or non-contact visit?"

"Non-contact."

She pointed. "That line over there."

I thanked her and got in the long line. When the guard motioned me forward, I turned my pockets inside out and walked through a metal detector. On the other side, an officer checked my ID and handed me forms to fill out. I waited another thirty minutes before hearing my name. The officer pointed to double doors. "Number six."

The visitation room was much larger, cleaner, and brighter than the jail's. Visitors occupied at least twenty of the stools. Ten guards monitored the area.

The surrounding walls and floors were white, and the inmates wore white pants and shirtsleeves. Conversations wafted toward me—some happy, some not. Needing something to moisten the Sahara Desert that was now my mouth, I walked toward a soda machine in the back.

"You buying one for a convict?"

The question surprised me. "Am I allowed to?"

The guard smiled a toothy grin. "Aww. First time? If you wanna buy something for a prisoner, take it over there." He gestured toward a hinged gate in metal links separating visitors from inmates. "Deuce'll give it to the lucky guy for you."

"Thanks." I bought two, then took Vincent's to the guard named Deuce. I found booth six and sat on the metal stool in front of the metal shelf, both of which were clean and free of graffiti. A six-inch wide section of mesh running horizontally separated the glass sections, allowing a more intimate conversation than the phones in the jail. If I leaned in close, maybe I'd be able to feel his breath.

My anticipation increased with each tick of the clock. Movement caught my eye. An inmate coming for visitation. My heart skipped a beat. Not Vincent.

I chewed on my nails and stared at the door. It opened again. *Vincent.* Euphoria rose from the pit of my belly. He walked toward me, and I melted. He was more handsome than ever. So gorgeous. Pleasure filled me as I imagined his strong arms around me.

He ran his hand through his hair. I liked the shorter style. He had the two-days-without-shaving thing going and his lips, moist and pouty, begged for a kiss. His sultry eyes caressed me.

Sliding onto his stool, he pursed his lips and sucked in air, then spoke through the inch-thick mesh. "There's never been a more beautiful sight than you sitting there right now."

I sighed, longing for his touch. "Too bad there's so much glass between us."

The first hour passed in a haze. With renewed declarations of devotion, we pretended to hold hands against the glass. But then the questions began. What had I been doing? Who was I doing it with? Had I been faithful? It took a half-hour of assurances to calm him down and get him to focus on enjoying our visit. He spent the last half-hour making it up to me.

As I walked toward my car, I thought about his unfounded jealousy. It was bad enough having to constantly deal with it in letters, but why did he have to waste our precious little time together with ridiculous accusations?

What would it take to get him to trust me?

[CHAPTER SIXTEEN]

Proposal

Two hours with my handsome man. Grinning like a Cheshire cat, I purchased two sodas, handed one to the guard, and sat on the metal stool to wait.

Vincent finally arrived, but one glimpse wiped the smile off my face. He ambled toward me, shoulders slouching, head hanging, then slumped onto his stool.

He moaned. "I couldn't tell you this in a letter. Don't know how to tell you now."

Trepidation crept through me. "What happened?"

"I got a set-off." His chin trembled and his voice broke. "Didn't get parole."

"Wha..." I lost my voice. With thoughts of our future crumbling, I tried to process the news. It didn't make sense. "Why?"

"They didn't explain. Said I'd come up again in another eight months."

I clutched my chest. Eight more months of being apart. Of not getting to touch each other. Of driving long miles every weekend to spend a short two hours with him.

Angst crossed his face. "You're not gonna give up on me, are you?"

"Of course not."

He furrowed his eyebrows. "There's so many guys in the free world, and you could have anyone you want. It'd be easier to forget about me."

I placed my hand on the glass. "Not a chance. You're the only man I want."

He put his hand opposite mine. "I don't know what I'd do without you."

On the way home, I replayed our visit. I hated to think about the next eight months without him, but had to accept it. Set-offs happen. But what if the parole board denied him again? The idea settled on me with the weight of an elephant.

What could've gone wrong? His record while incarcerated was spotless. Not one disciplinary. He got along with everyone, including the guards. The warden called him a model inmate.

The next day, I made numerous phone calls. His set-off was a problem, and I was a problem fixer. Someone could tell me how to make sure it didn't happen again.

I discovered that parole came down to two things. First, the prisoner had to show remorse. Second, he needed to have a place to live and a support system once released. Knowing Vincent was more than remorseful, it became obvious I'd dropped the ball. Vincent having a place to live wasn't enough. The key, I learned, was for me to spell out his support to the board.

I called Vincent's mother to tell her the sad news, following it up with a suggestion that we both write letters on his behalf.

"Just tell me what to say and consider it done."

I shared the encouraging news with Vincent in letters and we discussed it more at our next visit. The thought of his mother helping excited him. "Baby, you're the best thing that's ever happened to me."

"I only wish I could do more."

He bit his lip and smiled. "Now that you mention it, there might be something." He leaned forward. "How much do you really love me?"

I smiled, lost in his eyes. "To the ends of earth and beyond."

"You'll always want to be with me?"

"Always and forever."

He licked his lips and gave me his incredible smile. "How much would it be worth to be able to hold and kiss each other again?"

I sighed at the thought. "Priceless."

"One more question." He clasped his hands as if praying. "Will you marry me?"

Shock waves raced through me. My mind froze. "*Marry?*"

He slipped off his stool, landing on his knees. "Marry me, baby. Make me the happiest man in the world."

Words failed me.

"Think about it." He moved back to his stool and leaned in. "It's the perfect solution. A buddy of mine said if we got married, the board'd be more likely to grant parole. And if we're married, we get contact visits. Imagine—contact visits."

Marry? "It's just so. . . unexpected."

"Why? You got someone else in mind?"

"Of course not. It's just—you're in prison."

"My buddy said it's no problem. Told me about marriage by proxy." He pouted. "Please, baby. Do this for me. For parole. For contact visits."

"It's such a big step. Don't you think—?"

He threw his head back and his fist slammed the metal ledge. "What I think is that I love you and if you don't marry me now, you might as well be telling me it's over."

I grimaced. "Don't be like that. I do love you."

"Prove it. Prove you love me by saying yes. Otherwise, I won't believe you."

His words stung. How could he not believe me? Needing to think, I rubbed my face.

"Please, Leigh Ann. I love you."

Would it be so bad? Surely we'd get married someday anyway. It *would* be nice to hold and kiss him. To visit without glass between us.

"Please, baby. Show me you love me and that I'm the only one for you."

I stood and paced. Would marrying him ensure parole? Could I forgive myself if I said no and he got another set-off? It would be my fault, like everything else. And if marriage finally proved to him how committed I was, he'd start trusting me.

I sat down. "How would I explain it to my family? They wouldn't—"

"Don't tell them. We can do it in secret, with only the parole board and the prison knowing. When I get out, we'll have another wedding. A big wedding everyone knows about. We'll have two anniversaries. One to share, and a private one just for us." He put his hands to his heart. "If you say yes, I'll never doubt you or worry again."

Tears slipped down my cheeks, my resolve falling with them. How could I deny the man I loved something that could earn him parole? How could I reject him and pass up the opportunity to erase all his insecurities?

"How do we do this?"

[CHAPTER SEVENTEEN]
Wedding

Two weeks later, I had the preparations in place: rings and marriage license in hand, Justice of the Peace at the ready, and Kerri, my "stand-in-groom," at my side—both of us watching the clock.

The phone rang. I picked it up with trembling hands.

"Collect call from Vincent Bayshore. Will you accept the charges?"

Warmth coursed through me and landed in the pit of my stomach like a flood. "Yes!" I felt my cheeks puff out in what surely looked like a goofy smile.

"Oh baby, I love you!"

His voice made me shiver. I imagined him standing at my side. "I love you too. I can't believe we're doing this. Are you sure?"

"Babe, I've never been more sure of anything. I want to spend the rest of my life with you. Don't tell me you're having second thoughts."

I twirled the phone cord. "No, sweetie. I'm ready."

In less than two minutes, I had a new name. A name I'd use only on weekends for visitation. The smile I'd been unable to wipe off my face all day vanished at the thought. I hated keeping my changed marital status from my family, but their vehement disapproval of Vincent was no secret. I had no desire to let them rain on my parade.

If only love didn't have to be so difficult—but for me, it seemed the only way to experience it.

That night, I lay in bed hugging my pillow instead of my husband. In spite of our legal ceremony, tonight was no different from any other night since Vincent got arrested. Tomorrow would be a regular day, too. No honeymoon or wedding night for at least five months.

Five months.

Loneliness crashed in on me. I cocooned my body in blankets, burrowing deep as if I could hide from my bleak reality, and wept myself sick.

That Saturday, a familiar prison guard motioned me toward the other line, the one for non-contact visits. "You know better than that."

"I'm in the right line." I tried to smile, but my mind raced with "what-ifs." What if they don't accept our marriage license? What if we don't get a contact visit? What if—? The knots in my stomach tightened.

"Oh yeah?" He furrowed his brow. "Since when?"

"Since Tuesday." I handed him the new marriage license.

His eyes went wide. "Hoo-wee. Married? Seriously?"

I nodded and braced myself.

"Well, I'll be. All-righty then. Let's get you signed up for a contact visit."

Every cell in my body tingled with relief and excitement. I took the clipboard and signed my new name. Bayshore. Running my finger over the letters, I smiled. *Vincent's wife.* The next thought wiped the smile off my face. *Wife of an inmate.* I swallowed hard and handed the clipboard back.

"Now, Mrs. Bayshore, do you know the rules for contact visits?"

Mrs. Bayshore. "No sir."

"You can kiss and hug at the beginning of the visit, but it must be brief. During the visit, you're to sit across from each other and have no contact whatsoever. At the end of the visit, you can again briefly hug and kiss. Other than the hugs and kisses at the beginning and end, you're not to touch or pass anything between you. You can visit inside"—he pointed to a large room crowded with round tables—"or you can sit at a picnic bench outside."

Because we loved the outdoors, I opted for that. The wind caressed my skin as I waited for my husband. *Husband.* Maybe his touch, his lips on mine, would allow that fact to sink in and feel real.

Without seeing him, I knew he was near. When he came into view, my heart leapt. I wanted to run across the prison yard to him, but fear of being mistaken for an escapee and shot made me stand and wait. Anticipation swelled as he moved in slow motion.

With him still two feet away, my skin tingled as if he'd already touched me. The back of my neck and shoulders heated up. I closed the distance between us. His hand took mine, sending thrills through every nerve ending. He drew me to his chest, wrapped his arms around me, and engulfed me in his love.

"Oh, baby." His hands ran up my back and into my hair. "You feel so good." He nibbled my lips before eagerly devouring them. My desire for him grew beyond what I'd ever known.

I wanted to melt into him, to become a part of him and never let go. My hands moved across his back, up his neck, encircled his head.

"That's enough."

Vincent's lips pulled away from mine. "Aw, come on, boss. Give a poor guy a break. We just got married."

The guard kept his stony demeanor. "Rules is rules. We got kids watchin'." He jabbed his thumb toward a nearby table. "Gotta keep it G-rated. Have a seat, convict."

Vincent bowed his head in submission. "Yes sir, boss." He unwrapped himself from me and sat down.

Over the next two hours, we stared into each other's eyes and talked while stealing touches across the top of the table and playing footsies under it. As much as I loved the contact visit, not being allowed to hold hands while sitting so close was torture.

When our time ended, we once again had the pleasure of feeling each other's hands and lips, and once again had to be stopped by the guard.

As I watched my husband leave my sight for another week, the realization I still couldn't truly be a wife gouged a cavernous vacancy in my soul.

CHAPTER EIGHTEEN

Parole

Had I done enough? Did the parole board understand how much I supported Vincent? The idea of waiting another eight months was unbearable.

It didn't matter that I lived in the free world. I felt as locked up as he was. Even though he promised he'd stop doubting my love if we got married, his out of control jealousy continued. He forced me to explain why I went out with a girlfriend, describe what we did, and swear nothing else happened. Seeing friends became more trouble than it was worth, so I kept to the mundane life of work, school, eat, and sleep. I put up with his insecurities because I knew he loved me and his abandonment issues were real. Besides, he would trust me when we could finally be together.

I drove to the prison buoyed by the belief I'd hear great news this time. My stomach twisted and turned as I sat on the bench waiting for Vincent.

He bounded toward me, his head held high. He kissed me as though his life depended on it. "I got it, baby. They gave me parole."

Chills covered my body in gooseflesh. I hugged him with everything inside me.

"That's enough." A voice interrupted us.

Vincent gave the guard his puppy dog look. "The parole board said yes, and my wife and I are celebrating."

The guard's face softened. "Just this once. But stay away from the X-rated stuff."

Vincent flashed his amazing smile and kissed me again, passionately and lovingly.

Breathless, I moaned. "Oh, how I wish the guards didn't monitor us so closely."

He ran his fingers down my arm and took my hand in his. We sat across from each other, holding hands in silent rebellion of the no-contact-during-visits rule.

Excitement flowed through my veins. Made me forget about the pain of the "intervention" my family had held when they found out I was visiting Vincent. They ganged up on me and forced me to choose. Them, or my husband. Even though they didn't know he was my husband. How could they be so heartless? But I'd made the right choice. And soon my husband would be home. "When do you get out?"

"A couple weeks. I don't have the date yet, but after what we've been through, this is nothing." He stroked my thumb. "There's one other thing. I'll be under house arrest for a while."

The silver lining came instantly to mind. "I want to spend a lot of time together at home anyway."

He pulled back. "A lot of time? You mean all the time."

"All our free time. But I work. And you'll have to get a job."

His eyes narrowed. "I guess. But you're not going anywhere else, right?"

I patted his hand. "Nowhere but work."

At the end of our visit, we kissed until the guard stopped us and took Vincent away.

I called after my husband. "Before long, no one will be able to take you away from me."

My heart fuller than it had been in a long time, I skipped toward the gate. How much better was life about to get?

[CHAPTER NINETEEN]

Out

The high redbrick walls topped with circular razor wire of "The Walls" Unit in Huntsville dominated my vision. Jittery with excitement, I pulled into a parking space. It had been six months since we said "I do," and tonight my husband and I would finally have our wedding night. Just thinking about it made me giddy.

Pushing open the brass double doors, I stepped into the throng of people crowded inside. I soon found the guest room, where I paced nervously back and forth, every noise grabbing my attention.

Thoughts of being alone with Vincent, with no guards interrupting us, filled me with anticipation. No one would be watching, waiting to scold us if we held hands or kissed too long. We'd do whatever we wanted without anyone stopping us.

Smiling, I remembered the piles of presents waiting for him at our apartment—all the birthday and Christmas presents I'd bought that had to wait for this special day.

Finally, the door opened and my gorgeous man walked through. He dropped his rucksack and ran to me, hugging me so tightly I thought I'd pass out from lack of air.

"I've never felt so much happiness as I do right now, right this instant, holding you, smelling you."

Lost in each other, we kissed long and hard.

Someone bumped into me, bringing the crowd into focus. I yearned to be alone with my husband. "Let's go home."

"*Home*. Wow, that sounds so amazing." He lifted his chin in the air. His smile lit up his entire face. "I'm going *home* with my wife! This is the first day of the rest of my life."

"Well, let's get on with it." I took his hand and led him to the parking lot.

He gently pushed me against the side of my car and leaned into me. "Should we get started now?"

I wrapped him in my arms. "This is our wedding night, and I want it to be perfect. We've waited this long—we can wait until we're home."

His chest heaved. "If we must."

As soon as I put the car in gear, he took my hand, caressing my fingers, moving them to his mouth, kissing them one at a time. His mouth moved to my palm, fingers tickling my arm. Pleasure coursed through me. The entire drive home, he caressed me with his eyes, his lips, his fingers.

Once home, he poured his passion into kisses, consuming me with his lips and hands. Although desperate for his affection, I wanted to do things right.

Talking through kisses, my words came out garbled. "Wait. . . champagne. . . candles. . ."

"Right now, all I want is you." His mouth found mine again.

"But we need to—wait." I pulled away from him. "This is serious."

He took my hand in both of his. "What is it, baby? What's wrong?"

"Remember what I told you about my migraines? I had to go off the pill. And we need to. . . " I held up protection.

He pushed my hand away. "Baby, I love you so much, it'd be wonderful to have a kid with you. Lets' leave it to chance. The way I figure it, if our love is strong enough to make a baby, we should welcome it." Our lips met, his hands tugging on my shirt. "Don't you want my baby?"

"More than anything."

Sweeping me off my feet, he carried me to our bed.

CHAPTER TWENTY

New Name

Feeling like a grade-schooler in the principal's office, I held Vincent's hand while his parole officer questioned him about his needs to leave the house.

Vincent cleared his throat. "I'd like to visit my family. I haven't seen them for a long time. Maybe go to my dad's for—"

"What about a job?" The man's voice was deep and accusing.

"Yes, sir. Absolutely. I want to find a job."

After a half-hour of negotiations, the officer handed Vincent a copy of his monitoring schedule. "If you leave the house outside the allowed times, you'll be in violation. We'll receive an emergency call if that happens, or if the ankle monitor is tampered with or cut off. Do you understand?"

"Yes, sir."

"Any violation will result in your arrest, and your parole will be revoked."

Vincent visibly swallowed. "There won't be any problems."

"Let's hope not." The officer leaned forward. "The paperwork sucks."

The following day, we went to Vincent's dad's for the allowed visit with his family. Otherwise, he only left the house to look for a job, which he did while I worked. On occasion, Vincent allowed me to go to the grocery store or to rent a movie, but other than that, we remained side by side in our apartment.

Within two weeks, Vincent had a job working on highways. Not a great job, but a job. Besides, my work as an emergency room RN brought in enough money for both of us.

Life had never been better.

Six weeks after Vincent's release, dizziness knocked me off balance one day while working. Faster and faster, the room spun until I fell against the wall and landed on the floor. As I contemplated the cause, one possibility loomed large and exciting.

Anticipation trembled though me as the lab technician watched my test. Three minutes later, she turned to me with a broad smile. "You're gonna be a momma!"

Pregnant.

Too excited to stay at work, I left early. During the drive home, I tried to figure out a creative way to tell Vincent.

As soon as I walked through the door, my husband rushed to me. "Why're you home early? You all right?"

I took him by the hand. "I'm fine—well, mostly fi—"

He pulled my hand to his cheek. "What is it? You sick?"

"Not sick. It's just—"

"Tell me what's wrong."

I laughed and pulled him to the bed. "I'm trying, but you keep interrupting. Sit down."

"Sit down? Baby, you're scaring me."

"Just sit." I playfully pushed him onto the bed, sat on his lap, and wrapped my arms around him.

He pulled away. "Why're you acting so strange? Just tell me."

"You're so cute when you want something." I giggled. "Okay, okay. Since we've met, you've had a lot of different names."

His face scrunched up. "What are you talking about?"

"Well, you were a friend, then a boyfriend, then a fiancé, and now you're a husband."

"What does that have to do with what's wrong with you?"

I ran my fingers through his hair. "Today, you get a new name. How about. . . Daddy?"

Recognition took over. "Did you say Daddy? I'm gonna be a daddy?" He jumped from the bed while holding me and turned in circles.

The room spun, turning my giggles into moans. "You're gonna make me throw up."

That night, we celebrated the gift of our love.

Still giddy from the news, my husband gave me permission to go shopping with my sister the next day. During our time together, Michelle figured out Vincent and I were already married.

My phone rang as soon as I arrived home. Knowing who it would be and wanting privacy, I went to the bedroom and closed the door.

"Married?" My mother sounded angry. "What were you thinking?"

"I'm happy." I paced the room. "We're both—"

"Obviously, you *weren't* thinking. This is by far the craziest thing you've ever done. But it's not too late. You can fix this."

"Fix it?"

My mother let out an exasperated hiss. "Divorce. Or annulment. You can't continue with this absurd idea of being married to him."

"But. . ." My pacing turned to stomping.

"We'll get you an attorney. This is—"

"No. We're staying married."

"Don't be ridiculous. There's no reason—"

"Yes, there is. Not only do we love each other"—I braced myself—"I'm pregnant."

Silence.

"Did you hear me?"

"How *could* you?" Mom sighed deeply. "I hope you don't expect me to be happy about this."

Her words fell like stones on my soul. "I have to go." Brokenhearted, I slammed the phone down, curled up on the bed, and wept.

The bedroom door opened and Vincent peeked in. "Baby, it's gonna be all right."

Shaking uncontrollably, I tried to sit up. "My mom hates me."

He sat on the bed and held me. "No she doesn't. Besides"—he wiped my face dry—"we have each other, and now our baby. That's all that matters."

I sniffed. My husband's loving comfort was just what I needed. "You're right. You and our baby. That's what matters."

He held my chin in his hands. "Let's show them how strong our love is by doing the opposite of a divorce. Let's plan our wedding."

[C H A P T E R T W E N T Y - O N E]

Honeymoon

Bright light filtered through my eyelids, waking me. I checked the clock and jerked upright. "Vincent, you're late for work!"

Rubbing his eyes, he sat up. "Oh, didn't I tell you? I quit."

"*Quit?* When?"

He reached for a cigarette, lit it, and blew smoke in my face. "It's okay, baby. That job was too hard. Besides, since we're having a kid, I need a better job."

"How can you think this is okay? What are you going to tell your parole officer?"

He looked at me with pity and used his soothing voice. "You worry too much. It's not good for the baby."

"You hardly gave that job a chance."

"I worked there two months."

Perturbed and wanting to escape the aggravating temptation of a cigarette, I got out of bed and went to the den.

"Where you going?" He followed me. "Aren't you happy?"

I thought about his question. His jealousy caused out-of-control anger, including yelling, name-calling, and throwing things across the room or smashing them to pieces under his foot. Accusations of infidelity came over a man giving me a nod at a stoplight or my arriving home from work five minutes late. He drove recklessly and lost every job he had, either by quitting or getting fired for doing something stupid, like cursing out a customer—or the boss.

However, even with the difficult times—which were infrequent and didn't last long—he made me happier than anyone else ever had. Vincent showed his love in thousands of ways. He wrote poems, painted beautiful pictures, and left love notes scattered all over the apartment. He brought me breakfast in bed and massaged my feet and back. His tenderness and attentiveness astounded me. For the first time in my life, I felt worthy and completely loved.

"I'm happy. I just wish you wouldn't do such impulsive things."

He sat beside me. "If you want something to think about, how about our wedding? I've been out of prison for months now, and you're gonna be showing soon."

My family's negativity toward my husband gave me pause.

As if reading my thoughts, he added, "Your family treated me fine at Christmas. They're warming up to me."

I remembered Vincent's promise of a big, beautiful wedding and two anniversaries. With him unemployed and a baby on the way, I'd begun to rethink the whole thing. I'd had the big wedding with Keith, and in the end, all it amounted to was a waste. "Everyone knows we're married now. It'd be throwing money away."

"But you're worth it. You should have everything you want."

I wrapped him in my arms. "We could still have a reception and honeymoon."

His face brightened. "That sounds great. When can we do it?"

Knowing my second trimester would be best for travel, I calculated dates in my head. "How about April? We can make the reception a wedding and baby shower."

He hugged me tight. "Perfect."

Plans for the reception came together easily, but the honeymoon was another story. Out of the blue, my uncle called with a surprise wedding gift—airline tickets to visit him in Hawaii. Excited, I rushed to Vincent.

"We can stay with him, too. And, he'll spring for two nights in a hotel so we can have some time alone."

Vincent lifted me and swung me around. "Hawaii? With my beautiful, pregnant wife? That's the best gift ever!"

"We could even go deep-sea fishing."

His eyes went wide. "Really? Oh, baby, that would be so amazing!"

Finalizing our plans included things most couples didn't have to worry about while going on a honeymoon. Vincent received approval from his parole officer, and my obstetrician okayed deep-sea fishing, as long as I felt up to it. At that same doctor's appointment, we also found out our bundle of joy was a boy.

It didn't take long for us to choose his name: Vincent Junior.

The night of our reception, we celebrated our marriage and baby-on-the-way surrounded by people we loved. We danced, ate, opened presents, and smashed cake in each other's faces.

After staying up late to enjoy the evening to the fullest, we woke before dawn to catch our plane. My uncle met us in Honolulu with leis. Vincent and I toured Oahu in a rented Mustang, swam in the Pacific, walked hand-in-hand along the beach, visited Pearl Harbor, and attended a luau. The best day, however, was spent on the ocean.

I couldn't have asked for a better day—deep-sea fishing with the best husband in the world, my son growing inside me, and a beautiful view of Diamond Head. The size of the lures, which were larger than most of the fish we'd ever caught, astounded us. After landing eight yellow fin tuna, I hooked a seventy-pound Mahi Mahi—the biggest catch of the day. Vincent helped me reel it in, but it was still my catch.

By the time we arrived back in Texas, I was tan, large with child, and giddy in love. As much as I hated our honeymoon to end, we had to come back to reality.

And while reality, in this moment, was wonderful, it felt too wonderful. And that made me anxious.

All my life, whenever I felt happy, something snuck in and snatched it away.

Prayer had brought me peace after Vincent was arrested, so I gave it a try again. "Please God, don't take my happiness away."

CHAPTER TWENTY-TWO

Dark Turn

The veins in Vincent's forehead bulged. Jaw muscles taut, his words hissed. "Who do you think you are?"

Apprehension skittered in my stomach. "I'm your wife. The mother of your son." My words came out weaker than I wanted.

He stomped toward me. "Well, I'm the man of the house, and I can do whatever I want."

His brewery breath made me turn away.

He grabbed my chin and jerked my face toward him. "If I wanna go out with my brother, I'm goin'." His words slurred. "You were working, so—"

Annoyance pushed the fear aside as I found my voice. "Exactly. I was at *work*. Something you seem to have given up on. Just how many jobs have you had since you got out?"

He glared and jabbed my chest. "Don't even go there." He jabbed me again. "Do you know how hard it is to get a job on parole?"

Perturbed by his painful poking, I backed away and ignored my throbbing sternum. "Getting a job hasn't been the problem. You just can't keep them."

He grabbed my wrist and pulled me close. "Those jobs were worthless."

"Whatever. Besides, this is about today."

"What? I'm not allowed to hang out with my brother?" He pushed my shoulders. "You jealous?"

"That's ridiculous and you know it."

His finger smashed into my chest again. "You wanna sleep with him?"

Weary of his absurd accusations, I swatted his hand away. "You really are crazy. Where do you come up with this stuff? You're an idiot. You know—"

"If anything makes me an idiot, it's trusting you."

"Can you hear yourself? I am not, will not, and never have cheated—"

"And I'm s'posed to believe you?"

"You know, I don't understand how your mind works. You come home drunk—"

He swung around, fire in his eyes. "I'm not drunk."

"It's not even eight. When did you start? Lunchtime?"

"Hell no." His body swayed. "After three."

"And then you drove. How stupid are you?"

He wrapped his hand around the back of my neck and pulled until my nose touched his. "Why is it whenever I ask about your cheating, you change the subject?"

I pulled away. "The subject is *you*. You're not supposed to drink with your medications."

"Give me a break. You can't tell me I can't have a couple—"

"A couple?" I laughed. "A couple of six-packs maybe."

"Why do you care?"

"*Seriously?* You're drinking and driving. On parole. You could go back to prison—"

He seized my arms. "You gonna call my parole officer?"

I tried to pull away, but his grip tightened. "Why would I do that?"

"I'll tell you why. To get rid of me." A dark shadow moved through his eyes.

I needed to diffuse this. Fast. "I love you. And I'm pregnant with your son. Why would I want you back in prison?"

"Because if I'm gone, you could sleep with one of those doctors you work with." His voice seethed. "But it'd only be sex. No one else could ever love you even half as much as I do."

Insults from my childhood echoed in my ears. *"Who would ever love someone like you?"*

I searched Vincent's face for love, but instead found anger and fear. Just like Keith the day I told him I wanted a divorce and he put a gun to his head.

"You hear me, you slut? No one else will ever love you."

If I could just do better. "I'm trying to be a good wife." My words, barely a whisper, went without response. I should appreciate his love more. He loved me when no one else would. But how could he doubt me so much? "If you love me, you'll believe me. I don't want anyone but you."

The glare disappeared. His face softened. "You know I love you. But you hardly ever want sex. You must be getting it from somewhere."

"I'm not like you. I don't need sex every day."

He snarled, and for a moment, his teeth looked like fangs. My heart raced. Every hair stood on edge. *Fight or flight.* I chose flight and moved away from him as fast as I could.

Arms flailing, he came after me. He grabbed hold of my shoulders and shook me until I thought my eyeballs would pop out.

Finally, the shaking stopped. Defeated, my arms hung limp.

His rapid breath fell heavy against my face. "Look at me, you slut. Look at me and tell me who you're sleeping with."

Slut.

My mind sank into recollections of my grandfather justifying his own degrading actions with words that still haunted me. "You're just a slut anyway. Even your father says so."

Tears dripped off my quivering chin. "Who would sleep with someone nearly seven months pregnant?"

He jerked me to him. "So you *tried* to sleep with someone and he rejected you? You whore." He threw me back. Hard.

As I flew through the air, images of my unborn son raced through my mind. How could I lessen the impact? My butt hit the ground with a thud, my shoulders and head slamming down next. Moaning, I curled into the fetal position and cradled my arms around my baby.

"If you ever cheat on me, you'll pay. You hear me?"

My head swam, but one thought was clear: *protect my baby.* I gripped my abdomen. A whisper escaped my throat. "Leave us alone."

"I'll leave you alone when you tell me who he is."

Unable to focus, I looked up at him through blurry eyes.

His foot smashed into my arms that guarded our son.

Shocked, I tried to sit up, but aside from the shaking sobs, I couldn't move. Through the sounds of my weeping, the front door slammed shut.

He kicked us. He threw me down and kicked us.

For what seemed like hours, I rocked my baby and sobbed. My mouth felt like a rag had been stuffed in it. I pushed myself to sitting, then used the couch to pull myself up. Caressing my belly, I talked to my son. "Don't worry, Lil V, Momma's gonna keep you safe."

What was I going to do? Vincent's craziness petrified me. I sat on the couch and wrapped my arms around my abdomen in an effort to soothe both my son and myself. "I don't understand your daddy. One minute he's loving and tender, and the next, he's hateful and harsh. But I've never seen him so angry."

I sorted through my thoughts as I talked. "Daddy would never leave us, so we'd have to be the ones to go. We'd have to run. And hide. And then he'd never give up until he found us." I tried to ignore the craving for a cigarette. Reminded myself it wasn't good for my baby. But surely if there was ever a reason to smoke, this was it. One wouldn't hurt—in fact, it'd probably be better for my son if I calmed down. I lit one and inhaled deeply. Immediately, my inner turmoil eased.

"We can't call the police, Lil V. They'd arrest him and revoke his parole." He'd make me pay if he went back to prison. He had friends who would do anything he asked.

Then it struck me: I still loved him. I crushed the cigarette out with more vigor than intended. Even with all he'd done, I didn't want anything bad to happen to him. He could still be a great husband and father. I wouldn't give up on my fairy tale dream of happily ever after.

Besides, what would it take to escape? I'd have to change my identity. Leave in the middle of the night without saying good-bye to anyone. Never see my family or friends again. Even if I could pull it off, I wouldn't know where to begin. I had no one to turn to—no one who could help me.

Trapped, I had only one option: stay.

When I married Vincent, I believed if I loved him enough, he would live up to that love and be successful and honorable. If I gave up on him now, I'd be a bigger failure than ever and worse, once again, I'd be worthless.

I alternated between crying, thinking, pacing, and arguing with myself. I wanted to rest, but every time I tried, sleep remained out of my grasp.

Four hours later, the front door creaked open. Vincent entered, shoulders slouching, his puffy eyes laced with red. "I'm sorry, baby. I don't know what came over me." His voice broke with emotion. "I didn't mean it."

I glared at him, hoping my relief that he wasn't dead or in jail didn't show on my face.

"Please, baby. I love you. I know you're not cheating." He took tiny steps toward me. "You were right. I shouldn't drink and drive. I swear, I'll never do it again." He got on his knees and moved the rest of the way to me, then put his head in my lap, capturing my hand in his. "You and Lil V mean everything to me."

I yanked my hand away. "Lil V? Really? Then why did you kick him?"

His head snapped back. "What? I never—"

"You did."

He shook his head. "No, baby. I didn't. I wouldn't."

Fresh tears streamed down my face. "You threw me down and kicked me in the belly."

He buried his face in his hands, garbled words bursting through wails. "I'd never hurt you. Or Lil V. But the thought of you. Of another guy with you. It made me crazy. If I kicked you, it was an accident."

If he kicked me? How could he not know?

"Please, baby, say something. Anything."

Anger erupted from deep inside, shattering the remnant of calm I'd clung to. I spoke in a slow, firm voice. "If you *ever* hurt me or our son again—"

"Never. I'll never hurt either of you ever again. Please, let me show you. Let me make it up—"

"No." Numb all over and too tired to argue, I pushed away from him. "Right now, all I want is sleep."

He tried to help me up, but I refused him. In bed, his arm snaked around me. I pushed it off. "Don't touch me."

After only a moment, he dropped into a deep sleep. I remained awake, the bed vibrating with my sobs as I tried to figure out what to do.

How could I stay?

How could I leave?

[CHAPTER TWENTY-THREE]

Bleeding

Still groggy from my restless night, the sight of blood confused me. Streaks of red wove through the pink-tinged water in the toilet, reminding me of the many miscarriage patients I'd taken care of in the emergency room. Please, God, no. Don't let anything happen to my baby. "Vincent, wake up! There's something wrong."

The sheets rustled. Feet hit the floor. "What's going on?" Two seconds later, he entered the bathroom rubbing his eyes.

Swallowing hard, I found my voice. "Bleeding. Call the doctor."

In five minutes, we were on our way to the hospital, Vincent behind the wheel like a NASCAR driver. Trees blurred by the window as we raced down the road. Worried about our safety, I begged him to slow down.

"I know how to drive," he snorted.

I held on to the door. Couldn't he put aside his macho pride and think about us? "The doctor said to get there quickly, but I don't think she meant at ninety miles an hour."

"I don't need directions on how to take care of my wife and son."

Thoughts sped through my head. Was I bleeding because Vincent kicked me? Could it have been the emotional trauma? What if it was that single cigarette?

Arriving at the hospital, we rushed to triage. Mortified at the thought of anyone I worked with finding out what happened, I omitted details of the night before, only telling the nurse that I woke up bleeding. She wheeled me to the second floor for admittance to the labor and delivery emergency room.

In an eternity of minutes, another nurse had a fetal monitor on my belly and an IV in my hand. A third nurse brought a sonogram machine to my bedside. "Your doctor will be here soon. How much blood have you lost?"

I tried to calculate it. "I'm not hemorrhaging, but enough to scare me."

Vincent petted my head as if I were a dog. I wanted to push him away—but at the moment, I needed comfort.

The nurse looked at me. "Baby's heartbeat sounds great. Try not to worry. Any pain?"

"No." Not physical pain, anyway.

"How many weeks are you?"

"Not enough. Twenty-seven."

My doctor appeared out of nowhere. "Yes, it is too early, but don't worry—everything is going to be fine." She squirted sonogram jelly on my abdomen. As the ultrasound wand moved, she studied the monitor. Bringing the wand low, she said, "Just as I thought. You have a placenta previa."

Terrified, I tried to remember everything I knew about placenta previa.

Vincent's petting intensified. "What is placen. . .whatever you said?" His voice cracked with fear.

Dr. Smithe pushed the machine out of the way, pulled a chair near the bed, and looked at my husband. The corners of her mouth curved up slightly, her voice laced with sympathy. "Your baby is fine. The placenta is too low. Instead of being attached to the top of the uterus, where it should be, it's at the bottom, covering the cervix, or birth canal." She paused. "Since the placenta can't attach properly, it's vulnerable to tearing loose. For now, the tear appears small. But a large tear—"

"No." A whimper escaped, and I covered my mouth.

Pain shot through my hand as Vincent's grip tightened.

Dr. Smithe put her hand on Vincent's shoulder. "If the placenta tears away from the uterus, bleeding occurs. With a large tear, Leigh Ann could go into shock. She'd need blood transfusions." She looked at me. "It could mean a hysterectomy." Then to Vincent. "It could also mean death."

Tears slid down my husband's cheeks. "Death?"

My doctor continued. "Another possible complication is if enough of the placenta tears away, the baby won't get the oxygen he needs." She looked at both of us. "That could mean death or brain damage for the baby."

My entire body felt numb. I caressed my belly, trying to focus on the doctor's words. As if my son knew I needed to hear from him, he kicked and rolled in response. I closed my eyes and pictured my tiny baby safe inside me as I listened to his heartbeat on the monitor—strong and fast like it should be.

"Bleeding can also lead to early labor."

My eyes snapped open. "No! It's too early."

Dr. Smithe placed a reassuring hand on my arm. "I know it's a lot to take in, but worrying only makes things worse. If contractions start, we'll give you medicine to try to stop them. Right now, the important date is twenty-eight weeks."

Vincent stood and paced. "Why?"

Feeling sympathy for my husband, I blinked back tears and tried to sound strong. "Twenty-eight weeks is the age of viability."

"Age of what? Can't y'all just talk English?"

I tried to sit up, but the effort made me dizzy. "Viability. It's the age a baby is considered old enough to live on its own outside the womb."

"Right," Dr. Smithe said. "And you're a week shy of that important date. We'll make sure you hang on to him as long as you can. Every day makes a difference. For now, let's focus on that."

I laid a hand on my son. "Hear that, Little V? At least one more week in there. You can do it."

"We have two goals. One is to keep your baby snug inside Momma for as long as possible. The other is to minimize or stop the bleeding. The treatment of choice for both is hospitalization and bed rest."

Vincent sat up straight. "We'll do whatever it takes, right, baby?"

"Absolutely." I did my best to appear brave, not that I had a choice. Running and hiding was suddenly impossible. And although I was angry at Vincent, I needed him. At least the baby and I would be safe in the hospital. Vincent wouldn't hurt me here. But I'd have to be more careful about not talking back to him and work harder at keeping him from getting angry.

"What exactly does bed rest mean?" Vincent asked.

"It means Leigh Ann stays in bed. All the time. The only reason she's allowed out of bed is to go to the bathroom." My doctor folded her arms across her chest. "It's harder than you think to stay in bed week after week when you feel fine."

I lifted my chin with resolute certainty. "I can do whatever it takes."

"Good. It also means complete pelvic rest."

Tilting his head, Vincent asked, "What's pelvic rest?"

Dr. Smithe looked into my husband's eyes. "It means nothing in her vagina whatsoever. No tampons, no douching, and no sex."

Vincent's unblinking eyes bore into her. "No sex?"

Her eyes remained on his. "No sex. We need to do everything we can to stop the bleeding. No exertion. No stress. No sex."

"Whatever it takes," he said, sounding more than reluctant.

He moved toward me. "This is really serious, isn't it?"

The fear in his voice softened my heart. "Everything will be fine."

A frown puckered his forehead. "How do you know?"

Cupping his face, I said, "Because our boy is strong, like his daddy."

A tear slipped down his cheek. "You're right. He's gonna be fine."

Dr. Smithe walked to the door. "I'm going to get your admission papers started. Do you have any other questions?"

"My job. . . I need to let my manager know."

"Right," Dr. Smithe said. "No work until after he's born."

Vincent dropped my hand. "How're we going to pay our bills?"

I sighed. "We'll have to figure something out."

The doctor disappeared, and Vincent began pacing again. "I can't believe how bad this is. What are we going to do?"

Not sure what to say, I shrugged. My biggest concern, of course, was my son, but other considerations weighed me down. What if my bleeding became heavy and I had to have a hysterectomy? What if I died? Would Vincent be able to raise our son without me? How would my husband handle not having sex for so long?

And the biggest question: Could I forgive Vincent and trust him to never hurt either of us again? For our son, I had to try.

In my hospital room that night, Vincent crawled into bed beside me and took my hand. "I'm really sorry about yesterday."

"I know."

"We're going through so much right now. It's hard enough without us being mad at each other." He rubbed my fingers with his thumb. "Can you forgive me and love me again?"

A lump rose in my throat. "I never stopped loving you, but you scared me. You hurt me and—"

"I promise, I won't ever do it again." He kissed my fingers, one by one. "We need each other, and our son needs us as a team."

Swallowing my pride, I allowed our fingers to intertwine. "We're still a team."

"You won't regret it." He kissed my cheek, then moved his lips to mine. His soft kisses grew more passionate as his hands began to roam.

"Remember what the doctor said. No sex."

He cupped my chin in his hands and kissed my nose. "I just need you to show me you forgive me. There are other ways you can do that."

I pulled back. "Are you serious? In the hospital?"

He narrowed his eyes. "Why not? There's nothing wrong with *me*. Just because you can't have sex doesn't mean you can't do anything." He kissed me again, his hands traveling.

I tried to stop him, but nothing deterred his amorous appetite. Feeling as if I had no choice, I relented and comforted him in the way he best understood.

[C H A P T E R   T W E N T Y - F O U R]

Unhappy

"Happy Mother's Day," I told myself, since there was no one else to say it.

Nothing like spending your first Mother's Day in the hospital, worried your baby might not make it. I forced a smile, determined to celebrate the day. After all, I might not be a mother the next time this special day rolled around.

Would I still be a mother if my son died before being born? What if he was born alive, but died because he was too early? Unable to stop the morbid thoughts, I shook away the chill creeping up my spine and caressed my belly. At least we made it past the all-important twenty-eight week mark.

Some people said being pregnant didn't make you a mother, but my son kicked and moved inside me, stirring overwhelming feelings of love. I'd do anything—give up anything—for him.

"We can do this, Lil V. Just hang on. Every day makes a difference."

"That's right. Listen to your momma." Doctor Smithe entered the room and came to the side of my bed. "Happy Mother's Day."

I sat up. "Do you believe I'm a mother, even though my baby's not born yet?"

"Of course you are. And how's Momma doing this morning?"

"Worried." I sighed. "And wishing I was home instead of here. But I'll do anything to keep my baby safe."

"And you wonder if you're already a mom. You sure sound like one."

Her words comforted me. "I do, don't I?"

She placed her experienced hands on my abdomen to measure, examine, and inspect. "He sure is active."

I laughed. "You're telling me. Constant motion. And so strong. I think he's going to be a kicker, like his daddy."

Noticing her strange expression, I wondered if she'd put it together—my husband's kick put me in the hospital.

"Where is Daddy?"

"He'll be here soon." I looked at the clock and shrugged. "It's still early."

She completed her exam and pushed my breakfast toward me. "Eat up. I'll see you tomorrow morning."

Just like that, I was again alone. "Well, not really alone, right Lil V? I wish your daddy would hurry, though. Everything feels like it'll be all right when his arms are around me, and I could use some of that today."

Finished with breakfast, I still hadn't heard from him. Growing concerned, I called. When he didn't answer, I paged him.

My apprehension grew. He'd been so attentive and loving since I'd been admitted, taking care of my every need. Surely he wouldn't forget Mother's Day. I rocked back and forth as I dialed again.

Hours passed. Worry and anger battled. Something must be wrong.

I called everyone who might know where he was. No one had a clue.

Nervous energy flowed through me, making my legs shake and hands fidget. Not allowed to pace, I tried knitting, but frustration and unsteady fingers made it impossible. Nothing on TV held my attention, and none of my books were good enough for a second read. The tedium left my mind fretting over possibilities.

An image of Vincent lying in a ditch, the victim of a hit and run, brought fear to my belly. Could he be in an emergency room? Unconscious and unable to call?

But the pager. Someone would see my number.

My body ached for the feel of his touch.

My hands longed to wring his neck for doing this to me.

Finally, he answered the phone at eleven p.m.

"Are you okay?" I said, my voice infused with anxiety.

"Hey, baby. How you doin'?" He had his sexy voice thing going, and it irritated me.

"Where have you been?"

"Me and Ron went fishing."

"Seriously?" My words came out loud and slow. "Why didn't you return my pages?"

"Sorry. Left the pager in the car. Saw it at lunch, but there weren't any phones."

His sweet, calm voice made my blood boil. "Are you kidding?"

"What do you want? I said I'm sorry." Now he was getting annoyed. "We've been wanting to fish at Lake Whitney for a long time, and today was such a beautiful day, we figured—"

"Lake Whitney's over two hours away!"

"Yeah. So? What's wrong with that?"

I shook my head in disbelief. "What if something happened to me or the baby? I could have gone into labor. Or bled to death."

He scoffed. "Well, it didn't, did it? Why do you make such a big deal out of everything? Jeesh." He exhaled annoyance. "You're fine. Our son's fine. What's wrong with me fishing?"

My sobs made it nearly impossible to speak. "It's Mother's Day."

Silence.

"Did you hear me?"

He cleared his throat. "Well, technically you're not a mother yet, so it doesn't really matter."

I wanted to yank the phone out of the wall and throw it across the room. Hot pain rose in my chest like fire. Even my doctor said I'm a mother. "How *could* you?"

He sighed. "It's been a long day. I'm tired and want to go to bed."

If I'd known what to say, the words wouldn't have made it past the lump in my throat.

"Get some sleep," his voice purred. "See you tomorrow. Love you."

A click echoed in my ear.

I slammed the phone down, wrapped my arms around my belly, and wept.

[CHAPTER TWENTY-FIVE]

Making Up

Gentle caresses startled me awake. I opened my eyes to Vincent's face. He moved his fingers to my lips and tenderly kissed me. Then he placed a bouquet of flowers under my nose. "Happy Mother's Day."

The flowers, resting in a vase I already owned, appeared to be cut from someone's yard. But they were my favorite—Stargazer Lilies. I didn't want to like them, but I did. "You remembered."

"I remember everything about you."

Little Vinny kicked inside me, reminding me he was the only one there for me yesterday. Still mad, I wanted Vincent to feel my pain. "You didn't remember Mother's Day."

"I didn't mean to hurt you." His voice threaded with remorse and tears filled his eyes. He moved the vase to my bedside table and then held up a package he'd brought with him. "I have other things, too." He reached into the bag and produced a picture of a hummingbird feeding from a lily. "I drew this for you."

The details and infused symbolism of his drawings never ceased to amaze me. Why couldn't he have done all this yesterday? Why did he have to be so irresistible? I wanted to stay mad, but there was no use. Past experiences warned me. If I didn't forgive him and let him love on me, he'd get mad. Better to avoid his wrath and accept his penance.

"It's beautiful."

He smiled mischievously. "I have something else." He pulled out another gift, replete with silver paper and a bow.

I peeled off the wrapping. A box of Butterfingers. I smiled. Not generally a candy person, I craved Butterfingers with my pregnancy. Weird, but I wanted one every day.

Vincent scooted me over in the bed and lay down beside me. "I have one more thing for you—a poem I wrote. Wanna hear it?"

"I'd love to."

He sat up straighter and cleared his throat.

> *Will you take me in your arms forever?*
> *Will you whisper words of pleasure?*
> *Tell me things I need to hear,*
> *Tell me words of love, words that could bring a tear.*
> *Warm my heart by the things you say,*
> *I want to hear them often,*
> *I want to hear them every day.*
> *You're the only one I love in this special way,*
> *I promise I will never leave you,*
> *I will never stray.*

He knew all my buttons—the ones that brought on anger and pain, as well as the ones that melted my heart. For now, though, his gentle kindness gave me such joy. I put my head on his chest. "Thank you. What's the picture with the poem?"

He traced it with his finger. "A symbol of my love for you. It's my heart with your name written across it, and the hourglass chained to it means my heart is yours until the end of time."

I ran my hand over his chest and caressed his shoulder. "You have my heart forever, too."

His arms encircled me. "Does that mean you forgive me? Let me make it up to you."

"And just what can you do to make it up to me?"

He hugged me tighter. "You want a massage? Something special to eat? I could read to you. Or, I know"—he wiggled his eyebrows—"I could kiss you all over."

I giggled. "How about if you just hold me for a while?"

"That's easy. I love holding you." He formed his body around mine and snuggled into me. "We were made to cuddle each other."

A knock at the door awakened me. "Come in."

My doctor entered. "Good morning. You two sleep like that all night?"

I rubbed my face and sat up. "No. Vincent got here a little while ago."

Vincent slid out of the bed as the doctor walked toward me.

"Any bleeding? Cramping? Baby moving?"

"I feel great. Lil V must think he's at a rock concert or something the way he's in constant motion. I only wish I could go home."

She laughed. "Well, let me examine you." She measured, felt, and listened. "How serious are you about going home?"

"Can I? Is it safe?"

"You've had no bleeding for several days. However, there are still risks. Too much stress, picking up something, moving too much—doing anything I've warned you against could cause the placenta to tear away. If that happened and you weren't given blood immediately, you and your baby could die."

I nodded gravely. "Right."

"I want to stress the importance of following all the rules. Complete bed and pelvic rest. No cheating. Only out of bed to go to the bathroom. No laundry, no housework, no cooking, no getting up to make yourself food or even to get a glass of water." She looked pointedly at Vincent. "And no sex."

"A shower's okay, right?"

She scrunched her face in thought. "No more than once every three days."

The seriousness smothered me. I gulped. "Got it."

"As for you." She turned to Vincent. "You have to pick up the slack. You have to do the laundry, cooking, cleaning, everything. You bring her food and drinks. If you have to leave, put an ice chest with food and a pitcher of water by her bedside. Understood?"

He bent down and kissed me. "I'll be there for whatever she needs."

"You must both promise you'll call me immediately and head straight to the ER at the first hint of bleeding. Time is crucial. One drop of blood—you pick up the phone. Agreed?"

We nodded. "Promise."

"Good. I'll get the discharge papers going. You'll be in your own bed today."

Finally, after two weeks in the hospital, my own bed. With Vincent taking care of me. I felt like the luckiest girl alive.

Vincent packed my things with a bounce in his step and a song on his lips. I wondered how long his excitement would last. Would his zeal ebb and flow like all his other emotions? Would he be able to keep his word this time?

[CHAPTER TWENTY-SIX]

Bliss

Vincent moved around the apartment like a chief in charge of a sting operation. He packed my lunch into an ice chest and placed it on the floor next to me. Next, he arranged the coffee table with anything I might need for the day: a pitcher of water, remote control, cordless phone, books, paper and pen, my cross-stitch materials, even a box of tissues.

"Did I forget anything?" He surveyed his work.

I'd never felt so special, so well taken care of. Overwhelmed with love, I smiled and held out my hands. "A kiss good-bye."

He kissed my lips, then sat on the couch and kissed my belly. "You sure you and Lil V are gonna be okay without me?"

"We'll be fine. You thought of everything."

"I'd die if anything happened to you or our son."

I put my hand on his. "Nothing's going to happen."

He patted the beeper attached to his belt. "Be sure to page if you need anything."

"Don't worry. We're going to read and watch TV and be totally bored without you."

"Good. Oh, I have something for you." He went to the bedroom, returning with a box.

Curiosity tickled me as I opened the package. Inside, I found a folded piece of paper and six Butterfingers.

"Since you can't go to the store, I figured you'd need a stash." He grinned and pointed to the paper. "Read it."

I unfolded the note.

> *To the love of my life,*
> *My purpose in life is to please you. Leigh Ann, I'll do any-thing to make you the happiest person alive, even if I'm the most miserable person. I want to grow old and gray with you, loving you forever and ever.*
> *Till death do us part.*
> *With all my love, heart and soul,*
> *Your husband.*

Confused, I looked up at him. "Do I make you miserable?"

He sat next to me. "Just the opposite. You make me happier than I've ever been. The only thing that would make me miserable is losing you."

I hugged him tight. "You're not going to lose me, but if you don't get going, you might lose your new job."

Nine hours later, Vincent bolted through the door. "How was your day, angel?"

"Boring. Yours?"

"Terrible. I was at work and away from you. But I'm much better now." He gave me a kiss, then filled my glass with water and took my trash and dirty dishes to the kitchen. "Can I get you anything before I make dinner?"

"Hmm." I tapped my finger on my chin as if in thought. "How 'bout another kiss?"

"You can always have that." Returning to my side, he planted one on me.

I sighed. "Much better."

After dinner, he sat behind me on the couch and massaged my shoulders, then gently brushed my hair, braiding and unbraiding as we talked. With each brush stroke, pleasure coursed from my scalp to my toes. I loved it when he played with my hair, and it overflowed my heart knowing he enjoyed indulging me. "You sure know how to make me feel loved."

He gathered my hair into a ponytail and kissed me on the neck. "Remember that. No one else could love you like I do." He moved his hands to my shoulders and massaged them.

Over the next few days, Vincent turned the long-suffering boredom of bed rest into bliss. Even though sex was not allowed, we became creative in our ways of showing love. Romance intertwined with consideration, leaving me feeling more loved and appreciated than I ever thought possible. He cooked, cleaned, shopped, and even learned how to do laundry.

A week later, however, Vincent came home from work angry. I did my best to calm him, but his rage exploded.

"That jerk has no right to talk to me like that. Who does he think he is, anyway?"

"I guess he thinks he's your boss."

He held his fist in the air. "I'd be glad to take him down a peg or two."

Alarms rang in my head. "Vincent. You can't be serious. There's no reason—"

"No reason? He can't treat me like dirt just because I'm on parole."

"Parole's a good thing to keep in mind. Last thing you need is—"

"You're taking his side?" Vincent glared at me. "You think it's okay for him—"

"I'm not taking sides, I'm just trying to help—"

"I don't need your help." He turned away and stomped to the bedroom, slamming the door behind him.

Shocked, I called out to him, "Vincent?"

Silence.

"Vincent! Come back out here."

Silence.

Tears welled in my eyes. "I don't want to fight."

Silence.

Worry slithered up my spine. I pushed myself to standing, went to the bedroom, and opened the door. Vincent, sitting on the bed with a cigarette, gave the impression of smoke coming out of his ears.

"Sweetie." I put my hands together like a prayer. "Please don't be mad."

"Don't be mad?" He scowled and threw his lighter at the wall next to me.

My mouth fell open. Tears broke free and ran down my face. "Vincent, I just don't want you to get into trouble."

"Right. Now you pretend you care—"

"Pretend? You're crazy if you—"

"Crazy?" His eyes glazed over. "You think I'm crazy?" He picked up a book and threw it at me. "Get out!"

Sobbing, I ran from the room and fell onto the couch. I snatched tissues from the box and wiped my eyes, but the tears continued to fall. I finished off my glass of water in one gulp. Still parched, I decided to wash my face and get another drink.

Once in the kitchen, I realized my son needed food. Fixing dinner was apparently up to me. After putting together a sandwich, I grabbed some fruit.

Too afraid to upset Vincent further, I decided to sleep on the couch.

The next morning, a slamming door jolted me awake. "You don't love me anymore?"

I wiped the sleep from my eyes and tried to focus. "What? Of course I love you."

Vincent towered over me. "But you won't sleep with me?"

Terrified of saying the wrong thing, I tried to think. What did he want to hear?

He yanked my chin up. "You don't want to sleep with me?"

"I didn't"—my voice came out low and halted—"think you wanted me."

"I always want to sleep with you. You must want my boss, since you're on his side."

"Your boss? Stop being ridiculous. I've never even met him. Why do you say such things?"

"Guess I'm gonna have to show him who's really in charge."

Anxiety sliced through me. "What are you going to do?"

"I'm gonna tell him where he can shove his worthless job."

"Vincent, no. Please. You need that job."

"*Pfft.* I don't need anything from anyone. I'm gonna do what I want to do. You're on your own today." He stormed out the door.

Hours later, he still hadn't returned. After lunch, panic slammed me when I took a bathroom break and saw what I most feared.

Blood.

[C H A P T E R   T W E N T Y - S E V E N]

Again

Unable to decipher the images on the ultrasound monitor, I turned to Dr. Smithe. I studied her face, but couldn't read her thoughts. Finally, I blurted, "How is he?"

She moved closer to the screen. "The tear seems to be small, but we can't take any chances. Looks like you're coming back into the hospital."

"My baby's okay?"

"He's doing great."

Relieved, I let out the breath I'd been holding.

Vincent moved closer. "He's fine? You sure?"

Dr. Smithe said, "Yes. But we need to keep the bleeding to a minimum."

He reached over to take my hand, but I pulled it away. His head and shoulders slumped as he stepped back.

My doctor looked at me. "You weren't ignoring my bed rest order, were you?"

I swallowed. "Well—"

"Of course not." Vincent interrupted. "She stayed in bed or on the couch the whole time. I took care of her, and she didn't have to get up for anything but to go to the bathroom. Right baby?"

Something in his eyes frightened me. My mouth opened. I paused. "Right. Strict bed rest."

"Okay." Dr. Smithe wiped the jelly off my abdomen. "I'll get your admission going."

When she left, I turned to Vincent. "You left me. I took care of myself. You didn't—"

"As soon as you beeped me with 911, I rushed home. It never occurred to me—"

"*Never occurred to you?* Dr. Smithe explained it in simple terms. You promised."

"I know." His chin and lower lip quivered. "It won't happen again. Nothing's more important than you and our son."

"And you quit *another* job."

"It was a lousy job."

His absence of understanding brought on a riptide of exasperation. "Just leave me alone."

He pulled up a chair and sat three feet away. "I won't bother you, but I'm not leaving."

Wanting solitude, I rolled to my side and ignored him. Behind me, Vincent shifted in his chair. Rustling sounds brought the image of him rummaging through my purse. Sounds of pen on paper became apparent. Was he writing or drawing?

Bleary-eyed and emotionally drained, I covered my head with a pillow, but distress kept me from sleep. Veiled in my private misery, I had no idea how much time had passed when the nurse entered and told me my room was ready.

Clumsy from my large belly and depleted of strength, I needed assistance moving from one bed to the other. Vincent leapt at the chance. "Let me help her." He pushed the nurse out of the way and reached across to take my arm. "Here you go, nice and slow. Take it easy." Once I got situated, my husband tucked me in and fluffed my pillow, then slid his fingers down my face and cupped my chin in his hands. "How's that, angel? Comfortable?"

Alone again, Vincent pulled a chair next to my bed. "You have no idea how bad I feel. I wrote you a letter." He took a paper from his pocket, unfolded it, and handed it to me.

> *To My Dearest Leigh Ann,*
> *I remember the day we met, it was absolutely the most wonderful day of my life. Just the sight of you walking down the*

hall, sitting next to me in group, or standing in the class you taught, put the feeling in me that I never felt until we met. I saw such a confident woman who had dreams, goals, and a lot of love to give to the right person. I am that person. I saw so many characteristics in you that I wanted for myself. Now, thanks to you, I have dreams and goals, and that job wasn't going to get me anywhere. I'll get a better job. Also, like you, I have a lot of love to give, and you are the person I want to give it to.

Angel, you mean the world to me. You're the only person that has ever loved me unconditionally. You're the only person that hasn't abandoned me. Please show me you still love me and won't leave me by forgiving me. Please hold me and tell me everything is going to be alright. The thought of losing you hurts too much.

I'll love you forever and ever. Please love me back. Let me be your person, because you are mine.

Your Loving Husband

An ache grew in my chest. I understood his pain. He'd been let down so much by people he loved. How could I let him down, too? Hot anger began to dissolve into lukewarm disappointment.

He took my hand and kissed each knuckle, then intertwined his fingers with mine.

I pressed my lips together. He deserved my anger.

"Baby, you're my world. Don't you still love me?"

He was impossible to resist. Empathy welled from deep within. "Of course I do."

His puppy dog eyes implored me. "So you forgive me?"

Compassion took over. "Yes."

He jumped out of his seat, then bent over and kissed me. "Thank you, baby. You won't be sorry."

For the rest of the day, he showed his love for me in everything he did. He read to me, brushed my hair, massaged my feet, and talked with me.

Exhausted, I tried to give Vincent my attention, but drowsiness took over. With my third yawn, he climbed into bed and wrapped himself around me. His warm love completed me.

"I'll stay 'til you fall asleep."

Within minutes, the rhythm of his breathing and the pleasure of his caresses lulled me to sleep. When I woke up to use the bathroom, he was gone.

Over the next three days, Vincent made good on his word. He spent the daytime searching for a job, then concentrated his evenings on showering me with love.

On the fourth day, Vincent arrived with a bright smile and a special dinner. "I got a job."

"That's awesome! Where? Doing what?"

He opened containers and began setting up our meal. "Well, it's not my dream job. I'll be mowing for a lawn care company. But I should quickly advance to foreman."

"I'm proud of you." I smiled and took his hand. "I have good news, too. I've gone twenty-four hours without any bleeding."

"That's wonderful. Time to celebrate."

He darkened the room and lit two candles. Happiness bubbled up and poured out. What could compare to a romantic dinner with this man, whose love for me overflowed? Things really were better, just like he promised.

After dinner, Vincent climbed into my bed and tickled my neck with his velvety lips. The kisses grew passionate as his fingers roamed. My body heated up as if a flash fire exploded inside me. I wanted nothing more than to give in to my desires, but did my best to push them down. "Pelvic rest is so unfair," I said breathlessly.

He nibbled my lips, and his fingers began undoing my buttons.

I moved his hand away. "Baby, don't do this to me. It's hard enough as it is. I can't—"

His whisper filled my ear. "I want you so bad."

Instinct took over, and I returned his kisses with fervor. I pulled him closer, as though I could pull him into my body and let him experience my love from the inside.

When his hands worked at getting my pajama pants off, reality snapped me to attention. *This can't happen. It could hurt our baby.*

"This is dangerous. We have to stop."

"I live for danger." The words came out deep and sexy. "I want you so bad, and you want me too, I can tell."

I put my hands on his chest, trying to distance him. "We can't take the risk. Think of our son."

He refused to stop. "Right now, all I can think of is you."

Fright washed over me. "Then think of me—I could bleed to death. Please—"

He closed my mouth and put his finger on my lips. "Shhh. You have to say that, but your body says different. I know you better than you know yourself. This is what you want."

The pounding of my heart swished in my ears. "No, it isn't."

"You can't fool me. I feel your desire."

I tried to move away, but the side rail halted me. "We can't. Vincent, no—"

His hand muffled my pleas. "Don't worry. I'll be gentle."

My efforts to push him off failed. Hoping to minimize the risk, I remained as still as possible. Fear for my child numbed me as tears soaked my pillow. When he finished, I broke free and rushed to the bathroom.

After washing my face, I returned to Vincent. "You need to go."

He sat up in bed, his expression reminding me of a high school boy after he got what he wanted. "Any bleeding?"

"No."

He smiled. "See, I told you everything would be fine. You coming back to bed?"

I did my best to burn him with my expression, but he remained oblivious to the fire.

He got dressed and put on his shoes. "I'll see you tomorrow." He kissed me good-bye and walked out the door.

[CHAPTER TWENTY-EIGHT]
Discharged

Just as I fell asleep for the twentieth time, the door to my room opened, waking me yet again. Dr. Smithe.

"How are you doing this morning?"

I fixed a smile on my face. Should I tell her what happened the night before? What would she think of Vincent? Of me? "Doing well."

"Great. Any bleeding?"

What good could come out of telling her? It would only anger Vincent. A shiver passed through me. "No bleeding." *At least not yet.*

Dr. Smithe took out her stethoscope and listened to my chest and belly. "Let the nurse know if you have any problems."

I spent the day watching TV, reading, doing crossword puzzles. Anything to keep my mind off what had happened—as if I could forget. Maybe I was being too harsh. It wasn't really rape, was it? My husband loves me. But still, I tried to stop him.

That evening, Vincent entered my room as if everything was right in the world. "Hey, beautiful. How ya doin'?" He leaned over to kiss me.

I turned my face away.

"What's the matter?"

"You don't see anything wrong with what happened last night?"

Shock covered his face. "You mean us making love?"

"It wasn't making love. I didn't want it."

A smirk landed on his face. "Oh, yes you did. You're the one who got me all worked up."

How did I manage to get blamed for everything? "So it's my fault?"

"After what you did to me? Yeah."

I thought again about last night. I did do things to arouse him. "But I asked you—begged you—to stop."

"You didn't mean it. You wanted to make love as much as I did."

Although I knew he was wrong, maybe I was more to blame than I realized.

"You're not bleeding, are you?"

"No."

His fingers tickled my arm. "Then what's the problem? Nothing bad happened."

I pulled my arm away from his touch. "You risked our baby's life. And mine. What were you thinking?"

"That I love you. That I wanted to make love to my wife. Is that such a crime?"

"It is if I don't want to."

"I can't seem to do anything right. I didn't mean to hurt you."

Angry as I was, my husband's heartbroken face and pitiable eyes planted seeds of confusion. "Yet you seem to continually put us in harm's way."

Misery etched his face. "You can't be mad. You made me want it."

Could it really be *my* fault? Blinking back tears, I shook my head.

"Think of our son, Leigh Ann. He needs both of us."

Our son. He was right. What could I do? Kick our baby's father out of his life? "You just keep doing things—"

"But you've forgiven me. You can't bring up stuff you've forgiven me for."

"What you did last night is bad enough all on its own."

"You wanted it. You made me want you. You—"

"Please stop saying it's my fault." But a voice inside wondered if he wasn't right.

"I messed up." He lifted my chin. "I swear, we won't make love again until after our son is born." Tears streamed down his cheeks. "Baby, I love you. Please tell me you love me too."

He *needs* me. My heart betrayed me. "I forgive you."

But I knew, deep in my soul, that although I forgave him, things could never be the same.

After a few days of no bleeding, my doctor once again discharged me home with the same strict bed rest rules. Once again, Vincent treated me with love and cared for me with consideration and kindness. As much as his occasional blatant disregard for my safety and feelings astounded me, his ability for thoughtful tenderness overwhelmed me. I was married to Dr. Jekyll and Mr. Hyde.

Twice more I went through the cycle of Vincent's waxing and waning attentiveness and support, landing me in the hospital for bleeding.

Finally, at thirty-five weeks pregnant, my doctor greeted me with great news.

"Not only can we discharge you home, but we can take you off bed rest."

Joy pulsed through me. "Really?"

"The bleeding's under control, and I'm no longer concerned about contractions. You're far enough along that if they come, you're safe to deliver."

Vincent jumped from his chair. "So no more restrictions?"

"Not so fast," she said, putting up her hand. "The pelvic rest order is still in place. We don't want to push it. I still want her to take it easy and avoid chores and activities, but she doesn't have to stay in bed all the time."

His smile faded.

Elated, I thought about eating out. Maybe a movie or the park. Over the next joy-filled week, I avoided physical exertion or walking more than a few hundred feet, but enjoyed several outings, including a blissful day of fishing.

Then a phone call brought me down from the clouds.

CHAPTER TWENTY-NINE

Danger

The officer pointed to a visitation booth. "The inmate will be out shortly."

Being a veteran with jail and prison visitation, I knew the drill.

Vincent didn't. "I've never been the visitor. It's weird being on this side."

A headache threatened as I sat on the hard stool. "You'd better not ever be on that side again."

"No worries, babe. You're stuck with me." Vincent began to pace. "I can't wait to see him. I miss my brother."

"Me too." I shifted my weight. At thirty-six weeks pregnant, everything was uncomfortable, but the metal stool for jail visitors had to be the worst. Standing wasn't an option, though. My feet were too swollen.

Matt walked hesitantly through the door. He looked us both over before sitting down, then leaned toward the screen. "I wasn't sure y'all would come."

A flutter of compassion rose in my chest. When Matt had moved out in order to live with his biological mother, I hoped nothing but good would come of it. But he'd gotten into some bad stuff, on top of refusing to return Vincent's Mustang. I knew he had to live his own life, but I did miss his friendship.

Vincent moved toward the screen in the glass. "Bro, I'd never abandon you."

Matt's lip trembled. "Thanks, man. I messed up so bad. And I'm not talkin' about this stupid burglary charge they slapped on me. I mean what I did to you. I took your car. I thought you'd never want to talk to me again."

Vincent shook his head. "You could never mess up that much."

"But your car—"

"Forget it. I don't care about you moving out, I don't care about the charges, and I especially don't care about the car. All I care about is that you're my brother."

Matt bit his lip.

I put my hand on the glass and smiled. "We both love you. Now you need to get yourself straightened up and out of jail—you're going to be an uncle soon." I stood and turned to the side to show him my gravid belly.

His eyes went wide and then he laughed. "Dang, girl. You're huge."

I stuck my tongue out at him. "Gee, thanks."

The brothers needed some private time. Walking to the restroom, I wondered why the Tylenol I'd taken hadn't helped my headache. The pain had increased, making me nauseated.

When I used the toilet, a familiar fear raced through me.

Blood.

Again.

And we were an hour from home.

I felt like a ticking bomb. Worried the slightest jolt could separate my placenta, I moved gingerly as I returned to my husband. "Sweetie, we have to go."

Vincent's face went slack. "You don't look so good."

I spoke with a calm I didn't feel. "I'm spotting."

Vincent bolted from the stool. "Sorry bro, we gotta go."

Matt stood. "Go. Thanks for coming. And take care of my nephew!"

Once home, Vincent settled me on the couch. He propped my feet up and began rubbing them. "Your feet are so swollen. And your face, too."

Dread swept over me as the nurse in me put it together. Headache, plus swelling, plus nausea equals preeclampsia. The mother in me worried about potential seizures and what they could do to my baby. "I need to call Dr. Smithe."

When the doctor heard my symptoms, she ordered me straight to the hospital. "This is it, Leigh Ann. You're staying in the hospital until you've had your baby."

Vincent grabbed my pre-packed suitcase and practically pushed me to the car.

The triage nurse wheeled me to labor and delivery. Urine and blood samples were taken, an IV started, and an ultrasound machine brought to my bedside.

The privacy curtain parted for Dr. Smithe. "How are you doing? You still have a headache and nausea?"

I nodded.

She tapped the chart. "You have protein in your urine."

"What does that mean?" Vincent asked.

As I tried to focus on my husband, spots appeared before my eyes. A dangerous, late-stage symptom. Dread swept thought me.

"The protein is another sign of preeclampsia—"

"Even worse—I'm seeing spots."

Dr. Smithe folded her arms across her chest. "That's it. You're having this baby today."

[C H A P T E R   T H I R T Y]

Baby

Numbness flooded me. I swallowed hard and took my husband's hand, nervous excitement eclipsing my worries. "You're going to be a daddy. *Today*."

"We'll get the Mag Sulfate started to keep you from having seizures," Dr. Smithe said. "Then do an ultrasound to see if the placenta is off the cervix enough for a vaginal delivery. If so, we'll start the Pitocin to induce labor. If not, we'll do a C-section. Understand?"

"Yes," I said, hoping for the natural birth.

She sat next to me and slowly pushed the loading dose of Mag Sulfate into my IV, then turned on the ultrasound machine and studied the monitor. "It's close. If you want to go for a vaginal birth, we'll still need to be prepared for an emergency C-section at any moment."

"Let's give it a try."

She paused. "Now for the bad news. With so many complications, I don't feel comfortable doing an epidural."

Trepidation over the pain of giving birth gave my excitement pause, but the thrill of holding my baby soon pushed the worry aside. "Whatever you say. The only thing I care about is my son and his safety."

She tilted her head. "This isn't a little thing. Giving birth is extremely painful."

"I can do anything for my baby."

"All right." She looked at the nurse. "Let's get her started."

Vincent and I continued our private jubilation as they moved me to a labor room and hung IV drips of Pitocin and Mag Sulfate. I called my sister and shared the news.

By the time Michelle arrived around 1:00 a.m., the contractions had started. Because of my low-lying placenta, the nurses weren't allowed to check me. I had no idea how my cervix was progressing. But the contractions quickly grew stronger and came more frequently.

Around 6 a.m., something passed between my legs. I called to my husband in a pleading voice.

"What is it?"

"You tell me." I lifted the sheet so he could see.

"Oh, sh. . ." He gagged, then ran from the room yelling for a nurse.

Everything between my hips and knees felt wet and sticky.

The nurse rushed in and took a peek, then immediately dropped the sheet and pushed the call button. "I need Dr. Smithe. Stat! The patient's hemorrhaging."

Hemorrhaging?

The nurse moved fast, getting towels and pads and enlisting my sister's help. Everything was covered in blood. My blood. Seeing what passed—a blood clot at least five inches in diameter—I felt faint. Body trembling, heart racing, my mind clouded over with worry for my son. A metallic odor permeated the air, leaving the taste of pennies in my mouth. My blood so quickly saturated the pads and towels stuffed under me that the nurse had to replace them constantly.

Dr. Smithe appeared in my room, looking like she'd run a marathon. With one glimpse, she announced, "Time for a C-section."

My strength drained away. *Am I going to die?* I needed my husband, but no one could find him.

Dr. Smithe returned. "They're setting everything up. Let me check you before we go to the operating room."

As quickly as the bleeding had started, it stopped. Puzzled, Dr. Smithe said we could hold off and keep an eye on things. Too depleted to ask questions, I agreed.

The doctor moved a tray table to the side of my bed so she could be close while writing furiously in my chart. My sister sat on the other side holding my hand. Just as concerns about dying or losing my son gave way to worry over my husband, he strolled into the room.

"You okay, babe?"

I wanted to scream at him for leaving me at such a crucial moment, but held back. "Where'd you go?"

"Thought I was gonna throw up. It was too much. I needed a smoke."

I could have died. Was about to be wheeled in for surgery. And he went to smoke?

Alarms rang out, announcing my spiking blood pressure. The nurse returned and helped me roll to my side in an effort to bring it down.

He petted my hand. "I'm not used to seeing blood like you are."

I wanted to understand, but his running out while death stared me down infuriated me. The strengthening contractions blanketed me with fatigue, keeping the anger at bay. 7:00 a.m. Twenty-four hours since I'd slept. Twelve since I'd eaten. My stomach raged with nausea and hunger pangs, making my headache worse.

With my increasing headache and rising blood pressure, Dr. Smithe offered something for the pain, saying it would help both. As soon as the nurse injected the contents of the syringe into my IV, relief came, enabling me to rest between contractions.

An extra-hard contraction startled me awake. "Vincent?"

My sister took my hand. "He said he needed a shower and a nap, so he went home."

"Home?" Irritation pricked me again. "What if something happens?"

She shrugged. "He said to page if we needed him."

"But we live forty minutes away."

Over the next few hours, the contractions continued to strengthen. Dr. Smithe checked me at noon and decided to break my water. My breath caught when she brought out a tool resembling a huge crochet hook.

She gave me a sympathetic look and went to work. I closed my eyes and tried to imagine Vincent holding my hand. After five minutes of what seemed like a procedure from a medieval torture chamber, warm liquid poured from me. After that, my contractions came much stronger and closer together, ripping through me like trembles from an earthquake.

An hour later, Vincent sauntered through the door as though he'd missed watching me cross-stitch. He took my hand, acting like he'd never left my side.

After four more agonizing hours, I felt the urge to push. Michelle left to find my again-vanished husband. When they returned, the nurses moved us to a delivery room where everyone took their places. Vincent on my left, Michelle on my right, and the doctor at my feet.

I pushed for so long, I didn't know if I'd have the strength to continue. Finally, from Dr. Smithe, "There's his head. Okay, Leigh Ann, one more good push."

I took a deep breath, held it, and pushed as hard as I could.

My sister held my hand as she counted. "Four, five, six—"

"Stop pushing!" My doctor's shrill voice broke in. "No pushing. Breathe."

Alarmed, I did my best, but the need to push was impossible to suppress. Battling my body's instincts, I blew quick puffs of air.

"No pushing."

"Trying!" My body fought me as I did my best to obey. "What's. Wrong?"

"Hold on. Almost there."

An enormous sensation of pressure overpowered me as I struggled and fought. "Get him out," I cried. It felt as though my insides would explode if I didn't push. Eighteen hours of difficult labor didn't compare to the engulfing pain of not pushing.

A splashing sound filled my ears, as if someone turned over a bucket, drenching the floor with a gallon of milk. Panic poured through me with the realization it was my blood.

"The cord was wrapped around his neck," my doctor said. "He's fine now."

The sounds of my baby's newborn cries saturated me with blessed, euphoric bliss.

"There he is." My husband squeezed my hand. "Our son."

Tears ran down my cheeks. "We did it."

Dr. Smithe placed him on my belly, and my hands flew to him as he screamed and wailed. He felt soft, wet, sticky—and splendid.

After cutting the cord, Dr. Smithe held him high for me to see. His tiny, perfect body wriggled as if dancing with joy for being set free. The nurse took him away, and my empty arms reached for him. All I wanted was to hold my baby. Snuggle him. And sleep.

Vincent moved toward him. "Five fingers on the right hand. Five fingers on the left. Five—Ten toes." A broad grin covered his face. "He's got all his parts."

I'd never seen him so happy.

The nurse swaddled our new son and handed him to Vincent. "Born at 7:01 p.m., he weighs five pounds, eight ounces."

Pain ripped through me, and I yelped.

"Bear with me," Dr. Smithe said. "This is going to hurt, but I need to clear the blood clots from your uterus."

The room faded in and out as it felt like the doctor was performing a tonsillectomy through my birth canal. I had control over my screams, but not my tears. Words and images blurred in and out as darkness took over.

A prick to my leg snapped my eyes open.

The nurse hovered over me. "A shot to stop the bleeding."

A jolt of pain woke me. The room looked unfamiliar and dark.

Someone near me moved. "How are you feeling?"

Dad? "Where am I?"

His hand covered mine. "ICU. You lost a lot of blood, but you're going to be fine."

I tried to sit up, but pain made it impossible. "Where's my baby?"

"In the nursery. I'll get someone." My dad left the room, then returned with a nurse.

"You need some pain medicine? I have some pills if you want them."

Eager for relief, I took them. "Please. I need my son."

"He's fine. You can see him when you're stronger."

Rage erupted, empowering my weakened body. I threw off the sheets and tried to get out of bed, demanding until the nurse agreed and took me to the nursery in a wheelchair. From twenty feet away, I spotted him in the arms of someone else.

"Let me have him."

The nursery attendant laid him in my arms. Holding him tightly, I covered him with kisses. I'd never felt such consummate love. His tiny fingers wrapped around my thumb, and my tears once again flowed. "My sweet, sweet son. I'll always fight for you."

[C H A P T E R   T H I R T Y - O N E]

Home

"I can't take my baby home?" Indignation stirred strength into my still weak body. "I'm not going anywhere without him."

The nurse hesitated. "It's the pediatrician's decision."

"This is ridiculous. I want to talk with him."

I faced the doctor and explained my reasoning. "I'm a nurse. I can take care of my baby."

"He's lost too much weight," he said, compassion on his face. "I can't let him go home until he weighs at least five pounds. Besides, you're too weak to care for him."

"I'll have help. I'm going to stay with my sister for a few days, and my mother will be there too."

We agreed on a plan. I could take my son home, but would bring him to the hospital each day to be weighed until he reached five pounds.

Over the next two weeks, happiness and joy defined our lives. I loved being a mother, and nothing compared to the bliss of nourishing my son from my own body. Love for my husband also grew. Watching him tenderly care for our child warmed my heart.

Soon, though, Vincent's warm affections grew into hot passion. I tried to put him off, but he wouldn't hear it.

"It's been a month and a half." He pouted. "And we've only done it once in over three months. Don't you love me?"

"The doctor said six weeks, and it's only been three. My body needs to heal."

He embraced me and kissed my neck. "I'll be gentle. Promise."

Horror unfolded as I realized he was serious. "Vincent, please, I still have stitches."

He did his best to court me with kisses and caresses. "Come on baby, I won't hurt you."

I tried to think of something that would dampen his lust. "I'm still swollen."

He pulled away and narrowed his eyes. "Can't you think of me for once? I kept my promise to not make love until after you gave birth. I've waited long enough."

A sense of powerlessness crushed me as the truth sank in—nothing I could say would deter him. Defeated, I gave in. If he noticed my whimpers, cries of pain, and tears running into my ears, he acted as though he didn't.

After my six-week checkup, it was time for me to return to work. Matt's girlfriend needed a place to stay and we needed a babysitter, so she moved in. Her presence was a welcome help and brought Matt, who'd recently been released from jail, over more frequently. But we'd outgrown the apartment. We spent a month searching, then chose a cozy three-bedroom starter house in a quiet neighborhood a block from my sister. My parents helped with renovations and the down payment, but I qualified for the loan all on my own.

As soon as we got settled, Vincent again lost his job. Although happiest while unemployed, his parole officer insisted he work. With minimal effort and a month's time, he was hired to sell vacuum cleaners. Unfortunately, since it paid commission only and he failed to sell one vacuum cleaner in two months, it was as though he remained unemployed. After several discussions about his career goals, he began working as a waiter. Then in January, when Lil V was six months old, Vincent enrolled in classes at the local junior college.

Upon returning from registration, he danced through the door with an exuberant smile. With the excitement of a child on Christmas morning, he showed me his new textbooks and school supplies.

"I'm so proud of you."

He picked me up and twirled me around. "I can't wait to get started."

Three nights a week, Vincent gathered his schoolbooks and kissed me good-bye, practically skipping out the door to college. Because of his classes, we agreed he should work part-time. Even with sparse hours, he brought home more money as a waiter than he had with any other job.

But life was far from perfect. Vincent's moods twisted and churned with the ferocity of a tornado. Trying to predict his behavior was like approaching a mirror in a fun house and wondering if I'd be thin, fat, short, or tall. Would he be tender or vicious? Would he cherish and adore me, or accuse me of cheating and call me names? Bring me a love note, or throw something at me in a rage? He switched from alluring affection to abusive anger in the time it took the heat of a tongue to destroy a delicate snowflake.

When Vincent wasn't angry or jealous, he lavished his love on me until I was overwhelmed with its beauty and power. But add that same passion to his insecurities, and it became an obsession that suffocated me under a blanket of irrational suspicions. If I received permission to go somewhere, he had to approve my outfit before I left the house. Upon return, I faced endless questions, as though on trial for the crime of adultery. His distrust was so enormous, he wouldn't allow me to check the mail or answer the door or phone.

Early in our relationship, Vincent persuaded me he had the right to snoop through my purse and pockets, but the longer we were together, the less privacy I was allowed. He began going through my car and old boxes in the garage, then added my dresser, closet, and bathroom drawers to his list. Hunting for any hint of unfaithfulness, he would sometimes spend all day searching inside the house and out.

Then he began performing random strip searches, a humiliating practice where I had to stand before him, naked, while he examined my body and clothing for signs of betrayal. Protests over his invasions of my privacy only increased his distrust, so I kept my irritation to myself.

Still, Vincent was desperate to be happy. For us to have a happy marriage. And I was determined to give that to him. I gave everything within me to love the insecurities out of him, but it was never enough. No matter how hard I tried to please him, something always set him off.

When he lost control, I could sometimes settle him down by cupping his face in my hands, looking into his eyes, and saying the words he needed to hear. Other times, the only way I could prove my love was by taking my clothes off and insisting I wanted him, right then and there. Often, there was no way to diffuse his outrageous reactions.

Frequently while driving alone, I'd see him following in my rearview mirror. He popped in at work unannounced to check on me.

One day, a co-worker told me she saw Vincent in the halls. When I got home and asked him if he'd been at the hospital, he said he had. Confused, I asked why he didn't come see me.

A sly smile grew on his face. "I did. I was watching you."

"Why would you watch me?"

"Isn't it obvious? To see how you behave."

Thinking of my husband lurking sent a shiver down my spine. His diagnosis from the psychiatric hospital came back to haunt me. *Sociopath.* The hairs on my neck pricked a warning. Could they have been right?

He leaned forward and narrowed his eyes. "Always assume I can see what you do."

"I have nothing to hide. Do what you want."

He laughed. "Try to stop me."

A shudder moved through me, then concentrated on my left hip. The vibration was more than fear. I pulled off my pager and studied the unfamiliar number.

Vincent snatched it from me and glanced at the display. A smile spread across his face.

"Who is it?"

"Someone I met in treatment years ago." He hooked the pager onto his belt. "We lost contact, but reconnected last month."

"Does this person have a name?"

He looked away. "Roxanne."

My mouth dropped open. "A *girl* paged you?"

"Don't make such a big deal of it." He sat next to me and caressed my arm. "We're just friends."

Right. What would he say if it was me being just friends with some guy? "What does 'reconnect' mean?"

"We ran into each other. Talked. That's it." He kissed my nose and took my hand in his. "Baby, it's nothing."

His affection made me suspicious. What was he hiding?

"Remember when I went with your brother to that bachelor party? She was working there—"

I jerked away from him. "*What?*"

"As a hostess, not a stripper. We talked for like two minutes, and I gave her my pager number."

"You mean *my* pager."

"I just wanted to tell her about my beautiful wife and our amazing son and how wonderful my life is now."

I stood and paced. Turned to him and crossed my chest with my arms. "You'd go ballistic if a guy talked to me."

"Yeah, but guys only want one thing. Roxanne and I are *friends.*" He frowned. "Don't you trust me?"

His ludicrous reasoning made no sense. "So, you're saying all guys except you only want one thing, and I'm supposed to trust you, even though you don't trust me?"

He nodded. "That about sums it up."

Although I hated his tyranny and double standards, neither was as bad as his fury. But how could he expect me to trust him so completely when he had no trust for me? Maybe if I showed him what trust looked like, did my best to be a good wife, he'd learn how to trust too?

A few weeks later, I came home from work to find candles lit and the table set for dinner. Vincent still made me feel wonderful when he showed his love in such tangible ways.

He came out of the kitchen carrying a tray of food, a smile beaming when he saw me. "How's the best wife in the whole world?"

"Wow." I gave him a kiss, then sampled a morsel of steak. "You've been busy."

"Anything for the love of my life." He put the tray down and turned his attention to me. He pulled out a chair, helped me be seated, and placed a napkin in my lap.

When we'd finished eating, Vincent took my hands in his. "I have something to tell you."

My stomach dropped as the pieces came together. I hadn't wanted to think about the real reason behind his romantic gesture. But the distress in his eyes told me this dinner hadn't been just a show of love.

"Remember when I was sick a few weeks ago? How I missed a week of classes? Well, I . . . got behind."

I breathed a sigh of relief. "It's okay sweetie."

"I didn't think I could catch up. Oh, baby. . . " He bent over and cried into my hands, his body trembling with sobs.

Like a solar eclipse, my relief vanished behind a wall of dread. "What did you do?"

He looked at me, his face a mess. "I was too embarrassed to go back, so I quit."

"*Quit?* But you've been leaving the house to go to school. Where have you—? Have you been seeing Roxanne?"

"No. I swear. I've been going to the park."

I paced. "Why didn't you tell me?"

He wiped his face on his shirt. "Don't be mad, baby. I'll still take the classes." He stood and moved toward me, but I stepped out of his reach.

I wanted to scream at the injustice. "This is incredible. You demand an accounting of my every minute outside your presence, and then you pretend to go to class and do who-knows-what three times a week for a month."

He put his hands together under his chin as if praying. "I told you. I went to the park."

"And I'm supposed to believe you? You'd never accept that from me."

He got on his knees and pleaded. "I'd never cheat on you."

All I could think about was Roxanne.

"Please don't stop loving me. I won't ever lie to you again."

I turned my back on him and stormed to the bedroom, throwing myself onto the bed. The love and affection he lavished on me outweighed his anger and jealousy, but the double standard? This was beyond belief.

One thought eased my aggravation—he loved me too much to cheat. But how could he lie for so long and expect my blind faith? The idea of modeling trust for him once again struck me. Maybe if did that, and if I could somehow be a better wife, he'd learn to trust me.

Although angry, confused, and hurt, I went to bed consoling myself with the fact that even though he was hard to love, at least he'd never once hit me.

CHAPTER THIRTY-TWO

Shift

Gentle caresses on my cheek awakened me.

Vincent smiled at me from the side of the bed. "How you feeling this beautiful day?"

I rubbed my eyes, images filling my mind of Vincent heading out the door with an armload of books, pretending to go to school. "Tired."

"I have breakfast." Vincent set a tray on the bed beside me. "Lil Vinny's up, changed, and fed, and now he's in his playpen. We have some time for the two of us."

In spite of our fight, I appreciated his efforts. He'd prepared a feast—orange juice, scrambled eggs, bacon, toast, and the thing I needed most, coffee. "I'd gain ten pounds if I ate all that."

He ran his hand down my arm. "No way. Your body's perfect."

Smoothing my tangled bed-hair, I grinned shyly. "Thanks."

Vincent buttered a piece of toast and handed it to me. "Wanna go fishing?"

"Now?" Thinking of my many waiting chores, I hesitated.

"Please? Boo and I already packed the fishing stuff."

I laughed. "Oh really?" As if Lil V could do anything.

"Yep. It was all his idea."

As always, Vincent made it impossible for me to stay mad. "In that case, I guess we'll go fishing."

His grin melted my heart. "I want us to have a real family day. After we fish, we can fly kites. I'll pack a picnic."

Within the hour, we unloaded supplies at our favorite spot. Too late to catch the dawn-feeders, we managed to reel in a few perch. When Vincent helped our little Boo catch his first fish, we celebrated.

Taking out the camera, I encouraged my tiny angler. "Show me your big catch!"

He giggled and clapped his hands with each picture I snapped. The sight of my husband interacting so fondly with our child reminded me of how much I loved him.

Next, we pulled out the kites and watched them soar. Our son jumped up and down, tugging on the string as he laughed. The glorious sound of his sweet excitement made me want us to be like this forever. The only thing that mattered was Lil Vinny's joy. Whatever Vincent pulled, it didn't compare to the importance of keeping our family together and happy.

With the sun warming our faces, we enjoyed our lunch. Afterward, Vincent cradled me in his arms as we watched our baby nap, peace slipping over me like a glove. Could anything be better than a perfect day with my boys?

Once home, Vincent placed the baby in his crib. As I put away the leftover food and dishes, he came into the kitchen and hugged me. A smile formed on my face. "I really do love you."

He kissed my neck. "I love you more than you could ever know."

The phone rang, and Vincent reached out to answer it.

"Hello?" His jaw tightened. "Who is this?"

He slammed the receiver down, then picked it back up and smashed it on the counter until it shattered. Turning to me, he glared. "Who was that?"

"How would I know?"

He grabbed my hair. "Was it your boyfriend?"

A thread of fear laced around my heart. Reminding myself to remain calm, I reached for his arm. "You're my only boyfriend."

He pushed me away and glared, fire in his eyes. "Then why did that guy hang up on me?"

What does he want to hear? Contemplating the broken phone, I worried he'd break me in the same way. "Sweetie, you're the only man in my life. I'm sure it was just a wrong number."

"We'll see about that. Star 69 will tell me who called." He stomped from the kitchen, picked up the den phone, and dialed. "Did you just call my house?"

A moment of deafening silence in which the world stood still.

"No problem." He hung up and returned to me. "Guess you were right. Wrong number."

I touched my heart to calm its rapid beating. "See? No worries."

He returned to the kitchen and picked up the battered phone, throwing the pieces into the trash. "Sorry, babe. Didn't mean to get so mad."

I thought about how bad it could have been. Relief sighed through me.

He swept me into his arms. "You're the best wife a guy could ask for."

Later that night, after I rocked Boo to sleep, Vincent had a movie set up. "Now it's time for us."

I joined him on the couch. Just as he hit play on the VCR, the phone rang. Like Pavlov's dog salivating in response to a ringing bell, my heart jolted with foreboding. Vincent answered it.

"It's for you." His words came through clenched teeth.

I hesitated before taking it. "Hello?"

Diana was desperate to talk about her troubles. Although I wanted to help, Vincent appeared less than pleased, watching my every move as we talked. Knowing he could hear me, I kept my end of the conversation short. Even so, his growing agitation became obvious when he stood and paced. I'd gone too far.

"Sorry, Diana, but I have to go." I hung up and turned to face Vincent.

His arms crossed his chest. "Is she more important than me?"

"No, of course not. She's having problems with her ex again."

The muscles in his jaw bunched. "Well, you spent *our* time talking with her."

"It was only a couple of minutes." I sat on the couch and motioned him to sit beside me. "Let's watch the movie."

His head shook as he continued pacing. Suddenly he changed course, walking to the phone and smashing it into pieces.

Razor-sharp nails clawed at my insides. "What are you doing?"

He sat next to me. "I'm through with interruptions." He pressed play on the remote. "Now we can watch our movie."

Too afraid of saying something to stir his fury, I sat in silence as he acted as though nothing had happened.

The next morning, I gingerly approached the subject of our demolished phones. "Sweetie, we're too broke to replace phones on a whim."

He smiled and shrugged. "Then we won't."

"But. . ." I searched for words. "We have to. With the two you broke last night added to the others you've broken, all we have left is the speaker phone."

He ran his hand along his chin. "Perfect. Now I can hear both sides of your conversations."

For an hour, our words escalated. We went from arguing about my privacy to fighting over money. I complained about our lack of it, his failure to make it, and how fast he could spend it.

He jabbed his finger into my chest. "Are you saying I suck at being a waiter?"

"I never said that."

His eyes darkened, a thunderhead brewing on the horizon. "You said if I was a better waiter, I'd make more money."

My heart pounding against my throat, I began to tremble. "I said we don't make enough money to cover our bills. We need to spend less and make more. We *both* need to pick up more hours."

Vincent grabbed me by the shoulders, shaking me. "I can't ever do enough for you, can I? Why can't you be happy?"

"I am happy. I just hate it when our checks bounce. You spend money like we have a ton of it. I'm just asking you to stop spending money on stuff we don't need."

He put his finger in my face. "Are you saying it's all my fault?"

I swatted his hand away. "Don't do that."

The finger returned, closer than before. "What's wrong? You don't like this?"

"No. Please stop it."

He poked my nose. "Aw, poor baby doesn't like a finger in her face." His voice mimicked a schoolyard bully.

I reached up to bat his hand away again, but he moved it and I accidentally hit his face instead. Everything inside me froze.

His eyes went wide, then narrowed into slits. "You. Hit. Me."

My hands covered my mouth. "I didn't mean to."

His lip curled like a growling dog. "You're gonna pay for that, b*@#*."

Adrenaline racing through me, I ran. As I reached the bedroom door, his hands caught my shoulders. He spun me around and backhanded me, sending me flying. I landed hard on my backside, but noticed only the searing pain in my jaw.

I held my already swelling face with both hands and cried.

He rushed to me. "Baby, are you okay?"

Not wanting to move my hands, I tried to push myself away from him with my legs. "Leave me alone." My words came out garbled.

He moved toward me, relentless. "Oh baby, I didn't mean—"

I tried to open and close my mouth, but couldn't. "I think you broke my jaw."

[CHAPTER THIRTY-THREE]

Struck

Ashamed about the real reason for my bruised jaw, I agreed to tell people Vincent's made-up version of what happened. In spite of the pain, I couldn't afford a sick-day. I stocked my purse with ibuprofen, packed broth for lunch, and left for work rehearsing the story. "Vincent and I were playing catch with a football. He threw an especially hard one and I missed. It hit me in the jaw."

Everyone bought it.

One doctor I worked with, however, recommended an x-ray. She examined the film with a magnifying glass. "I don't think it's broken, but can't be sure." She handed it to me, then sent me to a faculty doctor for his opinion.

Dr. Rosenburg studied the x-ray and asked me what happened. Something inside me stirred. He didn't know me, so he'd be a safe person to tell. I took a deep breath and blurted, "Someone hit me."

My heart raced as I waited for his next question—who? Would I have the guts to admit the truth? My heart hammered as I worked at forming the words. *My husband did it.*

He stared at me. After a moment, his mouth opened.

Here it comes. I can do this.

"Wow," he said. "You were hit really hard."

That's it? I wanted to yell at him, to ask him if he cared. Instead, I remained silent.

He handed the x-ray back. "No break. Just a really nasty bruise. You'll need to take care of it."

My soul deflated.

Emboldened by my near confession, I decided to confide in my co-worker, Mahasti. Although my husband wouldn't let me have friends, he couldn't keep me isolated at work. Mahasti seemed to care, so maybe she could be trusted.

I had to take the chance.

Had to tell someone.

At lunch, I confessed why I sipped broth instead of eating solid food. Mahasti frowned and gave sympathetic nods as I described being struck and landing in a crumpled, sobbing heap. Relief and fear simmered inside with each word I spoke, making me tremble.

"That's terrible. I'm sorry he did that." Mahasti patted my hand. "You know, you can talk to me anytime." Her eyes moved to her watch. "Oh, time to get back to work." She left me sitting alone.

Why had I even bothered? Defeat drowned my desire to ever reach out again.

No one cares.

Not the doctors or nurses.

Not the one person I considered a friend.

My mother's words from long ago rang in my ears. "You made your bed. Now you can lie in it."

For two days, I iced my jaw and did my best to ignore my husband. But no matter how hard I tried, he worked harder at earning forgiveness. Still, even the flowers he bought me seemed colorless. Helplessness set in, and every time my mind flashed back to his blow, his incriminating words accompanied it. "You hit me first."

It was true. I had hit him first.

In Vincent's relentless pursuit of absolution, he'd managed to convince me of one important fact: it was my fault.

[CHAPTER THIRTY-FOUR]

Separation

Sunlight poured through the window, but my world appeared as dark as the inside of a sealed casket. I tried to move, but my bed was like wet cement. The agonizing reality of my life sucked every drop of hope from me. Maybe if I stayed in bed long enough, it would harden into a concrete grave. Death would bring the peace and freedom I longed for.

But where would that leave my son? He needed his mother.

I had to fight for him.

If only Vincent would get help. Instead, he got angry and refused when I pleaded with him to call his counselor. Continually insisting I was the one with the problem, he said him getting help wouldn't improve our situation.

Many of my husband's words stabbed me with accuracy. Nothing I ever did was good enough. I was worthless. No one else could ever love me. No one but Vincent.

But his love was too hard.

I'd told my mother things weren't going well, and she encouraged divorce. A hopeful sound in her voice, she offered to set up a secret checking account for me to hire an attorney. But Vincent would be angry if he found out—and he *would* find out—so I told her no. She insisted anyway and said she'd send the money to Michelle.

It would take a lot more than money to get a divorce. Explaining what my marriage had become would be too humiliating after defending

Vincent like I had. Besides, between Mom living in Haiti and Vincent's constant monitoring of me, our conversations were brief and rare. Plus, I wouldn't put her life at risk—Vincent vowed to kill anyone who got in the way of our marriage. In light of his past criminal activity, his current topics of conversation, and his escalating violence, his promises deserved credence.

No one could help me.

I squashed the thought of involving the police. Vincent had made many threats about what would happen if I did: "You'll pay dearly"; "If I have to go back to prison, it'll be for murder"; and "If I'm locked up and unable to take care of you, my prison friends who are now free would be more than happy to do it for me."

Tears ran down my cheeks and pooled in my ears. I rolled over and buried my face in a pillow, recalling stories he'd told me throughout our marriage. Appalling when I first heard them, his tales now paralyzed me. His desire for revenge knew no bounds, and neither did his appetite for the adrenaline rush he got from criminal activity.

Once, he told me, he retaliated against his drug dealer for shorting him. He said he and a couple of friends loaded themselves with weapons, covered their faces with pantyhose, and broke down the guy's door. Not deterred by a houseful of armed and dangerous people, Vincent claimed he and his buddies held them up at gunpoint. It felt amazing to pull off the heist, he said, recounting how they laughed later about the shocked faces of the dealers and the amount of money they'd gotten.

He told me he'd gotten his kicks scaring people "for the fun of it" and gave accounts of robberies, expressing joy over seeing fear in people's eyes as he jacked their car or held a gun on them at an ATM. He even bragged about his ability to hot-wire a car in less than sixty seconds. My stomach had twisted and lurched as he described the thrill of creeping through houses to rob. It was the biggest blast when the people were at home, asleep in their beds, he said, because, "The heightened danger increases the adrenaline high."

Vincent told me the "best part" about being chased by the police after robbing a business was when they shot at him.

Not only was he capable of bringing terror and pain, he enjoyed it.

And he loved to scare me. Like the time he sneaked up on me with black pantyhose over his head and I screamed. Or the times he'd jump out at me, making me gasp with alarm. Each time he put a knife to my throat or thrust a blade into the wall near my face, I did my best to hide my panic, but then he taunted me all the more.

One night, Vincent told me about starting a fight during a drunken night at a roller rink as a teenager. A fight that ended with a gunshot. He laughed as he described it. "Getting me angry is a mistake. When that guy tried to leave, I followed him outside and fired my gun. He went down. With all that blood, I left him for dead."

My stomach tightened and twisted. His words disturbed me bone deep. I married a crazy man.

Vincent was definitely capable of murder.

And so were his friends.

Calling the police was off limits.

A throbbing in my head signaled the start of yet another migraine. I rubbed my temples and continued ticking off the checklist of my dreary dilemma.

Should I take my son and run?

Vincent had convinced me he held powers of omniscience and omnipotence. I believed his proclamation that I could never hide from him—he'd find me no matter what. And if I had any doubt about that, I believed his threat to force me to come home.

"After all," he said, "you'd come home for your sister's funeral, wouldn't you?"

My only choice was to somehow persuade Vincent to divorce me. Perhaps we could start with a separation. Getting him out of the house would be a victory. Baby steps to untangle the mess of our relationship. And maybe baby steps, through a trial separation, would be all we needed to rekindle our happiness. Rekindle our love.

Lil Vinny's cries snapped me out of my desolate trance.

Beaten down by despair—my demoralizing marriage, my depressing life, my dismal options—I dragged myself out of bed and trudged to the nursery.

For days, I tried to bolster my courage. How to best approach Vincent? The ideal words to say? I needed to do it when he was calm, and I had to put a positive spin on it.

Finally, the right time—if there could be such a thing—arrived. I poured us each a cold drink and sat next to him on the couch. "Sweetie, we need to talk."

He took his glass, raising it to his lips. "What is it, baby?"

"You know I love you." A lump grew in my throat, and I tried to swallow it down. "But you make it so hard."

His expression sagged along with his shoulders. "I can't help it. You make me so angry sometimes."

I took a steadying breath. "I'd like to stop making you angry, and I may have an idea." I tilted my head and put on my sweetest smile. "We should remember why we fell in love. We need time to miss each other."

He looked at me, his face contorted with confusion. "What are you saying?"

No way he'd take this well. I braced myself for an angry reaction and said it anyway. "I think we should try a separation."

He shot up from the couch, spilling his drink. "Separation?" He threw the glass against the wall, shattering it. "Are you crazy? You'll never get a divorce from me."

My stomach twisted. "Separation, not divorce. I'm trying to find a way to make us happy again."

He paced the room like a caged lion. "Oh, I see. You want a separation so you can screw around guilt-free. That'll make *you* happy."

"No. I want to look forward to seeing you. To anticipate spending time together. To be reminded of the reasons we fell in love."

He picked up my dime bank—the one that resembled a quaint country cottage—the only thing of my Gran's I received after she died. "I've always loved this."

Confused, I wondered what my priceless bank had to do with anything.

"I know you love it too. And for even suggesting I give you a chance to mess around with other guys. . ." He threw the bank at the wall, destroying it. Dimes scattered across the floor. "That's what you get. If I can't have you, no one can."

My brain raced for a way to fix this. "You don't understand. I don't want someone else. I want us to stop fighting and enjoy being together—because we want to, not because we happen to live in the same house."

His face softened slightly as he leaned toward me. "You really want us to have a better marriage?"

A seed of hope sprouted. Maybe it could actually happen. To have a loving marriage with him was all I'd ever wanted.

He squinted, apparently reading my thoughts. "Thanks, but there's no way I'm moving out."

I did my best to keep the peace after that, trying to read his moods and slip in ideas of how nice it would be to miss him. With each remark, however, he'd insist he wouldn't leave.

One morning, I brought Vincent a cup of coffee and sat next to him. "I've been trying to figure out how to make things work without either of us having to leave." I took a steadying breath. "Do you think we'd have a chance to miss each other, to fall in love again, if we slept in separate bedrooms?"

Bewildered by the ease with which he agreed, I nevertheless rejoiced over my victory. Even though his move to another bedroom equaled only a tiny piece of freedom, I'd take what I could get.

Within two weeks of his changing beds, however, Vincent's behavior became even more erratic and out-of-control.

CHAPTER THIRTY-FIVE

Means to Protect

Shrieks yanked me out of my dreams. I jumped up and raced to the nursery. Lil Vinny stood in his crib, tears streaming down his red face as he clung to the side rail. I scooped him up and held him tight. "Shhh. It's okay, Boo."

His sobbing calmed, but didn't stop. I tried everything on the Mom check-list, changing his diaper, checking his body for anything that might be irritating him, and giving anti-gas medicine. I gently bounced him and caressed his head, singing our song, "You Are My Sunshine." Then I fed him a bottle while we rocked, watching the digital clock move from 2:02 to 2:17 a.m.

Why hadn't Vincent come to see what was wrong? His bedroom was only a few feet from the nursery. He couldn't have slept through our son's fit. Still holding my baby, I went to Vincent's door and knocked. No answer. I turned the knob and pushed on the door, but it wouldn't open. "Vincent?"

Worried something was wrong, I called even louder. "Vincent? You okay?"

Silence.

After searching the house, I carried my son outside. Vincent's car was gone. The screen to his window leaned against the wall. Anger surged through me. My husband had secured his door and, like a rebellious teenager, sneaked out his window and taken off.

When my precious Boo finally settled down and fell asleep, I moved him to his crib and slipped back into bed. Three-thirty, and Vincent hadn't come home yet.

At 7:00, my son's cries woke me again. This time, I found my husband asleep in his bed. When he emerged from his room at noon, I asked where he'd been.

"Out."

I put my hands on my hips. "Out where?"

He made a face like he smelled rotting fish. "Just out."

If I gave him an answer like that, I'd be flat on my back with a knife to my throat before I could say the second word.

As the days went by, I saw less and less of Vincent. I enjoyed the freedom that came with his absences, but the double standard perturbed me. He frequently came home during the middle of the night, and a few times didn't bother returning until morning. No wonder he hadn't protested separate beds. Why *not* do whatever he wanted, while at the same time controlling my every move?

And then there was his parenting. Vincent could be a great daddy, but when a bad mood took hold, he'd snap at Lil V and say cruel things. Some days I'd come home from work and find our son still in his pajamas—his diaper weighing ten pounds—crying for food and love. When I'd ask Vincent what he'd done all day, he'd mutter something about getting caught up on his soap operas.

Although he insisted he was still taking his meds, I didn't believe him. After convincing myself I had the right to know, I searched his room.

When Vincent burst through the door that night, I braced myself to confront him.

He stomped into the den, kicking our dog out of his way. "You're not gonna believe what that jerk of a boss did. Fired me for no reason whatsoever."

Frustration and anger joined forces. How many jobs could one person lose? "What happened?"

He shrugged. "Who cares? I was tired of working there anyway."

Did I dare mention the pills? Trying to figure out what to say or not say and how to say it while watching my tone wore me out. "What are you gonna do?"

He glared at me. "You can't even give me half a second to breathe, can you? Can't you give me a frickin' break for once?"

"Tell you what, I won't mention the job again tonight if you'll explain something." Steeling myself, I held up the full prescription bottle. "You're not taking your medicine."

He snatched it from me. "What the hell were you doing in my room?"

My words tumbled out with a soft, beseeching tone. "Sweetie, I'm worried. I can tell by the way you've been acting that you're off your meds. You promised you'd take them."

He threw the bottle at me. "If you think there's too many pills in there, maybe you should take 'em." He sat on the couch, grabbed the remote, and turned on the television.

Weary of dealing with him, I turned to my son and cleaned smashed peas and carrots from his face and hands. Lil Vinny toddled straight to his father, arms reaching out to be picked up. Vincent shoved him to the floor. My baby, crying before he hit the ground, landed with a thump.

Vincent leaned forward and got in his face. "Shut the f*** up! I'm not in the mood."

"Vincent!" I ran to pick up my child and held him tight. "What's wrong with you? Don't ever do that again."

"Then make sure he doesn't bother me."

After a few days of trying to convince my husband to talk with his counselor and take his meds, I gave up. Forcing Vincent to do something he didn't want to do was like trying to stop a hurricane from reaching landfall.

At the behest of his parole officer, Vincent began his next job search. Despite minimal effort, he landed a new position within a week. Another sales job paying commission only, he was hired to sell pre-need funeral arrangements.

The next day, Vincent, in a rare mood of happiness, kissed me good-bye and headed out for work. That afternoon, as Lil Vinny and I played with a ball, I reached under the television to retrieve a stray throw. My hand landed upon something hard and rectangular.

My voice-activated recorder, set to record.

Unbelievable. My suspicious husband found yet another way to spy on me. All the times I'd seen him lying on his bed wearing a headset suddenly made sense. It wasn't a growing love for music— he'd been listening to tapes made from strategically placed recorders.

Even when I thought things couldn't get worse, Vincent continued to surprise me with erratic, outrageous behavior. Paranoia took him over. He believed people were trying to kill him. A hang-up call, a noise outside, a car driving by too slowly—all would-be assassins. Given the type of friends he had, anything was possible. But when he refused to eat Taco Bell because the unknown guy behind the counter might want to poison him, I knew things were seriously wrong.

Along with the delusions, his love of knives escalated to an obsession. Never without at least two blades on him, he constantly whittled, threw knives into the wall, and waved them in my face or held them to my throat. Once when I entered his room before receiving permission, he ran at me with a large hunting knife and buried it to the hilt in the wall, mere inches from my ear.

One day at work, I broke down and told my boss that my home life had gotten impossible. She handed me a business card for an attorney with instructions to call him.

Vincent found the card. Convinced I was planning a divorce because I was having an affair, he kicked our dog across the room. Rowdy smacked against the wall with a yelp, then fell in a motionless, silent heap.

"Rowdy!" I ran toward him, but Vincent grabbed my arm. He threw me to the ground, sat on me, and put a knife to my throat. He moved the knife with expertise, never quite breaking the skin, yet making me hold my breath for the moment he decided to press down and slash me open. With thunder in his voice and the curve of amusement on his lips, he threatened to kill me along with the imagined guy.

The pressure of his weight on my chest suffocated me. His now daily ritual of pinning me down and threatening my life with a knife to my throat stole my desire to live. The cold steel pressed so close to my carotid, I wished he'd slice through it and end my misery. My eyes moved to my dog. Was he dead? "Rowdy. . ."

"You've got bigger things to worry about than a stupid dog. If you cheat on me or leave me, I'll make you pay." His knees dug harder into my arms, the blade tighter against my skin. "If you hurt me, I'll hurt you worse. I'll bring you more pain than you could ever imagine."

I wanted to scream, push him off, spit in his face—do something, anything—yet my body and vocal cords remained frozen.

He leaned into me, breathing my air, touching his nose to mine. "If you don't believe me, try me. I'll kill your son."

Terror I'd never known ripped through me. *My* son? He's *our* son. Even though Vincent had proven the horrific things he was capable of, how could he even consider such a heinous thing? Our eyes locked. I knew he meant what he said. He could. He would. A startled gasp escaped my lips. "He's *your* son. . ."

"How do I know that?"

As if he knew it was needed, Vinny began to cry.

My husband removed himself from me. "Go take care of your brat." He went into his bedroom, slamming the door behind him.

I ran first to Rowdy. As I examined his body, he began to move. I put together pillows and a blanket and laid him gently on the makeshift bed, petting him softly as he licked my face. Then I picked up my sweet son and took care of him with all the tender love I had. "Shhh. It's okay, Boo. Mommy's here and she won't ever let anyone hurt you."

My mind raced. What *would* it take to protect him?

I had no new ideas, and none of the old ones had worked. I couldn't call the police, solicit help from someone, or run away. The only person I could rely on and trust to put my son first was me. I had to find a way to be in control. In fights with Vincent, I had as much strength as a rowboat has over the ocean. I needed something that would, for once, give me power in Vincent's eyes.

Only one thing I knew matched that description—a gun.

I'd had a gun once before. The gun Vincent had found and used during his manic crime spree. Because of the guilt I felt over him wielding my weapon and landing in jail, I promised myself I'd never have a gun in the house again. But this was different. Now I had a little boy.

I convinced Vincent I needed to go to the store before I could make dinner. On the way, I stopped at Michelle's. Her husband, Ryan, had told me several times he'd do what he could to help me. Could I trust and rely on him? Gathering courage, I told him I needed protection. I described the hang-ups, drive-bys, and noises outside our house, all contributing factors to Vincent's paranoia and my fear of his friends. I begged for a gun.

Ryan didn't like the idea, but must have seen the desperation in my eyes. Finally convinced, he handed me a .22 pistol. "Do you know how to use it?"

The tiny gun felt heavy and cold. "No, but it's not like I'm going to shoot it."

He took the weapon back. "You don't get it unless you learn how."

The need to protect my son pushed down my trepidation. "All right, then. Teach me."

"One other thing. You have to promise you will not, under any circumstances, let Vincent—either of them—get it."

An image of Vincent holding the gun on me flashed in my mind. I blinked it away. "Promise."

Then he taught me about the safety and how to load and shoot it.

[CHAPTER THIRTY-SIX]

Lost

Vincent's finger poked my chest. "Tell me where you really were."

Weary from his hour-long interrogation, I exhaled deeply. "I told you. I got lost."

He closed the space between us, his breath hot on my face. "You're lying. Someone saw you miles from there. Said you drove by on Beach Street near Alexandria."

"That's impossible." I furrowed my eyebrows. "I wasn't there. Who saw me?"

He put his hands on his hips. "Someone I trust."

"Someone who's a liar. Don't you trust me more than whoever fed you that load of bull?"

"Trust *you*?" He scoffed, then lit a cigarette and sucked on it as if trying to finish it off with one inhalation. "There's an eyewitness who saw you right near where your ex-boyfriend lives."

Exasperated, I rubbed my face. "The eyewitness is the one you can't trust."

"I always believe Matt." He blew smoke in my eyes. "Why would he lie?"

The combination of smoke and fear brought tears to my eyes. "Your brother?" An ominous feeling crept through me. Matt wouldn't lie. "Then he's mistaken. I may not remember every street I turned down, but I was nowhere near Beach and Alexandria."

He laughed. "You think Matt wouldn't recognize you?"

It didn't make sense. I hadn't been in that area for months. My brain fought to find an answer to the riddle.

"Nothing to say, huh? Because you know he wouldn't mistake someone else for you." He took another drag and again blew his smoke at me. "What were you doing there?"

His eyes, like the dark-green clouds of a brewing tornado, stirred fear in my belly. "I wasn't there. Didn't do anything. I don't know why Matt says he saw me, but I promise, he didn't."

He crushed his cigarette, then walked circles around me like a leopard assessing its prey. "You're such a whore. You went to see your ex so you could have a roll in the hay for old time's sake."

His stalking coiled my stomach tight and made me want to disappear. I couldn't fight his absurd obsession with finding me guilty of infidelity, which left no room for truth. But I opened my mouth and defended myself anyway. "You're being ridiculous."

He grabbed my wrist and twisted my arm behind my back. "Maybe the ridiculous part is thinking it was for old time's sake. Maybe you never stopped seeing him."

His words seared my heart like acid. "I haven't even talked with him since you and I started dating." His nails pierced my skin and I whimpered. "How many times do I have to tell you? I haven't been with anyone."

"Right. Not even me." He let go of my arm and studied me, his eyes roaming up and down my body. "Maybe the reason you don't want to be with me is that you're hiding something." He grabbed my blouse, ripped it open, tore my bra off. "You got a hickey or something?"

Blazing anger fueled my insides. I wanted to cover myself, but instead stood there and let him search me for signs of betrayal. Wishing he could feel the burn of my glare, I asked. "Find what you're looking for?"

"Just because there's nothing there doesn't mean you're innocent."

In a flash, I was flat on my back with him sitting on my chest. Cold steel touched my neck. The tip of a large knife glinted in my peripheral vision. My heart skipped a beat before pounding in my ears.

"How often do you sleep with him?" He clenched his jaw. "Maybe I'll kill both of you."

I wanted to shake him off, but fear held me still. One move in the wrong direction and my blood would be everywhere.

He leaned in, his nose touching mine. "Why won't you sleep with me?"

Most of the time the thought of sleeping with him was less appealing than sleeping with a bed of snakes. The months of strip searches, coerced sexual encounters, and hours of watching porn so he could try new and humiliating things had taken their toll. Instead of making me feel loved, his touches violated me.

But if I told him that truth, he'd slice the life right out of me.

My brain scrambled for something to say. A part of me did still love him. Which part or why, I didn't know. "Maybe I need a little romance." The words tasted like poison, but I forced them out. "How about you let me make us a nice dinner, and we'll watch a movie together? Then you can sleep in my bed tonight."

His face relaxed. "Really?" He moved the knife and set it down, then stroked the neck he'd nearly slit. "Is that what you want?"

I swallowed and molded my lips into a smile. "Yes. I'll make those enchiladas you like."

He climbed off me, kissing my neck as he did, then gave me a hand up. "I'll go shower." Grinning like a diplomat who'd broken the law but knew he couldn't be punished, Vincent sauntered to the bathroom.

I ran my hand across my neck. The lack of blood sent a sliver of relief through me, but a tsunami of fear smashed it to bits. How would I get through this night in a way that made him believe I wanted him?

Letting him slit my throat would be so much easier, but for my son's sake, I had to find a way.

[C H A P T E R   T H I R T Y - S E V E N]

September 15

I answered the ringing phone. When Matt's voice greeted me, anger rose. "Why would you tell Vincent you saw me when you didn't?"

"What? I told Vincent I wouldn't go along with that crap."

Confusion dampened my anger. "What do you mean, 'go along with it'?"

He sighed. "Vincent wanted to catch you in a lie, so he asked me to say I saw you near some ex-boyfriend's house. Said he figured you'd come clean if you knew you were caught. But I told him I didn't want any part of that. Told him to leave me out of it."

"Well, he didn't leave you out of it. That really ticks me off."

"Ticks me off, too." He groaned. "Dang, Leigh Ann, why don't y'all get a divorce?"

"If only it was that easy. I can't even get him to give me a separation."

"He's obsessed."

I knew it was true, but hearing Matt say it made my stomach turn. "Is he there?"

"You think I'd answer the phone if he was?"

"Good point. Have him call me."

When I gave Vincent the message, he pushed me outside so I couldn't hear their conversation. A few minutes later, he slammed through the back door, waving his fist in my face.

"Don't ever talk to that traitor again! Do you hear me? I'll kill you both if you do."

His threats on my life came so often, they no longer registered unless accompanied with a knife. Even asphyxiation meant little without a weapon. "Fine. Don't lie to me about something he supposedly said again, either."

The next day, on September 15, I was in the kitchen when I heard a knock. "Vincent! Someone's here." Afraid to answer it, I called to him twice more, but he didn't respond and the knocking continued. I reluctantly opened the door.

Matt searched me, his eyes pleading. "I'm so sorry about everything."

I backed away. "I'm not allowed to talk to you."

Matt moved past me and found Vincent in the garage. Vincent's voice came through the walls like the horn of a freight train. "I told you to never talk to her again."

Matt's much quieter voice came through just as clearly. "I didn't. I came to see you. What's your problem anyway?"

"You and that whore of a wife of mine. You're both my problem." Crashing noises. "You're not my brother anymore. Get out of here and don't ever come back."

Not wanting Lil V to hear the fighting, I took him to my bedroom. A few minutes later, the front door opened and closed. I held my breath, hoping Vincent had gone, but the bedroom door flew open and he came at me with a knife in his hand and crazy in his eyes.

"I swear I'm gonna kill you. Why can't you obey a simple command?"

My heart hammered and a chill ran through me. Knowing I had to put distance between my precious son and his raging father, I jumped off the bed and moved away. "Stay there, Vinny. Stay on the bed."

Vincent grabbed me by the arm with his free hand and slammed me against the wall, then leaned his body against me and put the knife to my throat. "Now you've gone and done it. I don't have a wife *or* a brother." He threw me to the ground, sat on my chest, and ran the knife along my cheek. "I'm gonna cut your face off, you stupid b*&@#."

My son's cries collapsed my heart. I wanted to comfort him, but Vincent's weight held my trembling body in place. Tears snaked down my face, landing on the knife. "Please. Think of our son. He's watching you."

He grabbed my hair and pulled my face toward his, then banged my head on the ground. "Did you have that traitor come over here so he could kill me? So you two could be together?"

"No." I squeezed my eyes shut. What could I say that would calm him down?

He banged my head again and shook me. "Then why'd you let him in the house? What'd you two talk about?"

"Nothing." My voice sounded far away. "He was here for you."

He moved the knife to my throat. "If he shows up again, I'll kill him before he has a chance to kill me. And I'll kill you too, right after I kill your son and make you watch."

Rage stirred within. I wanted to push him off, grab my baby and run, but the knife held me in place. I gulped down a sob and closed my eyes. Death would be so much easier than the torture of his insanity. "Why don't you just kill me now? *Please.* End my misery."

Vincent's grip on me loosened. The knife fell away from my throat.

"Someday," he whispered into my ear. "For now, I have somewhere to be."

He leaned over and kissed me. A hard, violent kiss. "You know, all you have to do is be good. If you'd be good, I'd be good. When you misbehave, it makes me crazy. Makes me want to do terrible things." He let go of me and moved to the door. "If you can't act right, I'll have to keep trying to find ways to make you learn. Better behave while I'm gone, because I have ways of knowing what you do."

As soon as he walked out of the bedroom, I rushed to my wailing son. "It's okay, Boo. You're safe now."

The front door slammed shut.

I held my baby until he fell asleep. What would it take to keep him safe? Maybe if I pretended nothing had happened, everything would be fine. Vincent would calm down and come home begging for forgiveness, like he always did.

Still trembling, I covered my son with a blanket and left him to sleep.

I moved through the messy house picking up dishes, papers, and overflowing ashtrays. I emptied my hamper, then went to Vincent's room to gather his dirty clothes. The sight of his squalor filled me with disgust. How could anyone live like this?

So much junk covered the floor that only a few spots of carpet peeked through here and there. And he'd spilled something on his bed. His sheets would have to be washed first. I kicked clothes out of the way and picked up his pillow. When I shook it out of the case, papers scattered to the floor. One was a receipt from a pawnshop. Rage bubbled up and boiled over. His wedding ring? He pawned his wedding ring?

Incredulous, I flipped through the other papers. What I saw shattered my world.

[CHAPTER THIRTY-EIGHT]
Evil Plans

Should they be killed?

Should *who* be killed? The terrifying words uncoiled and reared off the page. I felt the blood drain from my face and goose bumps erupt across my skin. I slid down the wall until I hit a pile of dirty clothes. My husband hadn't written those words. He couldn't have written those words. But it was his scrawled handwriting under the letterhead of the funeral home where he worked. This was bad. Worse than bad. This was nightmare wrapped up in reality with no chance to wake up.

> "Does back seat come down in car? Hide in trunk and come through back seat?
> Knife attached to wrist or leg?
> What to do about video cameras? Stall? Destroy? Static interference? Frequency diffuser?
> What can put in road to flatten tires. Definitely! For sure!
> What kind of distraction can use, schools, churches, houses, cars. Bomb! Fire? Where? How?
> Should I just flatten tires and get them in the parking lot, because there are no cameras.
> Places to hide.

Who carries money? Driver or passenger?

What should do with them? Flatten tires and tie up? Out of commission? Find out what car go in. All cars used.

Should I get them at their car? Hide under? Use walkie-talkies.

Will Kyle participate? Will he sit in car and listen to scanner and tell me what's going on, if anything?

Are cops involved in fires?

Look at place; figure out easy route to go to and from; figure out best way to get it, to hide; a punch from auto part store."

There was also an inventory list, with all but four of the items crossed out, as though he had already obtained them:

"Boom mike; scanner; something to flatten tires while driving; tight black gloves; license plate, rigged; change of clothes—bright colors, white; black sweats, black shirt, black shoes; gun, or (word illegible); binoculars; handcuffs, grey tape; black pantyhose; wire cutters; flashlight; change of shoes; spray paint black."

There were no detailed action points, but the overall picture was clear. What I held in my hand amounted to a six-page kidnapping plot. My husband was planning some horrible things, and I couldn't sit back and pretend like he wasn't.

Should I call the police? Again, too afraid of the potential outcome, I nixed that idea.

Call Ryan? No, too dangerous to get someone else involved.

Vincent's parole officer? As bad as calling the police, and less effective.

I had to confront him. Maybe if he knew I knew, he'd drop the whole thing. I put the notes and pillow back in the case and returned it to the bed.

CHAPTER THIRTY-NINE

September 16

Late in the evening on September 15, I heard a car door slam, jolting me to attention. My heart picked up the pace. I grabbed a novel and jumped onto the couch, opening the book to a random page. The door opened. Vincent.

Would he kill me, or kiss me?

"Hey, babe. Miss me?" Vincent sat next to me and took my hand. "I learned so much at the Amway meeting. We could make a lot of money selling this stuff."

Good mood. Maybe we could have a rational discussion about earning money legally and he wouldn't go through with his plan. "That's great. Glad you had a good time."

He put an arm around me. "Sorry about earlier. I've been so stressed out about our money problems. I want to be a better husband and provider." He sat back. "Wanna watch a movie?"

My mind reeled with his Dr. Jekyll and Mr. Hyde personalities. How did he switch so quickly from loving to vicious and back again?

He moved the pillows to the floor so we could recline in front of the television and then put a movie in the VCR. I took my place and he lay next to me, wrapping his body around mine. He kissed, caressed, and fondled me as the movie played in the background.

If a blowup doll could feel, surely this was what it would experience at the hands of its owner. Unable to concentrate on the movie, I tried to think of ways to confront him about the papers.

"Can you believe that?" His hand tightened around mine, crushing it. "That slut's cheating on her husband. If you *ever* cheat on me. . ."

"Sweetie, it's just a movie. I'd never cheat on you."

Vincent jumped up, once again barraging me with accusations. His face twisting in a myriad of emotions, he yelled obscenities and paced back and forth, screaming what he'd do to me if I embarrassed, shamed, or hurt him. Then he disappeared into the garage.

The familiar sound of knives repeatedly stabbing the wall thumped in my ears, each one another emotional blow. I cringed as I pictured the wall, already perforated with thousands of holes from previous outbursts.

Finally, the noises stopped. I tip-toed to the war zone. "What are you doing?"

Vincent glanced up at me, a large knife poised over his school yearbook, shredded pages hanging in all directions. "None of your business."

"We need to talk."

"Leave me alone." He resumed carving his yearbook.

I put my hand over my heart, wishing it would slow down. "Please come inside."

"I'm done talking with you." He hurled the knife in my direction. Seeing the knife buried to the hilt just inches from my face, I recoiled. I ran back to the living room, lit a cigarette, and tried to think past the sound of knives penetrating the wall.

Shortly after the cuckoo clock struck midnight, his assault finally ceased. It was now early morning, September 16. Mustering my courage, I again went to the garage. "Please. You're scaring me. You're acting crazy, and I don't know what to do."

"Crazy?" He came toward me with the knife in his hand. "I'll show you crazy."

Stupid. Why did I say crazy?

In a flash, he stood inches from me, eyes narrowed. "You want to get me committed or something?"

I froze. *Gotta fix this.* "No, sweetie. I just want you to get better. Maybe you could go back to your psychiatrist."

"Why do you always put everything on me? There's nothing wrong with me."

I shifted the subject. "Why don't you wear your wedding ring anymore? You say you love me and want our marriage to work, but you never wear your ring. Don't you love me?"

His face and posture relaxed. "I love you, but I'm not going to wear my ring until you let me sleep in our bed again. I'll act married when you do."

I forced a smile. "So, if I let you sleep with me tonight, will you wear it?"

His eyes studied me. I knew that expression. Had seen if many times before. He wanted to know if he could get sex and, if so, how many times.

"It would take more than once."

Stuffing the dread, I swallowed. "Okay. Do you know where your ring is?"

"In a safe place." His face darkened. Grabbing my hair, he yanked my head back. "Why you so focused on my ring? You been in my room?"

Pain shot through my scalp as he ripped hairs out. "You're hurting me."

"I'll show you hurt." He moved behind me, wrapping his left arm around my neck, choking me. "Why'd you go in my room?"

My hands clawed at his arm, trying to loosen his grip on my throat. "To do laundry."

"I told you to not go in there without my permission." His right hand came around, cutting my left forearm with the knife. "Tell me what you know."

The sight of my blood sent shivers of foreboding through me. He'd never actually drawn blood before.

He's going to kill me.

"Please. Vincent, stop." My vision faded in and out. Tears spilled down my cheeks.

He squeezed tighter, jerking my body. The knife moved to my face. "Tell me what you know, or I'll make you watch Lil V die."

Terror pulsed through me. Fix this. Gotta fix this. "Please, let's talk. I want to help. I saw your plans. I don't want you to hurt anyone. We can figure out how to pay our bills without you risking your freedom. You don't—"

"Did you call my parole officer?" Another slice to my arm. "Remember what I told you? If I go back to prison, it'll be for murder."

My mind raced. What words would make this right? "No, baby. I didn't tell anyone. It's just between us. We can work this out together."

"I don't believe you." His arm still coiled around my neck, he walked backwards, dragging me along. "I'm gonna make you pay." Cursing, he pulled me toward the dining room, my heels dragging on the carpet, then threw me on the floor between the table and couch. He sat on my chest, putting the knife to my throat. "Who'd you tell?"

"Nobody!"

He made another cut that left warm wetness trailing down my neck.

My lungs convulsed for oxygen, but the air seemed thick as mud. How could I fix this? What did he want to hear? "Vincent, stop. I love you. I swear. You have to believe me."

He moved his face to mine, sucking the air out of me with his heavy panting, his voice raging in a piercing pitch of profanities. "I don't have to believe nothing." He sat up, grabbed a drinking glass off the table, and shattered it on my head. "You're gonna tell me the truth, or you're gonna die."

Sobs punctuated each word. "Didn't. Tell. Anyone."

"We'll see." Hatred flooding his eyes, he held a pair of pantyhose. "When I get up, you're going to get under the table. If you don't"—his knife nicked my face—"I'll cut your face off."

My heart kicked like a rabbit, threatening to explode through my chest. Too afraid to make him angrier, I obeyed.

He tied my arms to the legs of the table with the pantyhose. "Tell me who you told, or watch your son die."

He really will kill him. He'll kill both of us.

My mind scrambled. *Fix this. Fix this now.* What if I told him someone knew? Would fear keep him from murder? Ryan was the only person he was afraid of. "I told Ryan, but I can fix it. Promise. Just give me—"

"I knew it." He dragged his knife across my leg. "How could you do this?" A nick to my arm. "You're gonna burn in hell." Lacerations to my other leg. "I'm gonna make you pay while I sit back and laugh." He cut the front of my shirt, then began pulling my shorts off. "I'm gonna have sex with you, and it'll be your last time." He slit my panties down the middle.

Numb. Everything went numb.

Cries erupted from the nursery, waking everything inside me.

"Vincent. Please. Let me fix it. I can do it." The words came through panicked hiccups. "Give me a chance. Listen. Our son. He's upset."

He leaned back and sat on his knees. Shaking his head, he ran his hands through his hair. "You can't fix this. No one can."

"I can." Tears ran into my mouth, garbling my words. "Let me call Ryan. I'll tell him I made it up. He'll believe me. It'll be okay."

He stared at me for a long moment, fiddling with the knife. "You fix this, and fix it good, or everyone dies. You call Ryan, and if you say one thing I don't like. . . " He leaned forward and dug the knife deep into my left thigh, gashing it wide.

A scream escaped with the searing pain. It was now nearly one in the morning, and my son's cries increased to wailing.

"That's what I'll do to your neck, right after you watch everyone you love die."

Every thought, every emotion, every action focused on one thing— the means of survival for me and my baby. "I can do this. I can fix it."

He leaned forward and cut me loose. I scooted out from under the table. My shorts, clinging to my leg wound, blossomed red.

I took three deep breaths and forced words through my constricting vocal cords, trying not to blow my one chance to get the gun from the nursery. "Can I settle Lil V down first? Ryan will know something's wrong if he hears him screaming."

Vincent's face tightened, and so did his grip on the knife.

I held my breath awaiting his verdict.

"Fine, but be quick." He stood and helped me up.

My heart rocketed faster and faster with each step I took toward victory. But one look at my baby standing in his crib, tears streaming down his face, broke my heart. I wanted to hold him, comfort him, but had to protect him from his homicidal father in the other room. "Sorry, Boo. You have to hang on." My eyes locked on the closet. Fingers reached for the hiding place. Cold steel brought comfort as I wrapped my hand around the gun.

With shuddering breaths and jerky limbs, I advanced down the hallway in a trance. Pointed the gun at my husband. "Get. Out. I'm calling the police. "

Still holding the knife, Vincent's eyes went wide, then just as quickly he relaxed into a smile. He took a step toward me. "You don't have the guts."

The weight of the weapon gave me courage, but not enough to keep my hands from trembling like fine china in a stampede. "Don't want to shoot you. Just want you to leave."

He laughed. "I'm not going anywhere. Give me the gun, or I'll take it. You don't have it in you, but I do."

"Leave. Now. Please." Sobs broke my voice.

Still laughing, he continued toward me. "You wouldn't."

Wanting some control, to make him feel fear, I pointed the gun away from him and pulled the trigger. The loud noise, the kick to my hand, the fire that shot out of it shocked my senses, making me almost drop the gun. Vincent stood still, eyes big as silver dollars.

In a split second he went into action, coming at me fast. "You crazy. . . You could have killed me."

Don't let him get the gun. Don't let him get it. Don't let him. . . My hands locked onto the weapon. He tugged at it. I squeezed my eyes shut and yanked. He pulled. Time moved in disjointed fragments, like a radio station going in and out.

An ear-splitting noise.

And another one.

My son's screams pierced through the ringing in my ears.

Too afraid to move, the gun still in my hands, no one threatening to tear it away, I opened my eyes. Vincent leaned against the wall, his back toward me. A quick move, and he ran toward the door.

The front door crashed open.

I dropped the gun and collapsed.

My baby crying. *My baby.* I picked myself up and ran to the door. Fast forward and slow motion all at once. Slammed it shut. Locked it. Bolted to the nursery. "Boo!" Cradling him in my arms, I sat with him in the rocking chair, snuggling, kissing, shushing him. As his cries calmed, I heard my husband.

"Help. . . Leigh Ann. . . help me. . . Leigh Ann."

I put Lil V back in his crib and scrambled to the front door, grabbing the cordless phone on the way. The lifeline in my hand, I peered through the peephole. My husband lay crumpled in the front yard, the ten feet between us inches and miles at the same time. Afraid it was a trick, I cracked the door, bracing my foot behind the hollow aluminum barrier.

Shock injected itself like anesthesia into each beat of my runaway heart.

"Help. Me. Leigh Ann. . . *h-e-l-p.*" Vincent's voice, a low, wheezy whisper, strained across the porch.

Instinct took over. I staggered outside. Dropped the phone. Pulled on his arm. Tried to make him stand. Why was he so heavy?

His breathing was wrong. His skin was pale. His lips were blue.

"Vincent?" I fell to my knees, fumbling in the dim light of the waning moon, my hands frantic, racing across his body. Seeking. Searching for something. Anything.

Wet. His shirt was wet. I ripped it open.

My fingers settled on a perfectly round hole in his stomach surrounded by blood.

Dear God. A gunshot wound.

"Vincent, no!" The stabbing pain of nerves coming to life shook me. My mind blurred. "Vincent? Stay with me. I'm getting help."

He coughed. "Leigh. . . Ann." His voice sounded far off. Strange.

Every cell in my body shuddered. "Stay with me." I grabbed the phone and dialed.

"Nine-one-one. State your emergency."[1]

"Please! Help! Need"—my breaths came out in frantic panting—"police. Ambulance."

"What's your problem, ma'am?"

No, no, no! Desperate. Panicked. On full speed forward. "I gotta go." Every breath fast, short, clipped.

"Ma'am, don't hang up on me. I need to know why you need the police."

"I've gotta go." My voice near hysteria, my mind already there.

"Ma'am. . ."

Oh my God, my husband's. . . "shot." I wasn't sure where my frenzied thoughts ended and spoken words began.

Think, think. What can I do?

"Who has been shot, ma'am?"

"Husband." I applied pressure to his wound with shaky hands.

"Calm down, ma'am. How did he get shot, ma'am?"

"I cannot do this. . ." and stay on the phone. Vincent's eyes rolled back. His face grew gray. Moans, groans, and gurgles emitted from his open mouth, barely audible above my own agitated movements and heavy panting.

"I need to know how he got shot, ma'am."

"What?" No, no, no. Oh my God, this is bad. So, so bad. Please, no. Clutching the phone as though I could force help through it, I rocked back and forth on my knees.

"How did he get shot?"

Pant, pant. Why did that matter? We need an..."ambulance" *now.* "Okay? I gotta go. I have to go. My husband is dying."

"What is your name?"

"Leigh Ann Bayshore. I have to go." My husband needs me. I need to take care of him. I have to fix this.

"Where is your husband now?"

Why so many questions? Why couldn't she let me get back to him? "Front yard. In the front yard."

"Where was he shot? Where on the body was he shot?"

"Abdomen." His moans increased. My own groan of agony bursting from deep within.

"Ma'am, you need to calm down and we'll get an ambulance now and the police."

"I've got to start CPR." Have to be with my husband.

"Who shot him?"

"What?" *Why is she keeping me on the phone? My husband needs me.* "Listen, I have to go. I have to do CPR."

"We'll get the ambulance out there."

"Okay, okay, thank you." I hung up and shook Vincent. "Vincent! No! Stay! Vincent?"

His moaning increased through gurgling and sputtering breaths. Then out came a horrible gurgling sound.

The death rattle.

I gathered my husband in my arms. Clutched his lifeless hand. No, no, no! "No! Vincent! Don't die. I love you. Hang on. Help's coming."

Vincent moaned again, but his body remained still.

What do I do? What do I do? Ryan's words came back to me. "Call me if you need anything, day or night."

Shaking fingers dialed the number. Ryan's sleepy voice answered.

"Help... called 911."

Silence.

"Ryan? Hello?"

Pink foam dribbled from Vincent's mouth. I dropped the phone and put my face to his. He blew his last breath onto my cheek.

"No! Vincent!"

I moved his head from my lap and leaned over him, filling his lungs with my air.

No pulse.

I slammed my fist onto his chest, hoping to restart his heart.

Still no pulse. "Vincent, no!"

Kneeling beside him, I began compressions. "Can't. Do. This. To. Me." Pump, pump, pumping his chest, I begged him to live. My heart beat fast enough for both of us, but his remained still. "Our. Son." *Please live, please live.*

My tears wet his face as I tried to breathe life back into him.

Back to his chest. "No, no, no." Pumping, pumping, pumping with everything inside me. "Baby. Sorry. So. Sorry. I. Love. You."

[C H A P T E R F O R T Y]

Lies

Flashing blue lights pulsated, stabbing the darkness. I leapt to my feet. "Help! Over here. Please help."

The police officer hustled toward me as I bent over my husband to continue.

He kneeled next to me. "Does he have a pulse?"

I filled my lungs and forced air into Vincent's lungs. "No." I sobbed. "Please help."

He pressed his fingers to Vincent's neck and leaned over his face for what felt like too long. "You breathe. I'll do compressions."

With someone there to help, something inside let go. As if I'd been robotically doing what needed to be done because I was all Vincent had, my automated responses fell apart. Reality pressed me down, my insides imploding into shattered bits.

"Breathe for him!" The officer's voice commanded. Angry.

I bent over Vincent again. Moved my mouth to his. Smashed our teeth together. Sat up and watched in a daze as the officer pumped Vincent's chest.

"Breathe!" The officer pushed my arm. "Give him a breath!"

Vincent needs you. Two more breaths, this time managing to keep our teeth apart.

We continued the exhausting rhythm until red lights finally arrived.

Firefighters removed equipment from the truck and raced toward us. One of them pulled me away from my unmoving husband. "We've got this, ma'am."

Numbness invaded, throbbing through me as the men took over.

"Who shot him?"

Where had the voice came from? I looked around. "What?"

"Ma'am." An officer waved his hand in my face. "Who shot your husband?"

Lost inside myself, I stared openmouthed. *Who shot him?* I swallowed and tried to think, but fog clouded my brain. I looked at my husband. So empty. So hollow. Pretending to be harmless. But he couldn't fool me. He'd find a way to make me pay if I told what he'd done.

"Ma'am? Can you hear me?"

An image formed in my head: Vincent handcuffed to a hospital bed, ranting and raving about my betrayal and how his friends would take care of me. *Even if he dies, I'll never be free. He'll haunt me forever.*

The images evolved into one of my son. My innocent baby all grown, crushed and broken with thoughts of what his father had become. Angry at me for shooting him. How could I tell him? How could he live with the truth?

Hands shook me. "Ma'am, who shot your husband?"

Words wouldn't take shape. *Think.* What do I do? Another image formed: Handcuffs on my wrists. Taken into custody. Away from my son. What would happen to my baby? My mouth, a dried-up sponge, refused to let me utter the words the officer wanted to hear.

"Ma'am, was it the same guy who cut you?"

Cut me? My eyes moved to my legs. Blood. Lots of blood. I remembered the large slash Vincent made on my thigh, the nicks to my neck, face, arms. I couldn't tell them he did this to me. He'd make me pay if I did.

The fog lifted. *That's it.* The guy who shot my husband was the same guy who cut me. Someone else did this. My husband was the hero—not the bad guy. My mouth opened on its own. "Yes." The story formed in my head so clearly it felt real. Words found their way out. "Yes. The guy who cut me."

"Where is he?"

Confused, I stared at the officer. "Where's who?"

"Where's the guy who shot your husband?"

"He"—I waved my arm—"ran away. Gone. Out the back door."

"Wilson," he called to another officer. "Let's check the house."

"My baby." Sobs escaped as tears flowed down my cheeks. "I need my baby."

"Where's your baby?" the second officer asked.

"His crib. The nursery."

The officers drew their guns and entered my house, followed by two other armed men in blue. I watched my husband as four firefighters worked on him. My chest pounded with each compression. The ambulance arrived.

I rubbed my eyes. Nothing felt real. This couldn't be happening. Could it?

A hand grabbed my arm. I stared at it, then traced it to its origin, the officer who had helped me with CPR.

He began walking me, helping me move my feet. "My name's Officer Stiles. What's your name?"

"Leigh Ann."

"Okay, Leigh Ann. Let's go inside so we can talk."

Three officers were there, one holding my son. I moved toward him, but a hand pulled me back.

"I want my son."

Another officer entered the house. "Her sister's here."

Michelle? How? A tingle of comfort brushed through me. *The phone call to Ryan.* "Can I see her?"

Officer Stiles shook his head. "Not yet. Can she take your baby?"

Aside from me, no one loved Lil Vinny more than Michelle. "Yes. Of course."

The officer holding my son took him toward the front door, making a wide arc to keep distance between us. I tried to reach out to him, but he was too far away for my touch. "Mommy loves you, Boo." My mouth so dry, the words came out sticky. I blew kisses at him as he disappeared.

I began moving to the kitchen, but once again, a hand stopped me.

"What are you doing?"

I tried to swallow, but my tongue stuck to the roof of my mouth. "Drink of water."

"Have a seat." Officer Stiles edged me onto the couch. "Officer Kline has some questions for you. I'll get you water."

The cool wetness felt good, but when I emptied the glass, the dryness remained. I held the glass up. "More please?"

From across the room, I saw my cigarettes. I stood to get them, but once again a hand stopped me. I spoke to the new cop, Officer Kline. "I need a cigarette."

"Where are they? I'll get you one."

Irritation pricked me. "Why won't you let me. . . why are you treating me like this?"

He cocked his head. "Like what, Leigh Ann?"

"Like I'm in trouble or something. You won't let me do anything."

"You're not in trouble. Why? Should you be?" His voice held condescension.

"No." My nerves tingled. *Does he know I'm lying?* "But the way you're treating me. . ."

"I'm sorry." Officer Kline's shoulders relaxed. "I don't mean anything by it. You're not in trouble. Not at all. You're a victim. And a witness. And we don't want you to contaminate the crime scene." He placed his hand on my arm. "Now, where are your cigarettes?"

Crime scene? The words chilled my heart. "Over there."

He brought them to me, keeping hold of my lighter. I fumbled to remove one, to get it to my lips, to hold it steady as he lit it, then inhaled as if my life depended on it. The cool smoke worked its magic.

"Leigh Ann, I need you to tell me what happened."

I took another drag and looked at my bloody leg.

Officer Kline followed my gaze. "We need paramedics in here."

"No," I said. "My husband needs them. How's he doing?" A paramedic approached. I waved him off. "I'm fine. Help my husband. How is he?"

The paramedic flicked his eyes to Officer Kline before answering. "There are plenty of guys out there helping. Let's look at your leg."

I pushed his hands away. "How's my husband? You need to—"

"We don't know," Officer Kline interrupted. "But for now, you're bleeding. Let the guy do his job."

Giving in, I allowed the paramedic to bandage me, but refused transport to the hospital.

"You need stitches," the paramedic said.

"No." I raised my voice. "Later. How's my husband?"

The paramedic looked at Officer Kline again. "I'll go check."

"Okay, Leigh Ann, you were telling me what happened," Officer Kline said.

I closed my eyes and imagined the version where the violence hadn't come from my husband. So practiced at lying to protect Vincent, words tumbled out about an intruder forcing his way in, tying me up, cutting me, Vincent saving me. When I finished and opened my eyes, another officer was talking into Officer Kline's ear. Not able to hear him, I reached for my cigarettes. Before I could get one out, the policeman, still exchanging whispers with the other officer, had the lighter waiting.

Allowing the nicotine to soothe me as they whispered, I worried about Vincent. "How's my husband?"

The unknown officer walked away and Officer Kline ignored my question. "Leigh Ann, I need to ask some questions about your story."

Story? Did he know it was a lie? I gulped. "Okay."

He asked questions, and without any conscious thought, I spit out lies to fill in the holes.

"Leigh Ann"—he put his hand on my shoulder—"was Vincent abusive?"

A dagger pierced my heart. *He knows.* "Why. . . would you ask that?" My words came out weak and shaky.

He frowned. "Sometimes when an abusive husband gets out of control, the victim takes action. I'm wondering if it's possible that's what happened here."

My already numb body froze. My lungs wouldn't work, but my heart hammered. I wanted to run. To hide. But even if the room hadn't been occupied with armed policemen, my legs were paralyzed.

Time to tell the truth. Yes. I did it. My husband was crazy. I opened my mouth, but the words remained super-glued to my tongue. I closed my mouth and opened it again to try once more. "Am I a suspect?"

He leaned back. "No. I told you. You're a witness and a victim. That's all."

Although my body felt like it moved through molasses, my mind worked double-time. Surely if he thought I did it, if I were a suspect, he'd have to read me my rights. "You don't believe me?"

I watched his reaction for any sign of disbelief. All he had to do was give me one inkling of doubt or skepticism, and I'd tell him the truth.

His face softened. "I didn't say I don't believe you—I'm just asking what needs to be asked."

At that moment, I made a promise. If at any point anyone showed disbelief or read me my rights, I'd tell the truth. Swallowing, I spoke with tiny words. "I didn't do it."

"Okay then."

"Please. . ." I begged. "How is my husband?"

An elongated pause, an enduring stare, as if the officer wanted to make me wait for the words and study my reaction. "I'm sorry, Leigh Ann. He didn't make it."

I fell back, my heart ripped out of my chest and torn in two. I buried my face in my hands and wailed.

[CHAPTER FORTY·ONE]
Statement

"Time to go." Officer Kline touched my shoulder.

My mind and body separate, each moving independently in a dark, groundless, sphere. The edges of my vision dark as death, I looked at the officer. His lips moved, but sound didn't reach me. My ears hummed with eerie silence. *My husband is dead.*

Is this real?

He began to move toward my bedroom, then turned back. "Leigh Ann, did you hear me? We need to get you a change of clothes."

"Change of clothes?"

"We're going to need what you're wearing. Where can we find some clothes?"

I tried to think, but his words didn't make sense. *My husband is dead.*

Officer Kline grabbed another policeman, sending him into my room on the errand. "We need to go to the station now."

The policeman returned with clothes. Kline took them and lifted me by my elbow. "We'll go in my car."

He escorted me outside. What I saw brought my insides to a crashing halt. My husband, covered with a sheet, his sneakered feet poking out. Unable to move, I stared at him. At my dead husband. *How is this possible? How is my husband dead?*

Officer Kline stepped over his body and held his hand out. "Leigh Ann, come on."

My mind replayed the officer stepping over his body. My husband's dead body. "You. . . you didn't take him to the hospital?" They didn't even try to save him. An ache in my chest spread to my fingers and toes. I fixed my eyes on my dead husband. Imagined him bolting upright, pantyhose covering his face, grabbing my legs, laughing at my fear.

Instead of stepping over him, I walked around.

I sat in the passenger seat of the squad car, hugging my legs to my chest. *My husband is dead.* "Mommy"—I rocked back and forth—"I want my mommy." My voice broke and tears cascaded down my face, landing on the bloody bandage covering my thigh.

At the station, Officer Kline brought me to the forensics investigator for evidence collection. He added drops of something to a cotton swab and ran it along the webbing and back of my right hand, thumb, and index finger, then used another for the palm and fingers.

As he repeated the process for my left hand, my mind replayed the image of my dead husband, covered with a sheet, his feet poking out.

Next, the man took pictures of the knife wounds on my face, neck, forearms, and right leg. Then he had me remove the bandages on my leg and upper left arm to record the deeper cuts.

A female officer escorted me to the bathroom and handed me my clean clothes. "Change into these. We need everything you're wearing."

I looked at the T-shirt and shorts as though they were props from the Twilight Zone. "*Everything?*"

"Everything."

She took my bloody clothing and put them in brown paper bags.

Although uncomfortable and cold without panties and a bra, the idea of walking around barefoot did me in. I pointed at my naked feet. "Can't I keep my shoes?"

"We'll find something else for you."

She closed the bags and secured them, then wrote on the labels and handed the packages to the investigator. Another policeman walked me to an office where a man sat behind a desk.

He stood. "Hello, Leigh Ann. I'm Detective Dutch. I'll be taking your statement."

An overwhelming numbness gripped me. I needed Vincent to comfort me with his love like he always did after a fight. Aching for his hold, I wanted to lie down and shroud myself with a blanket. "My husband is *dead.*" Anguish warbled my voice.

The detective's face shifted. Softened. "Can I get you something? Coffee?"

I nodded. "And a cigarette."

He smiled. "You know, you're right. Let's get you taken care of."

Another officer poked his head through the door. "I know these aren't great, but here's some shoes." He handed me a pair of hard rubber slip-ons. "It's what we give the inmates."

I didn't like the idea of wearing something meant for a criminal, but put them on.

Detective Dutch thanked him and stood. "Let's go outside."

While I smoked, the detective told me how sorry he was for my loss. I tried to believe him, but as I stared at the prisoner shoes, his words seemed hollow.

Back inside, he got us coffee before returning me to his office.

I inhaled the aroma. Took a sip. The hot liquid traveled down my throat and splashed into my stomach. At least I could feel something.

Detective Dutch folded his hands beneath his chin. "Better?"

"I guess, but maybe I should get stitches now."

He glanced at the blood-soaked bandage on my leg. "We'll do that after I get your statement."

After? "Am I in trouble?"

He gave a slight smile. "Not at all. You're a victim and a witness, so we have to get your statement."

My voice listless with shock, I answered questions, gave details, made up lies. When my blood began dripping on the floor, I pointed it out to him. "Can I go to the hospital now?"

He handed me paper towels and masking tape for the bleeding, then refilled my coffee and suggested another break.

Too tired to argue, I did my best with the makeshift bandages and followed him outside, my feet shuffling in the awkward shoes.

He watched me smoke as he talked about my husband. The detective wondered, given Vincent's criminal record, how violent he was.

What could I say? *You don't know one-tenth of what he's done.*

"Did you know he had a warrant out for his arrest?"

That brought me to attention. "A warrant? For what?"

"A moving violation he never took care of."

Is that all? The night he got the ticket came back to me. He'd yelled and cursed at me and threatened to drive the car into an embankment in such a way that I'd get killed and he'd be spared. He'd sped up and pulled onto the shoulder to go around traffic, heading toward the concrete wall too fast, coldly telling me how easy it would be to make my death look like an accident. As I prepared myself for the impending impact, blue lights flashed behind us. I'd never been so happy to be pulled over.

I reminded him over and over to take care of the ticket. He told me he had.

Detective Dutch continued. "I'm curious to know what kind of guy would let a ticket go to warrant when he's on parole." He moved closer and looked at me with sympathy before confessing he and the entire police department believed I was better off without Vincent. In fact, he declared, the city was better off without him.

His words stunned me. Did he know I did it and was telling me it was all right? I crushed out my cigarette. "Why would you say such a thing?"

He shrugged. "Guess I thought you should know what people are saying."

I didn't want those jail shoes to be my fate, but wondered if it was time to tell the truth. So far, though, no one had read me my rights.

Back in his office, the detective continued asking questions. My answers came in a monotone voice, with flatlined emotions, as if giving a running commentary of a horror film I'd seen a long time ago. After another hour, I'd gone through the whole stack of paper towels, making a bloody mess. "I really think I need to go to the hospital now."

He finally agreed. "All right. I'll take you."

As we walked through the building, my brother Mike rushed to me and gave me a hug. His arm still wrapped around me, he turned to the detective. "What's going on?"

Detective Dutch gestured in the direction of my bloody leg. "She needs stitches."

"I'll take her," Mike said. "She's not under arrest, is she?"

Detective Dutch shifted his weight. "No, but—"

"Good. Let's go, Leigh."

The detective didn't seem to like the idea. "I guess it's okay. I'll follow you."

"Whatever." Mike led me to his truck, opened the passenger door, and helped me in. "You okay?"

His comforting protection touched my heart and made the tears start again. "No." My voice cracked and body crumpled with that one syllable.

His chest heaved. "Michelle said you shot Vincent."

My insides cringed. I wanted to tell him the truth, but couldn't. "That's not what happened."

As he drove to the hospital, I spilled out the story I'd told the police.

In the emergency room, a woman approached me with admission questions. After the usual name, address, and phone number, she asked, "Married, single, or divorced?"

Wailing, I buried my face in my hands and curled into the fetal position. What was I now? *A widow by my own doing.* I shuddered.

Detective Dutch responded. "Her husband was murdered tonight."

Murdered? I wanted to scream he was wrong. He died, yes, but it wasn't murder. All I could do was weep.

After the nurse cleaned my wounds and gave me a tetanus shot, the doctor examined me. Too apathetic to react to the pain, I remained quiet as he dug his finger into my thigh wound to see how deep it was.

The doctor stripped his gloves off and threw them into the trash. "This should staple up fine." He donned sterile gloves and began his work—without first deadening the gashed area. Each staple sent a jolt of pain through my thigh. At least the pain was preferable to the detached numbness that had overtaken me. When he finished, twenty staples held my wound closed.

The still-bleeding wound on my arm also required stitches, but the busy doctor decided steri-strips would suffice. Before I left, the nurse handed me a prescription for pain medication and an antibiotic.

"All right," Detective Dutch said. "Let's get back to the station to finish your statement."

Mike scrunched up his face. "You're kidding, right? She's been there for hours, and it's six in the morning. My sister's been through enough for now and needs some rest."

The detective's face twitched. "I think we should finish."

"I'm sure that's what's best for you," Mike said, "but I'm thinking about my sister. So, unless you're arresting her, I'm taking her to my house."

Detective Dutch hesitated, but finally agreed after getting Mike's address and phone number. Before walking ten feet away, the detective returned, saying he needed a description of the intruder.

My mind froze. "I, uh, didn't really see him."

"Anything is helpful." He poised his pen over paper. "What was he wearing?"

Anxiety raced through me. I didn't want anyone getting arrested based on my description. Remembering what Vincent told me about crimes he'd committed, I described his gear of choice. "Black. He wore all black."

"Hair color?"

"He, um... had black pantyhose over his head. I couldn't see anything."

"Race?"

I thought of Vincent's friends. I didn't want any of them to be suspects. He had white friends and Hispanic friends, but no black friends that I knew of. "I couldn't really tell. I guess he could have been black."

"Hmm. Okay then. Thanks. If you think of anything else, let me know."

Why hadn't I considered the description of the so-called intruder sooner? And why did the police wait five hours to ask?

At my brother's house, I went to see Lil V. His sleeping form seemed so at peace. So oblivious to the devastation of the night, which for him was nothing more than a lot of yelling and crying, a loud bang, and his Aunt Michelle putting him to bed at his Uncle Mike's house. Not wanting to shatter his dreamy innocence, I knelt close and watched him, singing and caressing his back. Mike's wife, Shari, brought me a pillow and blanket. After thanking her for everything, I collapsed onto the couch. My heart troubled and restless, my mind confused between reality and fantasy, I tried but failed to sleep.

A loud knock resounded on the door. Mike opened it to Detective Dutch and another officer.

"We need Leigh Ann back at the station," Detective Dutch said.

"You said she could rest." Mike's voice was stern.

The detective stared Mike down. "But now we have more questions."

Mike's arms crossed his chest. "Is she under arrest?"

"No, but if she cares about solving this, we need her to come now."

Mike turned to me. "Leigh, you up for that?"

I was petrified, but wanted it to be over. "If it will help."

Although Mike and Ryan wanted to go with me, the officers said no.

While getting ready to sign the final draft of my statement, an officer poked his head into the detective's office. "Her attorney's here."

"Her attorney?" Detective Dutch looked at me. "Did you hire an attorney?"

Confused, I shook my head.

"She says she's your attorney and wants to talk to you."

The detective slammed his hands on his desk before telling the officer to let the woman know I didn't hire an attorney and she wasn't needed.

My mind tried to focus. Why would someone say she was my attorney? How would she know to ask for me? "Maybe I should find out what she wants."

The detective scowled as the door opened wide and the woman appeared, grim-faced. "I need to talk with my client. This interview is over."

Detective Dutch huffed as he left his office.

The woman, whose name was Anne, sat next to me. "Leigh Ann, you need to keep your mouth shut. Don't say another word to anyone, and don't sign anything."

"But why? I'm not a suspect. They told me so. They said I'm a victim and witness."

Anne peered down her nose at me like I was a slow-minded child. "Don't fool yourself. You're not only a suspect; you're the *only* suspect. I'm taking you to your brother's, and you seal your lips from now on. Especially when it comes to your family. They'll be the first ones called to testify against you."

Testify against me? This woman was crazy. "Why are you here?"

"Your mother wanted to hire an attorney. Since she's in Haiti, your brother took care of it. Called my husband, George, but he couldn't make it so he sent me. We're both attorneys." She stood. "Now, let's go."

Anne drove me to Mike's and went inside with me, telling my family to not ask any questions and not let me talk about what happened. Being mostly law-enforcement and government employees, they obeyed.

Alone in my misery, I kept the painful truth to myself.

CHAPTER FORTY-TWO

Arrangements

The dark-suited man sat across from me, asking question after question. How did he expect me to answer anything now? My hands shook, my stomach churned, and my head? It didn't work right.

When my mother and brother answered the next few questions, I gratefully stayed silent and let them and Vincent's parents take over. Until they got to the casket. And the man insisted on my input and led us all to a huge room full of boxes. Boxes for dead people.

I froze in the doorway. "Isn't there a catalog instead?"

"No," the man said. "Choosing the right casket for a loved one is an experience. You need to use touch and smell as well as sight."

My feet moved toward the beds of death only because my mother guided me. I didn't want to experience touching and smelling caskets. A horror-filled reality swept over me. I was here to shop for a box in which to bury my husband. His death was my fault. The caskets taunted me with whispers.

Do you want brown, gray, or maroon for your dead husband's new home? The home he needs because you killed him.

Are you going to go cheap? Or get a nice one to ease your guilt over killing him?

Each casket had something to say. Their accusing voices overwhelmed me.

My breathing and heart rate galloped faster and faster, as if racing each other to a finish line I hoped not to cross. I wanted to faint, to vomit, but forced myself to go deeper into the macabre room. Then I spotted it. A tiny, blue casket meant for a baby. *I could have been here for that one.* My knees buckled—I had to either fall to the ground or run.

I bolted. Out of the oppressive room, down the hall, past the receptionist with her mouth gaping open, through the double doors. Outside, I collapsed. I buried my face on a concrete seat and took a lungful of fresh air. Sobs rushed from me as I shook. I yanked open my purse, frantically digging for cigarettes. Lipstick, compact, wallet, I turned the purse over, dumping the contents. Just as my quivering fingers managed to get a cigarette out of the pack, my mother-in-law stepped through the door.

Mara sat on the ground next to me and held me in her arms. Rubbing my back and rocking me gently, she gave comfort with her words, saying everyone was there for me.

I lit my cigarette and took a grateful inhalation. Let it out. Would she be here for me if she knew the truth?

We cried together before returning inside. My mother approached and said all I had to do was sign some papers. I nodded and looked at my hands. Hands that had taken my son's father away from him.

Suit-man put his elbows on the desk and made a steeple with his fingers. "We have a bit of a problem. Since there's an ongoing murder investigation, the life insurance company won't release the money for the funeral."

Shock waves pulsed through me. "What?"

"This is fairly common." He tilted his head. "I'm sure they'll come through in the end, but for now, we need some sort of payment."

Tens of thousands of dollars in debt already, the best I could do was write a hot check.

Before coming to the funeral home, my sister had suggested I call my husband's employer. Since Vincent had sold funeral arrangements, maybe there would be some kind of employee discount. Besides, they needed to know he wouldn't be returning to work. Brushing aside thoughts of how morbid it was, I'd called.

The lady who answered took Vincent's name. After a pause, she said, "Ma'am, he hasn't worked here for over a month."

"Mrs. Bayshore?" The suit-man cleared his throat, dragging me back to the business of my dead husband. "Do you have your checkbook?"

In spite of the coolness of the room, the air was stifling, suffocating, still, as if it came from the bottom of a cave. "I, uh"—my voice cracked—"I'm broke."

Suit-man's lip twitched. He looked at each person in our group, then back at me, waiting.

Awkward silence filled the room, broken only by my whimpering. My mother put her hand around my shoulder. "Don't worry, sweetheart, I'll take care of it."

I'd never be able to repay her. Not only did she fly home from Haiti to be with me through this, she was paying for Vincent's funeral.

Back at Mike's house, Mom forced me to eat. After three bites, I ran to the bathroom and threw up.

Michelle agreed to watch Lil V while my mother and her sister, Ursula, who flew in from New York, took me shopping for the wake and funeral. When we had purchased what we needed, we drove to my house. A crime scene for two days, the police had finally released it back to my custody. I didn't want to go in, but convinced myself it'd be better to get started now with my family's help rather than tackle it alone later.

Noxious odors assaulted me. Chemicals, blood, and gunpowder swirled together, combining into an ammonia-coppery-sulfuric stench.

Fingerprint ink blackened doors, walls, countertops, furniture, and toys. Near the back entrance, someone had cut out a section of sheetrock six-inches wide that ran the entire height of the door.

The vacuum lay on its side, its bag missing. Drawers had been pulled out and dumped everywhere. The items from my coat closet covered the couch, while the cushions haphazardly littered the floor.

Papers lay scattered across the kitchen table. Patches of carpet had been ripped up. Kitchen cabinets stood open, their contents strewn about the countertops.

In my bedroom, more fingerprint ink—on the bed, the sheets, the dresser, the safe, my makeup table, and mirrors. My personal belongings were splayed out on the bed, floor, and dresser, and my tangled clothes hung from the drawers as if strangled.

Overwhelmed by yet another violation of my life, I wanted to curl into a ball and weep, but couldn't find one square foot not covered with debris. Instead, I buried my face in my hands and filled them with anguished tears.

For hours, my mother and aunt helped me do laundry, fold clothes, file papers, return dishes to cabinets, and wipe surfaces as clean as possible.

Gathering my courage, I opened the door to Vincent's room and peered in. Unable to distinguish Vincent's usual chaos from damage done by the police, I dug in. I found eight knives, four flashlights, a twelve-pack of beer, and another dozen empties, plus paraphernalia for shooting up drugs. Surprise filled me when I located the papers that started all of this. How had the police missed them? Unsure what to do with them, I decided to hide them under his mattress.

There I discovered a bottle of Vicodin containing thirty-two pills. Rationalizing my emotional suffering was worse than the pain from the knife wounds, I took two. Knowing the emotional pain wouldn't stop anytime soon, I emptied the rest into my pocket, figuring I'd add them to the bottle I'd received from the emergency room physician.

Thirty minutes later, just as a comforting numbness began circulating through my blood, my mother announced it was time to get ready for the wake. We went back to my sister's, and I got myself and my son dressed in our new black clothes.

On the way to the funeral home, I buried my face in my mother's chest. "I can't believe he's dead."

She lifted my face so that our eyes met. "I'm just glad it's over."

Over? This would never be over.

[CHAPTER FORTY-THREE]

Services

My heart thumped twice with each tick of my watch. Flanked by my mother and aunt, I stared at the doorway and swallowed the rising bile. "I can't do this."

"We'll do it with you," Mom said.

Unable to cross the threshold on my own, I allowed them to pull me into the room. I sensed people watching me. When we'd made it halfway to the open casket, my husband's face came into view. My feet refused to move closer, as though hands came through the floor and held them. "I can't."

Mom's grip tightened. "We're right here. You can do it."

I walked through quicksand, my mother and aunt moving one foot and then the other under the strength of their love.

From two feet away, Vincent's chest came into focus. My head swam as I watched for movement, but he remained still. *He's not breathing.* His serene expression gave the impression of sleep. But a sleeping person would breathe. *He's not breathing, and it's all my fault.*

Inches from his casket, I looked down at the man I still loved. Any second now, he'd open his eyes and sit up, strangling me or putting a knife to my throat. My lips trembled. I covered them with shaking hands. *He's going to make me pay for this.*

My mother hugged me and whispered into my ear, "He can't hurt you anymore."

I considered her words. He looked harmless, but I knew what he was capable of. Not only could he still hurt me, he would. I reached out and touched his hand. A hand both gentle and harsh. It felt cold, stiff, and completely unfamiliar. Could this be a wax likeness? The real Vincent hiding, waiting for the right time to make me pay?

I studied his peaceful face, running my fingers through his hair. Memories of good times swept over me, crumpling me to the floor.

My mother and aunt assisted me to the kneeling bench in front of the casket. Squeezing my shoulder, my mother leaned forward. "We'll give you some privacy."

Alone with my dead husband, I fell across him and wept. "Oh, Vincent, I'm so sorry. I'm so, so sorry." I spoke in a voice not even audible to myself.

On the morning of the funeral, I wanted to stay in bed snuggling Vinny. He, however, woke up early, ready to play. Even though the thought of food nauseated me, my son needed to eat. I hauled myself out of bed and took him down the stairs of my sister's house to the kitchen.

My mother and aunt, already up and holding coffee mugs, got one glimpse of me and offered to take care of my son. I thanked them and dragged myself back to bed. Imagining my husband in the bed next to me, I curled into the fetal position and cried as I talked with him, wishing he could embrace me. Tell me everything would be all right. Soothe me like he always did after a fight. Even though he was the one who made me miserable, he was also the one who comforted me. "Vincent, can you ever forgive me? I miss you so much. I'll tell our son all the good things about you and how much you loved him."

A knock on the door. Mom's head poked in. "You should start getting ready."

Two hours later, the funeral director led us to the family room where we could wait in privacy while the guests arrived at the chapel. A vast emptiness occupied a cavity within my chest. My entire body ached for my husband's love. For his comforting arms.

Lil Vinny toddled to me. I snuggled him tightly in my lap. As I ran my hand over his freshly cut hair, my stomach churned and twisted. Heat rose up the back of my neck. I put my son down and ran to the adjacent bathroom. No time to shut the door, I fell on my knees and vomited into the toilet. My insides contracted over and over.

Fingers pulled my hair away from my face. *Vincent?* A glimpse of my helper's feet told me it was my dad. Another heave, followed by three more. A wet cloth touched my neck.

Dad knelt beside me and handed me paper towels. I looked into his eyes, which held a sadness I'd never seen before. His tears said more than a thousand words. The only other time I'd seen him cry was when his mother died. Then I knew. He really did love me.

The funeral director signaled that it was time. I rinsed my mouth and wiped my face, then entered the chapel surrounded by my family. The cloying aroma of hundreds of flowers greeted me. Countless conversations ceased as we filed in. It seemed everyone who'd ever known Vincent had shown up. Over two hundred pairs of eyes stared at me. In an effort to avoid them, I studied the enormous chandelier hanging from the ceiling, its prisms sending particles of light into my dark soul. I sat on the front pew between my sister, who held Lil V, and my mother, who held me. I stared blankly at the casket twelve feet away.

The room filled with a recording of Vincent's father Stan singing a song I'd never heard before, "How Great Thou Art." How could anyone sing, at the funeral of a loved one, about God being great?

Although I didn't know him, the preacher who performed the service obviously knew Vincent. With my eyes fixed on the casket and my body paralyzed, I listened as the man recounted stories of my husband's childhood. Back then, Vincent's family went to this pastor's church and spent Sunday afternoons at his house.[2]

The preacher claimed assurance of Vincent's salvation—whatever that meant. With the exception of when Vincent talked about God and prayer while he was locked up, I'd never known him to be religious. But the idea that a man of God expressed certainty Vincent was a Christian in heaven awaiting a reunion comforted me in an inexplicable way.

Then he said words I wouldn't forget. "A Christian never dies by accident."

Never dies by accident? But this was an accident. I didn't want him to die. Did that mean God wanted him to die?

The preacher continued. "Nothing happens to a believer that doesn't pass by our Heavenly Father first."

So, God approved it and let it happen? Did He want me to kill my husband? Confusion swirled as I tried to make sense of the incomprehensible.

When the preacher concluded the ceremony, he prayed. "Daddy, kiss his family, his wife, his son, and make it all better."

No disrespect intended, but nothing can make this better. Not even God. And why would God kiss me?

At the graveside, my eyes refused to break their catatonic stare at Vincent's now-closed casket. Was he really in there? An urge to join him consumed me.

At the conclusion of the service, I remained seated as a long line of mourners expressed condolences.

Michelle approached. "I'll take Lil V home so he can nap."

My son rested his head on my sister's chest as she carried him away. One of his new shoes dangled from his left hand, and he rubbed his eyes with his right.

I couldn't move. Tears blurred my vision as I focused on the box holding my husband. I wanted to stay until they put him in the ground.

An arm patted my shoulder. "Sweetheart?"

Vincent?

"It's time to go," Mom said.

I looked up at a single dark cloud, sent for me alone, hanging in the otherwise sunny sky. My eyes moved back to the casket. "I'm staying."

"But they have to—"

"No. I won't leave until. . ." How could I explain my need to see him lowered into the ground? I didn't understand it myself, but something inside needed to throw dirt on him.

Her grip tightened. "I'll stay with you."

We sat together for several long moments, her presence keeping me afloat.

A man in filthy work blues approached. "Ma'am?"

I kept my eyes on my husband. "Yes?"

"You should be going now. We have to, uh, finish up here."

Finally breaking my gaze, I turned to him. "I want to be here for that."

He shook his head. "You're not allowed. Policy. We can't, you know, lower him, 'til everyone's gone."

My mother stood. "Come on, sweetheart, let's just go."

Overwhelmed with anger and grief, I didn't have the energy to argue. My mother helped me up, but instead of following her, I fell onto the casket. Draping myself over my husband's body covered in dark wood and roses, my body quaked with weeping. "Vincent, I love you. I love you so much it hurts. How can I raise our son without you?"

Mom pulled me off and led me to her car.

As we drove away, I watched the men prepare the casket to go into the ground.

CHAPTER FORTY-FOUR

Depression

"Are you sitting down?" Michelle's voice sounded ominous.

An inky shadow passed behind my eyes and, for a second, the room went dark. What now? Surely things couldn't get any worse.

"Sorry to beep you while you're working, but figured you needed to know right away. Mike got a subpoena for a grand jury."

Shock seized me. "Our brother, Mike? Grand jury?"

"Yes. They want to indict you for murder."

My chin dropped to my chest. *Murder?* I wagged my head, trying to make it go away.

"Did you hear me?"

Fingers twisted and squeezed my diaphragm, making it hard to breathe. I dropped the phone. The weight of a gorilla pushed me down the wall of my workplace break room, slamming my butt to the floor.

What did this mean? Were they going to arrest me? Here? Now? My mind snapped to the bag holding my own dark secret. I needed to get rid of it. Now. I'd planned to dump it on the way to work, but rain and unexpected traffic got in my way. Jumping to my feet, I ran outside into the downpour to retrieve the bag from under the driver's seat. Back in the break room, I buried it deep in the big trash can.

"Are you all right?" Candace's voice startled me.

"Yes. No. I need a minute." I ran to the bathroom. Wide eyes stared at me from the mirror. This was bad. Really bad. Turning on the water to muffle the sounds, I allowed myself a good cry. Then I washed my face and sat on the toilet seat lid, trying to calm down.

When I returned to the floor, another nurse said the manager wanted to speak with me. She must have heard I was upset. I hoped she'd let me go home.

My boss wore an unreadable expression. "Have a seat."

I sat.

"Can you explain this, please?" She held up my bag from the trash.

I froze.

"Candace saw you throw this away. Said you looked upset. Curious, she took it out. When she saw what it was, she brought it to me."

My mind raced. What could I say?

"You know I have to call the Nursing Board."

"No!" I jumped to my feet. "*Please.* You can't."

She stood and walked toward me. "I can't ignore that you had empty bottles of Vicodin with other people's names on them—all with Dr. Lunden as the prescriber. I called him, and he doesn't know any of these people." She sighed and put her hands on her hips. "You've been forging prescriptions, and if I don't call, my license is in jeopardy."

"No. No. No. Please. No." Heaviness pulled me to my knees. I folded my hands into a prayer.

"I'm sorry." Her eyes moved from me toward the door. "Todd, please help Leigh Ann clean out her things."

A landslide moved through me, making me collapse to the floor. "I'm fired?" My voice came out a whimper.

She stood firm. "Don't make this harder than it already is."

Todd walked me to my car and left me there, sitting alone in the driver's seat.

Vincent had forced me to teach him how to call prescriptions in, but after he died, I only found the one bottle of Vicodin. When they were gone, I wanted more. *Needed* more. It had been so easy to call them in for myself.

For a half-hour I wept, drowning in shame and despair. Driving home, I prayed for someone to run me off the road and end my torment. Tears fell harder than the torrential rains.

Somehow, I arrived home. I headed straight for my stash. Emotional pain hurt more than physical, and I needed more than my usual two Vicodin to dull the misery. I took three, stripped off my scrubs, and turned on the water almost hot enough to burn before stepping into the shower. I closed my eyes and tipped my head back, letting the water pour over me. I wanted nothing more than to be with Vincent on the sofa, his arms around me, comforting me.

Even when the pills worked their magic, numbing my pain and taking the edge off my agony, they could not ease my sense of being tainted. I stepped out of the shower unchanged. My problems couldn't be washed away. I got dressed and picked up my son from the babysitter.

The next morning, I woke in a daze, my body like lead. It took effort to move, to breathe. My eyes, swollen half-shut, stared out the window at nothing. The urge to vomit nagged, but since I hadn't eaten, the threat was as empty as my stomach. Desperate for deliverance from my pain, I picked up two Vicodin from the nightstand and swallowed.

The sound of my son's cries came through the intercom. I took a deep breath before beginning the long process of pulling myself out of bed. By the time I reached his nursery, the urge to let the floor suck me into a never-ending sleep gripped me. The sight of my precious baby stole my air, crushed my lungs.

He's fatherless, and it's all my fault.

I forced a smile. "Morning, Boo. Mommy loves you." Even my voice moved slow and heavy.

Lil Vinny stood on his new toddler racecar bed and reached for me. "Momma!"

I grabbed a diaper and wipes before lifting my son. Squeezing him tight, I carried him to the den and changed his diaper. Without wasting energy to snap his outfit closed, I moved him to his bouncy seat and turned on cartoons so I could take another break.

Gathering my strength, I dragged myself to the kitchen, sat on a chair in front of the stove, and scrambled two eggs. The effort of getting Lil Vinny strapped into his high chair with breakfast in front of him debilitated me. I rested on the couch while he ate.

With no energy left to make myself something, I nibbled on the remaining few bites of his eggs. Then I reclined on the floor near the playpen so I could watch my son and talk with him while he played. For the remainder of the day, rest breaks separated each necessary task. My sluggish body kept me from mundane chores, like showering, brushing my teeth, and eating. It didn't matter—as long as my baby was fed, dry, and clean and my dog had food and water, nothing else was important.

When nighttime mercifully arrived and I'd met Lil Vinny's needs, I tucked him into bed and lay next to him. Tears snaked down my face as I sang our song and snuggled him. While I caressed his back, his breathing slowed and deepened.

With him asleep, I whispered, "Boo, I'm so sorry. I didn't mean to take your daddy from you." My voice broke as the confession poured from my mouth. "I'm so, so sorry." Uncontrollable sobs wracked my body, and I held my son even tighter. "Please forgive me. Please keep loving me. Your mommy's a screw-up and your daddy's gone, and it's all my fault."

His rhythmic breathing showed he was oblivious to my suffering. I had to keep it that way.

Cold steel touched my neck. The glint of a knife caught my eye. I tried to move, but my hands were tied. A crazed voice spat at me. "I'll make you watch as I kill your son, and then I'll kill you."

"No!" My body jerked and I cried out. Panting, I bolted upright and twisted around in the darkness. Sweat covered me. "Lil Vinny!" A shiver ran through me as I frantically turned. My baby lay asleep next to me. Relief washed away the fear. Another nightmare.

I rubbed my wrists, then massaged my neck. Everything hurt. No surprise, considering I'd fallen asleep squished in the toddler bed. I contemplated my options: stay scrunched up in bed with him, or take the long walk to my large, empty bed? No big decision. Aches and pains were a small price to pay for the warmth of my son's nearness. I scooted Lil Vinny over, placing his splayed arms and legs back where they belonged, then wrapped my body around his.

For weeks, my life swirled around a vortex of depression, a whirlpool sucking me in. Unable to talk with anyone, I spent countless hours confessing to my sleeping son or crying out with remorse to my dead husband as I lay across his grave and wept.

Collectors called my house all day, every day. I had to get a job. But I was in no shape to work. Down to ninety pounds, I'd become frail. I couldn't sleep or eat, and paranoia ruled my life. Vincent came to me in nightmares, and every noise I heard was him, out of his grave, coming to get me for what I'd done. Sure, I'd seen him in his casket looking lifeless and harmless, but I knew him too well to believe anything could take away his power to hurt me.

Constant noises inside my house unhinged me. Was Vincent hiding in the attic, waiting for the right time to jump out at me with a knife? Several times I called the police after hearing strange sounds. Each time they'd arrive to find me cowering in a corner, holding a knife. Searching inside and out, they found nothing.

Vincent's friends also wanted revenge. Sometimes the noises outside were them, eager to kill me for taking his life.

My son kept my heart beating when I longed for death. He'd already lost his daddy. What would happen to him if I died, too? I needed help, but didn't know where to turn.

One night I opened my kitchen pantry and a pair of eyes stared back at me. I dropped the jar of baby food I held in my hand. Mashed squash and particles of glass splattered as I stood petrified, unable to move or scream. The mouse twitched and scampered away.

I cringed at having mice in the house, but at least it wasn't Vincent.

My brother Chris sent an exterminator friend to my house the next day.

Crawling into my attic, Glen scuffled around for several minutes before yelling down. "Definitely a mouse problem. But's there's something else up here too."

Trepidation crept through me. A stash of guns? Drugs? The makings of explosives? A body? "What is it?"

Glen came down the attic stairs and handed me some wires and a recorder. "It appears you had a tap on your phone."

A whimper escaped. Would Vincent's torment ever end?

I hit play on the recorder. Sure enough, the sounds of a phone conversation with my sister filled the room.

Glen made a face and pointed to the device. "Don't know what to do about that, but I can take care of the rodents."

The rodents. Oh yes, that's what he came for. "How'd the mice get in there?"

"Maybe you left a door open?"

I remembered driving by my house when the police had control of it. Yellow tape, chalk marks, officers milling around, cars lining the street—and my garage and front doors standing wide open. "The police did. Could that explain the noises I've been hearing?"

He nodded. "You've got a bunch of the critters. But I'll get rid of them."

His kindness comforted me. If a stranger could bring some peace to my frayed psyche, maybe I wasn't as alone as I'd imagined.

I picked up the phone and called Michelle. "Help me. I can't do this anymore."

[C H A P T E R F O R T Y - F I V E]

Hospitalized

I stared at the psychiatric hospital, clutching a bag filled with allowed items. This time, I wasn't a nursing student. This time, I'd not only be locked up twenty-four hours a day with the crazies, I'd be one of them.

That first time I'd arrived afraid and nervous, yet the experience had been positive and enlightening. I'd met Vincent there, and even though terrible things came out of meeting him, I couldn't ignore the good—especially my precious son.

Would this experience be good?

After my initial meeting with George's wife, Anne, George became my attorney. Now his words came back to me. "Be careful what you say. Every word and every action can be used against you if you're charged with murder."

Murder. The reality that I could be convicted of murder and spend my life in prison twisted inside me like a parasite feeding on my organs. How could I get help if I couldn't talk about what happened?

I wiped fresh tears with a trembling hand. "Thanks for bringing me."

"Of course." Michelle brushed away a stray tear of her own. "Anything else you need?"

She'd already done so much. Even though she didn't have kids, she'd taken on the responsibility of Lil V and assisted with moving his stuff to her house. She'd found someone to take care of my dog and promised to watch my house. She'd called the insurance company regarding my hospitalization—thank goodness for COBRA insurance, which my ex-employer was required to offer—and talked with the admissions people at the hospital. She helped me pack my suitcase. Then she'd taken me to my attorney's office.

Unfortunately, George had no interest in hearing the truth about my husband's death. All he did was warn me not to talk to anyone and promise to let me know as soon as he heard anything about the grand jury. Before I left his office, I gave him the pages of Vincent's kidnapping plan. When he'd asked what he was supposed to do with them, I told him decision-making was his job, not mine.

Now, I stood with Michelle outside the hospital with nothing in the way of me getting better. Nothing but the awful truths of what my marriage had become and the horrific night I'd shot my husband.

I killed my baby's daddy. Ended the life of the man I loved. And I couldn't tell anyone.

It would be so much easier to give up. To end my pain and suffering. But I'd dumped the remaining Vicodin into the toilet instead of my stomach. I had to get better for my son.

"I've burdened you too much already, Michelle."

"Don't worry about me. Or Lil V." She took my hand. "Just take care of yourself."

She escorted me into the hospital and stayed with me during my admission assessment. When it came time to say good-bye, she held me in her arms. "Everything's going to be fine."

The nurse walked me down a hall and used a key to open the door. It shut behind us, the lock clicking into place, sounding like a thunderous boom in advance of a storm. My insides rumbled with anxiety. Oh, how nice the comforting numbness of Vicodin would be right now.

On the way to my room, she pointed out the nurse's station, the off-limits hall for the men's rooms, the hall leading to classrooms, the dayroom, the outside smoking area, and the snack room. Once inside my quarters, I looked around. A nightstand and dresser matched the dark wood frame of the bed. Curtains the color of the yellow dress Vincent loved decorated the window.

How I missed my husband.

A small desk and cushioned folding chair stood bathed in sunlight. I sat on the bed, folded my shaking legs under me, and gripped fistfuls of the stiff comforter.

The nurse opened my suitcase. "Do you have any medication, drugs, pills, alcohol, or dangerous items?"

I wish. "No."

She held out her hand. "Shoelaces."

Removing them from my sneakers, I gave them to her.

She pulled my clothes out, yanking the drawstrings from sweat pants and pajamas. "Nothing you could hang yourself with is allowed." She put the ties in a pile with my shoelaces.

With expertise, she continued her search, opening, unzipping, taking apart, and feeling the lining of every item I'd brought. She added my compact mirror, razor, shampoo, mouthwash, and lighter to the pile.

Next, she searched me. With no regard for modesty or apology for causing embarrassment, she turned my pockets inside-out and ran her hands over every nook and cranny of my body. Finding nothing, she gave me a thin book. "This contains the schedule and rules. Familiarize yourself with it."

Another woman appeared in my doorway. "Her doctor's here."

My feet dragged as I followed her to an office off another hall.

"Come in." A man with kind eyes and a wrinkled suit stood and shook my hand before pointing to a chair. "I'm Doctor Jones."

He asked questions for an hour, his bushy mustache moving when he talked. He wrote in his notebook as I described the agony my life had become. A hopeless, helpless despair that begged for relief from the strangling torture of emotional pain.

When I refused to discuss what happened the night my husband died, his thick eyebrows bunched together and a scowl crossed his face. He sighed and closed his notebook. "We'll do what we can to help you given your limiting circumstances."

Worried he deemed me uncooperative, I fumbled for words in an effort to explain. "My attorney told me not to discuss it."

"It's obvious you're suffering with severe depression and post-traumatic stress disorder. You also have chemical dependency issues, so we'll add Chemical Dependency groups to your regimen." He rested his elbows on the desk and folded his hands. "I'm going to start you on an anti-depressant and an anti-anxiety medication. You'll be in group and individual counseling. I'll see you again tomorrow."

At the conclusion of our session, a tech escorted me to the dining room. Dinner consisted of noodles and sauce that hadn't harmed any animals in the making. Pushing the food around on my plate, I took inventory of the other patients. One woman carried on a loud, animated conversation with herself. A man three tables over seemed to be picking bugs from his hair and eating them. A pale girl with coal hair sat in the corner, staring into space with empty eyes. I wasn't the craziest in the dining room, nor was I the sanest.

That night, as I lay in bed aching for my son, a foreign feeling rested on me. Distress, despair, and desperation had debilitated me for so long, the names for positive emotions eluded me.

I rolled over and hugged Lil V's stuffed bear tighter. Smoothing the well-worn fur, I inhaled my son's scent. Then it hit me. *Safe.*

The locked doors keeping me inside this place would keep my husband out. And since the staff checked on me every fifteen minutes per suicide-watch protocol, even if he did find a way in, they would prevent him from hurting me.

I soon settled into a routine of group meetings, therapy, visits with my doctor, and "down-time," which included games, reading, and TV. I enjoyed talking with people without fear my husband would accuse me of cheating. Since Vincent had forbidden my friendship with Diana a year earlier, the only person outside my family I'd talked to was Mahasti at work—but I hadn't seen her for months.

I made small steps toward positive feelings, but the shame and guilt of killing my husband, the nightmares, the hopelessness and despair over the future continued to overwhelm me. Everything reminded me of Vincent, incapacitating me. I missed Lil V terribly, and the few short visits we shared did little to assuage his absence.

After a week of inpatient treatment, my doctor deemed it safe to switch me to intensive outpatient status. Although I believed his decision came more from the dictates of my insurance coverage than the state of my mental health, my heart rejoiced—more time with my Boo.

I now spent my days at the hospital and my evenings and nights with my son. The healing power of him falling asleep in my arms each night was the best medicine. Especially since I could confess things to him no other living, breathing person could hear.

I still felt helpless, but I'd learned I could live without Vicodin—and thanks to my antidepressants, I was able to eat.

On my last day of intensive outpatient treatment, a nurse approached me. "You have a phone call."

Who would call me here? I followed her to the nurse's station and picked up the phone.

"Leigh Ann, it's George."

My attorney. Fear and excitement warred inside. "Yes."

"Maybe you should sit down."

Not again. "What is it?"

"I don't know how else to do this but just tell you."

My heart stopped.

"You've been indicted for murder."

[C H A P T E R   F O R T Y - S I X]

Indicted

D a d   h e l d   t h e   h e a v y   d o o r   for me. Legs wobbling, I
entered the courtroom, followed by my family. Two aisles separated three
rows of pews. Pews like in the Catholic church I'd gone to as a child—but
this was no church. A waist-high wooden wall with a swinging gate split
the vast room in half. An elevated podium stood on the far side. It was,
after all, like church in one horrifying way—the judge on high would
hand down judgment.

My attorney walked toward us.

As I introduced him to my family, they shook hands.

"Let's go to the hall," George said, then took us back through the
double doors to the hallway lined with benches. "We're set for the bail
reduction hearing. As I told Leigh Ann, once the judge sets the new bail,
her dad can arrange paying it while Leigh Ann does a walk-through."

Dad looked at me, then back at George. "How long will the walk-
through take?"

"As much as four hours. They'll get her processed, take her picture,
fingerprint her. A walk-through is much faster than the typical arrest, but
the wheels of justice always turn slowly."

Four hours in jail. Surely I could handle that. My stomach churned,
making me grateful I'd skipped breakfast.

George turned to my family. "What we need from y'all is testimony affirming your support of Leigh Ann and stating how, especially

considering her son, she has no reason to run."

Dad put his arm around me. "We'll do whatever we can to help."

Ever since my husband's death, my dad's continued support brought comfort I'd never known. His presence and willingness to testify, along with the rest of my family, took the edge off my frazzled nerves.

"Okay, then." George clapped his hands together. "Let's get this done. Leigh Ann and I will go in, but the rest of you need to wait out here until you're called." He opened the door to the courtroom and gestured to me. "Let's go."

George waved toward the rows of pews as we passed them. "This part of the courtroom is called the gallery." He pushed open the hinged gate in the middle of the waist-high wall. "Since you're the defendant, you get to pass through the bar, like an attorney."

Was that supposed to make me feel special?

Next, he motioned to a long table on our left. "That's the prosecutor's table."

The prosecutor who wants to send me to prison.

Indicating twelve chairs surrounded by waist-high wooden walls, he said, "The jury box."

I gulped. Someday strangers would sit there and decide my fate.

He pointed to the high seat. "The judge sits there on the bench, and the witness box is next to it." He placed his briefcase on the table to our right. "We sit here."

Time froze as I stared at the bench. Numbness engulfed me, and a plea to an unknown God kicked in. *Please, let this go well.* I sat in the chair and my leg began to bounce, kicking the air with each beat of my heart.

A bailiff stood near a door in the back and called out, "All rise for the Honorable Judge Steve Burkhold."

George helped me up, steadying my swaying body.

The door opened, and a white-bearded man in a flowing black robe moved to his chair. "Be seated."

My foot once again began its own version of the quick step.

Preliminaries completed, George called my dad to the stand. Dad answered my attorney's questions about my family's support, my desire to be with my son, and his certainty I would never run. Then the prosecutor started in.

As soon as the interrogation began, I knew problems loomed. My dad had always told us anything to do with money was private, and now a prosecutor asked personal details about his finances in a public courtroom.

With each inquiry about his income, assets, savings, investments, and retirement, my dad's unease became increasingly palpable. I wanted to stand and tell them to forget it—I'd rather face jail than see my dad suffer this way. But my attorney held me in place and wouldn't let me speak.

After several more witnesses, the prosecutor closed, saying my family was capable of the original $50,000 bond.

The judge put his hands on his desk and leaned forward. "*Ms.* Bayshore," stretching out the word Ms. as though reminding me I was no longer married. "What *is* wrong with you? Certainly your predicament is one to cause nervousness, but I have never seen anyone act as agitated as you appear to be. Your leg has been bouncing like a Mexican jumping bean during this entire proceeding."

With all attention on me, my leg froze mid-swing.

The judge shuffled through papers. "From the information here, it appears Ms. Bayshore was released from a psychiatric hospital yesterday. Is this correct?"

My attorney half-stood. "Yes, Your Honor. Leigh Ann was treated for depression and post-traumatic stress disorder. Her doctor deemed her healthy enough to be released from both inpatient and intensive outpatient treatment, but she continues to need significant therapy. This is another reason a fair bond is so crucial."

"From the looks of it, she needs more help." The judge glared at me. "Ms. Bayshore, can you please stop bouncing your leg?"

I hadn't realized it had started back up. "Yes, Your Honor. Sorry."

The judge pushed papers together and moved them to the side. "While it is obvious to this court Ms. Bayshore continues to need treatment, what is not obvious is if her mental health supports comprehension of the charges against her. I'm ordering a drug test and a psychiatric evaluation to be performed before I make any other decisions. If Ms. Bayshore can show she's clean, and prove she understands the severity and possible outcomes of her situation, then at that point I will address bond."

With a motion from the judge, a sheriff's deputy moved to my side. Anxiety stabbed my chest.

"Bailiff," the judge's voice boomed. "Take Ms. Bayshore into custody. She will be held until the psychiatric evaluation can be performed."

Panic took over. I turned to George. "What's going on?"

"I didn't expect this." He smoothed his beard. "Don't worry. Everything will be fine."

"Fine? How could it be fine? *They're going to lock me up.*"

"Hopefully we can get the psychiatrist to visit you this afternoon, but. . ." He shrugged. "You might have to spend the night in jail."

My head dropped into my hands. *Oh, please no.*

"Ms. Bayshore?" The bailiff held a pair of handcuffs. "Please stand."

"No, no, no. Please God, no." I whimpered through sobs.

The bailiff put his large hand on my arm and pulled me up, spun me around, and slapped the metal bracelets on, sending pain through my wrists. He then pulled me toward a huge door, similar to the one I'd seen Vincent disappear through when he was the one in custody. But he'd deserved it. He'd committed a crime. I was a victim, not a criminal.

Another bailiff joined us, and the two of them dragged me to the place of my nightmares. A massive key opened a jail cell, and the deputies pushed me in.

[CHAPTER FORTY-SEVEN]
Custody

Not sure if my uncontrollable shivering was caused more by the frigid air of the tiny cell or my need to pee, I stared in disbelief at what passed for a toilet. Filth covered the stainless steel contraption, which housed a drinking fountain in back and a bowl with no seat in front. The roll of paper, shoved into a cubby in the side, looked wet.

Odors of urine and vomit burned the inside of my nose. I tried mouth-breathing, but that left me with a sticky, rancid taste. Harsh yellow lights magnified the grime and graffiti covering the cement walls. Sounds from other cells echoed off the impenetrable bars, floors, and walls.

My leg bobbed up and down, both from nervousness and in an effort to warm me. Frightened and emotionally drained, I wanted to lie down, but the metal bench was hard and as cold as if it had been stored in a freezer.

A jangling of keys. The gate to my cell opened. A female officer stood in the doorway. "Let's go."

I followed her through a maze of tunnels and immense locking doors to a large, brightly lit area. Deputies milled around the elevated work area in the center of the room, surrounded by a chest-high wall, as if emphasizing their power over the lowly inmates. Cells of all sizes and unmarked doors lined the outsides of the room.

She unlocked one of the doors and pointed to the back wall. "Stand over there and strip."

Strip? Memories of Vincent ordering me to strip crashed in on me. I walked to the back and swallowed hard as I began to undress.

The woman put on gloves, taking each item of clothing, searching pockets and linings—even the soles of my shoes. Next, she picked up a flashlight and walked toward me. "Spread your arms and legs and open your mouth."

She shone the light into my mouth. "Move your tongue up." She then inspected my body using the beam of light. "Turn around." After checking my backside, she squatted. "Spread your butt cheeks apart and bend forward."

More humiliated than ever, I did as she asked.

"Squat and cough."

As I did, she used her light to be sure she didn't miss anything. "Stand and face me."

She put the flashlight down and ran her fingers through my hair. Finally, she handed my clothes back. "You can get dressed now."

The officer took me past several large holding tanks—square rooms with cement walls, each with thick glass facing the hallway so anyone walking by could see inside. She stopped at one of the women's tanks and pulled out her massive key ring.

At least twenty women littered the room. Some sat on one of the two long metal benches that ran the length; some huddled on the floor. One stood at the pay phone mounted on the back wall. Uncertainty turned to panic when I realized the person on the phone was a man. "There's a man in there."

The officer looked into the tank and laughed. "Just get in." She shoved me into the room and slammed the heavy door shut.

The stench of body odor, urine, and who knew what else assaulted my nose and gagged me. Trying to avoid the man, I inched toward a vacant spot on one of the benches near a waist-high brick wall. A toilet filthier than the last stood on the other side, the low wall providing the only privacy.

A few of the women slept, but most of them stared at me, whispering and pointing. The man on the phone turned, and the sight of him reminded me of a mangy dog. Scrawny, short, and covered in tattoos, he smiled and hung up the phone. His eyes scanned me from head to feet, lingering at places in between. He moved toward me.

Disgust and confusion slithered through me. How could they let a man in here?

"My, my, my." He whistled. "You're prettier than my wife. What'd such a pretty young thing do ta end up in a place like this?"

Something about his voice sounded odd and out of place. Too high. Like a woman. Couldn't be—he mentioned a wife.

"Come on now, shuga', you don't need ta be afraid a me. I'm good ta pretty ladies."

I swallowed hard through my tightened throat. It really was a woman. No wonder the guard laughed.

"You look so innocent in yer sweet flowery dress. What'd ya do? Take candy from a baby?" She/he sat next to me. "Did ya smack a guy fer getting too close?"

All the non-slumbering women laughed. Some of them began talking to my space-invader, who seemed to be well-known. They all called her *him*.

Remembering what Vincent said about the dangers of appearing soft or afraid while locked up, I straightened and let out a laugh. "Nothing like that."

He smiled and leaned even closer. "Then what, sweetie? Whatcha charged with?"

I turned and looked him in the eyes. "Murder."

His jaw dropped. "Whoa, shuga'. Seriously?" He tilted his head to the side as if trying to read me, then smiled. "Who'd ya whack?"

"On the advice of my attorney, I can't talk about it." I gave him a quick smile. "Besides, I didn't say I actually killed someone, only that I'm charged with it."

He winked. "I like you. You got smarts on top a yer beauty. I always say, if yer gonna go down, go down big. Name's Lynn. What's yers?"

"Leigh Ann."

"So, Leigh Ann, who you *charged* with killin'?"

I paused. What difference did it make? My charge was public, and I wasn't admitting to anything. "My husband."

"Woohoo. Way to go." He smacked me on the shoulder. "Men suck." He stood and made a sweeping motion with his hands. "Everyun, this here's Leigh Ann, and yur all gonna be nice to her and make her feel welcome."

Within thirty minutes, the women in the tank accepted me as one of them. But now I had to do something I'd put off too long already. If I didn't pee soon, I'd wet myself.

Giving in, I used the toilet, trying to keep at least a modicum of privacy but not succeeding. While still hovering over the john with my skirt hiked up and pantyhose around my knees, the door to the tank opened. A guard entered and called ten names, including mine.

As the officer led us down the hall, passing by tanks crowded with men, the women went crazy, whistling and shouting to them. The men returned their catcalls with fervor, making a gaggle of construction workers seem mild by comparison.

The officer took us one by one to a machine for fingerprinting and booking photos, then returned us to the tank.

Eventually, the guards brought "sandwiches" for lunch—one piece of hard bologna on two pieces of stale bread—after which I had no choice but to drink from the fountain part of the toilet.

Several more times guards took me away for processing, including visits to a nurse who asked personal questions and an intake officer who wanted to know about gang affiliations, tattoos, and any enemies I might have in the jail.

Dinnertime brought a second round of bologna.

Hours later, another officer pulled twelve of us from the tank. Two female guards took us down several halls and then into a room with three open shower stalls. An officer pointed to three of us and told us to strip and get into a stall. Being one of the chosen, I took my clothes off and handed them to her, then stepped in.

Lynn's eyes scanned my naked body. "Hoowie, darlin'. Looking good."

"Spread your arms and legs," the officer ordered. She pumped a large canister like an exterminator would use, then sprayed us down, concentrating on areas with hair. Telling us to turn, she sprayed our backsides.

Bug spray dripped off me as I stood shivering in the frigid room awaiting orders.

"You three move out. You three"—the officer pointed to three more women—"strip and get in."

I stepped out of the shower and stood to the side, hoping to get some clothes soon. Instead, I waited, humiliated and degraded, for all four groups to be doused with bug spray. After all twelve of us had been sprayed, we reentered the showers in the same groups of three to rinse off in icy water. Next, the officer let us retrieve our panties, socks, and bras with no underwire. Then we received our jail clothes—stiff navy blue scrubs and a pair of rubber slip-on shoes. Although relieved I'd worn a regulation bra, I would've exchanged it on the spot for a pair of socks. I put on the clothes and slipped my naked feet into the shoes. The same kind of shoes I'd been given at the police department the night I shot Vincent.

Memories of that dark, horrible night rose from my feet to my heart.

A guard took us to another cell—the coldest one yet. My long hair hung down my back like icicles. I pulled my arms into the short sleeves in an effort to find even a hint of warmth. As I waited, my toes went numb. Exhausted, I lay down on the cold metal bench and snuggled myself, wanting to cry but not daring to.

Sometime later, a female officer stepped in. "Move out."

As we lined up, I noticed blue lips and fingers on my cellmates. The officer walked us down more hallways. Should I have been dropping breadcrumbs behind me?

The officer opened a large, heavy door. "Get a mattress and a crate."

The other women seemed to know the drill. They pushed each other out of the way like bargain shoppers at a mega sale, testing and choosing mattresses. Following their cues, I found a mattress and put one of the battered milk crates—which contained a worn blanket, rough mattress cover, towel, razor, bar of soap, comb, toothbrush, and toothpaste—on top of it. We lumbered down another hall, dragging our mattresses behind us, stopping at an elevator.

When we reached our floor, the officer dropped off inmates in singles and pairs at their assigned cells. At "E-Tank," she called out, "Bayshore, this is you."

The large barred gate slowly slid open, and I stepped into a small square area with two more gates. The first gate closed before the second gate opened, amid clatters of protest from the old, rusty metal.

Still dragging my mattress, I entered the tank. The large rectangle, about thirty feet long and twenty feet wide, was darker than the hallway but lit too brightly for nighttime. In plain view, a woman sat on one of two toilets facing me.

Next to the toilets, a curtain hid what appeared to be a tiny shower. Two metal picnic tables with attached benches were bolted to the floor near the bathroom area, and five women sat at one playing dominoes. Above the table to the right hung a television, turned off, and a clock, which read 2:45 a.m. Beyond that, two metal bunk-beds were attached to the left wall—women in the bottom bunks talked with each other. Three bunks were attached to the right wall.

A skinny black girl who appeared to be fifteen approached. "Tameka. What's your name?"

"Leigh Ann."

"Nice to meet you." She pointed at two bare metal beds, both top bunks, neither with a ladder. "You can have either of those."

"Thanks." Deciding on the one closest to a window, I heaved my mattress up, but it fell back on me, knocking me to the ground. The women giggled as I struggled with getting both the mattress and myself onto the top bunk. When finally successful, I collapsed onto the thin mattress, covered myself with the worn blanket that might barely succeed in warding off frostbite, and stared at the ceiling three feet above me. Depleted of all energy, I rolled onto my side and closed my moist eyes, wanting nothing more than sleep.

"S'cuse me," a tiny voice said.

I opened my eyes. "Yes, Tameka?"

She smiled and held up a crude cigarette that looked more like a joint. "You wanna smoke?"

I bolted upright. "Oh, that would be amazing. Thank you so much."

"Rolled it myself. Can't afford real ones." She lit it with her cigarette and handed it to me.

I took a drag. Not used to the stronger, unfiltered cigarettes, I coughed. At least it soothed my frazzled nerves. Thanking Tameka, I lay back down and allowed myself to cry, amazed at the comfort a kind smile and cheap smoke could bring.

The bright light blazed through my closed eyes. I rubbed them and sat up.

The gate opened with its loud clang, and an officer entered the tank. "Eyes, ladies. Everyone show me your eyes. Breakfast time."

As soon as the officer did a head-count and left, the women lined up at the bars. I jumped down awkwardly. The clock read 3:30 a.m. Inmates in white handed us trays through a rectangular opening in the bars.

I sat at one of the tables and studied the breakfast offerings. Watery grits, fake scrambled eggs, stale white bread, and an apple that made my mouth water. Leaving the apple for last, I ate the flavorless food with the appreciation of a man on a deserted island receiving dirty, lukewarm water.

After breakfast, I gave in to the fact my bladder needed emptying again. The reasonably clean toilets had a mist of condensation covering them from the freezing temperature. Hovering over one, I tried to ignore the feeling of being on stage, peeing for everyone's entertainment. Afterward, Tameka gave me another cigarette. Fog filled the air from nine women smoking.

Back in bed, my nose twitched with the smell of bug spray rising from my skin. The insides of my eyelids glowed red from the harsh lights. But the satisfaction of food combined with tobacco allowed me to sleep.

The call for lunch woke me at 10:45 a.m. I jumped off my bunk and stood in line at the bars with the other women. A trustee shoved a tray through the food pass. Staring at the mystery meat, runny mashed potatoes, slimy greens, and two pieces of dry white bread, I took my lunch and sat. Wondering about the strange meal times, I set aside the sugar cookies for later.

After eating very little, and still tired with only seven hours sleep in almost thirty, I lugged myself back to my bunk. Desperately wanting a cigarette, I toyed with the idea of asking Tameka for another, but decided to close my eyes instead. As sleep began to overtake me, an officer called me to the bars.

I jumped down and approached her. "Yes ma'am?"

"These were in your property." She held up my pack of cigarettes. "If you sign, you can have them."

My entire body tingled with anticipation. "Show me where."

I lit one with some sort of heating element bolted to the wall, then gave Tameka three to show my appreciation. Her excitement over real cigarettes gave me a reason to smile.

Exhausted, I feel asleep as soon as I extinguished my smoke.

"Bayshore!" A voice shouted over the intercom on the wall, waking me. "Visitor."

I shook the fog from my brain. Grabbing my toothbrush and toothpaste from my crate, I jumped down. By the time I finished brushing, the gate opened.

An officer led me down a hall and through a locked door. "Have a seat."

A middle-aged woman sat on the other side of thick glass holding the phone. I sat and picked up my phone.

"Ms. Bayshore, I'm here to evaluate your mental competency. Do you understand?"

"Yes."

She proceeded to ask questions about my comprehension of the charge against me, assessing my ability to stand trial and my understanding about the possibility of life in prison. Then she thanked me and said she'd notify the judge of her decision.

An officer returned me to the tank just in time for the 3:45 p.m. dinner. I accepted my tray, but ignored it until I could call my attorney collect. "George, I've been here a day and a half. When am I going to get out? It's December 22nd—"

"Be patient. There's nothing else to do at this point. We have to wait for the judge, and I imagine he's done for the day. Guess you'll be spending at least one more night in jail."

Anger boiled inside as I sat at the table and faced the jail food. Another night locked up? This was so unfair. After three bites of cold ham and bland beans, I pushed the tray away, distressed by a new thought.

What if I have to spend Christmas in here?

CHAPTER FORTY-EIGHT

Bond

The time had come to wash off the bug spray. Thanks to my real cigarettes, I'd been able to barter for shampoo so I wouldn't have to use bar soap for my waist-length hair.

I opened the curtain and stared in confusion at the tiny two-by-two stainless steel shower. A floor mat was stuck to the wall and the knob to turn the water on was nowhere to be found. Pushing aside my pride, I asked for help.

Tameka came to my rescue. "We rigged the button you have to push to get the water to run, so you don't have to keep holding it." She pulled the mat halfway down, revealing a water-logged book underneath. Under the book was an inch long button. "When you push the button with the book, the water comes on. Pull tight on the mat and bang on it so the suction cups stick to the wall and hold it in place."

"Genius," I said with a laugh. "Thanks."

"No problem. There's a lot to learn about a place like this." She point-ed at my slip-on shoes. "For instance, those are called shower shoes for a reason. You don't ever want to go in there barefoot."

"No chance of that. Thanks again for your help."

Since the shower was too small for undressing, I put the soap and shampoo on the ledge and undressed in the open, where everyone could see. Right in front of the shower was a window to the hall where any guard who happened to walk by—including male guards—could see the shower and toilets. I tried for privacy, but my efforts failed.

Bracing myself for freezing water, I pushed the button with the book and banged the mat into place. Surprisingly, the water turned warm. Within seconds, it didn't matter that I was in a tiny, dark space with shoes on. The heat and steam thawing my body made the experience blissful.

After a long dousing with liquid heaven, I peeled the mat away to shut the water off, then grabbed my hand-sized towel off the ledge of the window. With some ingenuity, I managed to get most of myself dry before stepping out and dressing, then tackled my unconditioned, knotted hair with the trial-sized comb.

Amazed at how good I felt being clean and of normal temperature, I accepted an offer to play dominoes. The ruthless women took no pity on my inexperience, and with each point earned, they slammed the "bones" on the metal table. At 10:00 p.m., the lights mercifully dimmed. I thanked the girls for a good time and told them I needed sleep.

"You can't go to bed," a lanky white girl, whose name I'd forgotten, said. "Nobody sleeps until after breakfast."

"I'd like to try," I said with a sigh. "I'm beat, and am hoping to see the judge in the morning."

She laughed at me. "Good luck with that."

Not sure if she meant sleep or seeing the judge, I lit a cigarette and said goodnight.

Before lunch the next day, a voice called my name over the intercom, announcing a visitor. An officer opened the gate. "Up against the wall."

"Excuse me?"

She put her hands on her hips and glared. "On the wall for a pat down."

As I leaned against the wall, she spread my legs with her feet, moving her hands over every part of my body. "All right, Bayshore, you have a date with your attorney."

Excitement and relief tingled through me.

One elevator, four heavy locked doors, and countless halls and tunnels later, she brought me into a familiar courtroom where George stood waiting for me.

"The judge wants to talk with you."

A guard led us to the judge's chambers—a large wood-paneled office where the judge sat in an ornate leather chair behind a massive cherry desk. "Have a seat, Ms. Bayshore."

"Yes, sir." Doing my best to appear normal, I sat with George on the plush sofa and willed my leg to be still.

"Ms. Bayshore, you passed your drug screen and psychological evaluation, so I'm prepared to offer bond."

I trembled with elation. "Thank you, Your Honor."

He leaned back in his seat and folded his arms, appraising me with his eyes. "Not so fast. This won't be easy. You get bond, but you will have severely strict bond conditions you must adhere to, or I'll yank your butt back in jail so fast, you won't know what hit you."

"Yes, sir."

"You will wear a monitor around your ankle and be under house arrest. You must stay in your house at all times unless you have permission to leave by your probation officer.

"You are not to take any drug not prescribed to you by a physician. You will report to a probation officer three times a week, and with each visit you will be screened for drugs. You will notify the court of any address or phone number change, and if you get a job, you will provide the phone number and address. You may have a surprise visit by your probation officer at any time. And you are not allowed to go outside the boundaries of this county. Do you understand and agree to these conditions?"

House arrest? Probation officer? Three visits a week? "Yes, Your Honor."

"Good." He waved to the guard in the doorway. "Take her back to her cell."

As soon as we exited the judge's chambers, my attorney told the guard he needed a moment with me.

When she stepped away, I asked, "When do I get to go home?"

"Hopefully today."

My stomach balled into a knot. "*Hopefully?*"

He shrugged. "Since you've been ordered an ankle monitor and visits with a probation officer, you have to be released to that department. It can take a while for the paperwork to go through. They should get to you today, but I can't promise you. In truth, they may not."

"So, tomorrow?"

"I'm afraid not. That department isn't open on Saturdays. If you don't get out today, you won't get out until Monday."

"But"—my voice fluttered—"Sunday is Christmas."

"Oh, that's right," he said impatiently. "So, the department will be closed Monday as well. Could be Tuesday."

The knot in my stomach tightened. "I can't spend Christmas in jail."

George tilted his head as if trying to convey sympathy. "I'll do what I can. The department closes at 5:00, so if they don't call you out by at least 3:45 or 4:00, you won't be going today." He turned to the guard. "You can take her now."

"But, George. . ." The guard took my arm and pulled me toward the heavy door leading to the jail.

He nonchalantly waved good-bye. "Call me when you get out."

Christmas in jail? The entire trip back to the tank, tears spilled down my cheeks.

I paced, watching the seconds tick by on the clock. *Please, they have to call me soon.* My pacing continued until 4:15 when Tameka told me to give it up. Angry and despondent, I sat on my bunk and cried. Christmas in jail.

At 4:25, the intercom squawked. "Bayshore. Roll it up all the way."

Jumping to my feet, I turned to Tameka. "What does that mean?"

A broad smile covered her face. "It means you're going home."

CHAPTER FORTY-NINE

Revoked

I lay on the now-level ground of Vincent's grave and imagined my head on his chest, his arms embracing me. Remorse and grief swept over me. Flooded my soul. "Oh, how I miss you. Why did this happen?" Tears watered the barren dirt beneath me. "Why did you have to get so angry? How did things get so out of control?"

Soft tinkling from wind chimes hanging on a leafless tree intensified the tranquil aura of the hushed cemetery. My weeping and pleading intermittently shattered that peace.

Although I'd visited him many times since his burial three months ago, this was the first time since being indicted for murder. His murder. "I'm so sorry, my love." The words caught in my throat. I wiped my face and blew my nose on a well-worn handkerchief. "You know the truth. You know it wasn't murder. Can't you help me?"

My fingers traced the dirt, longing to feel Vincent's silky hair. As if moving onto his lap, I curled into the fetal position, my ankle monitor jabbing my leg. The feeling of imprisonment returned. *At least my probation officer allowed me to come here.*

"Christmas was so hard without you. We'll never spend another special day together. Ever." Trying to find a dry spot on my handkerchief, I wiped my face again.

"Lil V misses you so much. He searches and calls for you all the time." Breathing deeply, I imagined Vincent's scent. "Wish I could stay with you longer, but they'll send out the cavalry if I miss curfew."

I bent down and kissed the ground where I imagined his lips lay before heading to my car.

Over the next several months, the stress of my tumultuous life increased my blood pressure and gave me daily migraines. Still unable to talk with anyone about taking my husband's life, depression settled in deeper. Thanks in part to inadequate treatment for post-traumatic stress disorder, thoughts of Vincent cycled between love and torment.

When not haunted by his ghost, I longed for his presence. Guilt and shame warred with my ache to be held by him. Memories of his cruelty pushed aside my yearning for his touch. Hunger for his passion supplanted defilement from his rapes and strip searches. Dreams of happy times with him lulled me to sleep, and nightmares of his torture awakened me with terror.

The circumstances surrounding my psychiatric hospitalization added to my legal woes, prompting an investigation by the Board of Nursing. Unable to add one more thing to my chaotic life, I decided not to fight and surrendered my RN license.

Logistics of my life deteriorated as I took on split shifts as a waitress in order to pay bills. Three times a week I opened at the restaurant, worked through lunch, drove thirty miles to report to Mr. Brown, my probation officer, to give urine, then drove thirty miles back and worked until close. My hectic schedule kept me from my one source of comfort—my son—who was now practically being raised by his babysitter.

One Friday, my boss offered extra money if I'd work through my break. Knowing the probation department was open on Saturday, I accepted. Upon arrival at the office the next day to report, I found it had closed early.

Fear and concern gripped me. Was I going to get arrested? Monday morning, I called Mr. Brown. Understanding the office closed early, he agreed it wasn't my fault and told me not to worry.

About a week later, my attorney paged me while I was at work. When I called him, he informed me I'd missed court.

"But you told me I didn't have to go. You said it was only a docket call. That you'd go but I didn't need to."

"I was wrong. The judge is infuriated you didn't show. Said if you don't appear in court within the hour, he's going to issue a warrant."

After making an excuse with my manager, I raced to court, making it just in time.

The judge—a new judge since my last hearing—laid into me with his harsh reprimand.

I begged for mercy. "Please, Your Honor. My attorney told me I didn't have to be here."

Judge Harris looked straight at me. "I don't care what your attorney says—if you're name's on my docket, your butt better be in my court."

"Yes, Your Honor. I'm sorry." My voice quivered. "This will never happen again."

"If it does, you will be taken into custody."

Thoughts of near incarceration mingled with anger at my incompetent attorney. As soon as I walked out of the courtroom, I collapsed on a bench. My head throbbed, and my vision blurred. Since I'd managed to get the rest of the day off work, I wanted to pick up my son. But on the way to the babysitter's, my headache increased and numbness and tingling began on my right side. Something was seriously wrong.

I drove to the emergency room.

A nurse took my blood pressure, her eyes wide.

"What is it?"

She took it on my other arm before answering. "Dangerously high. 218/152."

Unable to concentrate due to pain, I thought I misunderstood. But twelve hours, four pills, and six injections later, the doctor confirmed what the nurse had said. He then ordered bed rest for at least two days.

When I called my probation officer to explain, he told me no problem, as long as I brought in a doctor's note.

Three days later, I handed Mr. Brown the note, which also included a list of the medications given to me to explain what would surely be a dirty drug screen. He assured me everything was fine.

Then one afternoon my car wouldn't start. Once again, I called Mr. Brown. "I tried to find someone to drive me there, but no one can."

When he told me there wouldn't be a problem if I brought the receipt from the mechanic, a sigh of relief escaped. "Thank you. Do you think the judge will ever reduce how often I have to report? It's been seven months, and three times a week is so hard."

"As we've discussed before, several requests have been made to reduce your requirements." He huffed. "That's all I can do."

"Thank you. I'll get my car into the shop and see you Monday."

Ryan and Michelle were moving to another house, so on Saturday, Lil V and I went to their place to help them pack. While there, sheriff's deputies appeared with a warrant for my arrest. Without giving me a chance to kiss my son good-bye, they slapped handcuffs on me and escorted me to the door. My baby ran after me, his arms reaching out as he screamed and cried.

"Don't worry," Michelle said. "We'll take care of Vinny."

"This is a mistake." From the back of the squad car, I pleaded with the officers to let me go. "At least let me say good-bye to my son."

"Sorry, ma'am," one of the officers said. "No can do."

Anguished tears poured from my eyes as I slumped in the seat, trying to hide my face from anyone who might see me.

The officer drove me to the Tarrant County Jail, and once again I suffered through the humiliating intake treatment before making it upstairs to a tank twenty-four hours later.

As soon as I got my mattress and crate on a bed, I called my attorney. After several unsuccessful attempts, I finally reached him. "George, you have to get me out of here."

He sighed. "I'm sorry, Leigh Ann, but it's Sunday. There's nothing I can do."

"Why did they arrest me?" My voice pushed through gritted teeth.

"I don't know. Call me tomorrow afternoon."

My jaw locked tight. Not wanting to spend another night in jail, I slammed the phone down and smacked the wall with my open hand. "A whole lot of good that jerk's doing for me," I said to no one in particular.

"Are you okay?"

I turned to the voice and saw a young girl who looked more like a model than a criminal.

She pushed her long, blond hair off her slender shoulder. "Name's Alisha."

Alisha and I commiserated over our troubled lives. Her situation included a charge for capital murder, thanks to her boyfriend killing a woman and then robbing her while Alisha watched in shocked terror. Pregnant and fearing her life, she gave in to his threats and helped clean up the mess and hide the body.

She told me the heartbreaking story of giving birth to her son while incarcerated. "As soon as he was born, they took him from me and gave him to my mom." Tears rolled down her cheeks, wetting her full lips. "Giving birth while wearing handcuffs and leg shackles was so humiliating."

Compassion welled. She seemed too sweet and innocent for such brutal treatment.

Alisha, eight years younger, took on the role of mentor and helped me get settled. She explained how things worked in the jail, information I hadn't needed during my previous short stay behind bars. I'd be able to buy luxury items like roll-your-own cigarettes, paper and pens, and real soap and deodorant. "The commissary guy comes by with a cart each weekday, and you can spend money people put on your books."

"Books?"

"If someone wants to give you money, they put it into your account, called your books."

"I don't expect to be here that long."

A look of defeat covered her face. "That's what I thought when they brought me in nine months ago."

The next morning, heeding Alisha's advice, I approached the man with the cart on the other side of the bars. With his explanation that any money on me when arrested would be on my books, I bought tobacco and rolling papers.

Keeping myself busy, I rolled twenty cigarettes. Then I called my attorney.

"According to the warrant, Leigh Ann, you missed reporting several times."

I felt the blood drain from my face. "But my probation officer knew. He said it wouldn't be a problem. Told me to bring in the receipt from the mechanic, but I never got the chance."

"Well, I'll inquire into it, but can't make any promises. Call me tomorrow at noon."

Once again, my attorney hung up without bothering to get the full story. What kind of joker was he? I stormed to my bunk, wadded up my blanket, and vented my anger into it.

Alisha tried to comfort me, but I pushed her away and wallowed in self-pity. I ignored everyone else in the tank and focused on my indignation until it was time to call George again. "Did you fix it yet?"

"I can't get you out."

His words punched me in the chest. "Wha. . .Why not?"

"The judge refuses to give you bond." He sounded matter-of-fact, as if discussing what he ate for lunch.

"For how long?"

"Well"—he cleared his throat—"the judge says you'll stay in there until trial."

"*Trial?*" Heat flooded my face as fire burned inside. "You can't let that happen. I have a son. A job. A house. My trial's months away. What am I supposed to do?"

"Sit tight and do your time. There's nothing else I can do. In fact, since you'll be in jail until trial, I've requested the court to appoint you a pro-bono attorney."

My mind skittered. "Pro-bono? Why? You're my attorney."

"As soon as the judge signs the order, I won't be your attorney anymore."

"But. . ." Fury and disbelief boiled inside. "But you've been paid."

"That money's gone," he said without apology.

"On what?" My teeth gritted. "You haven't done anything."

"Leigh Ann." Impatience laced his voice. "If there's any money left, I'll give it to your mother. Now please, don't call my office again. You'll hear from your new attorney soon."

With that, he hung up.

I wanted to smash the phone. Kick the wall. Bang my head on the bars. Months. I could be here for months. What a jerk. Took the money and did nothing but leave me to rot in jail.

Stuck

On my fifth day of incarceration, Michelle told me over the phone that the apartment she and Ryan were staying in until their house was ready was too small to keep Vinny. She'd asked Vincent's sister, Katrina, and her husband, Andrew, if Lil V could stay with them for two weeks.

Concern overshadowed my gratitude. I had prayed for Vincent's family to want to be a part of our son's life, but this meant he was going to live with a woman who, it seemed to me, blamed me for her brother's death.

After two more days of pleading with everyone to do something—anything—to get me out of jail, I began to get the sense my ex-attorney was right. I'd be locked up until my trial. No longer able to deny reality, bitterness and rage took over. I occupied my time by alternately lying in bed feeling sorry for myself and writing letters full of fury to my mother.

Anger, frustration, and depression ruled my life, but my sister's generosity did provide some comfort. Michelle put enough money on my books to allow me to buy the best of what the commissary guy had to offer. I purchased tobacco, shampoo, and my own drinking cup. I also got instant coffee and enough cup-of-soup to have one each night, as well as a "stinger" to heat water for them.

In addition to the money, Michelle gave me two things to concentrate on to keep me from despair. First, she promised to visit. Second, she told me my son would be with her each Sunday and I could call and talk with him then.

On top of all that, Michelle brought me the allowed clothing, which included three pairs of white granny-panties, three white, wireless bras, three pairs of white socks, and one cotton nightgown—long with no pockets, buttons, or zippers. With the freezing temperature of the tank, I was most grateful for the thick socks, and usually wore all three pairs at once.

Missing my son was by far the most distressing part of my incarceration. I longed to hold him, touch him, even change his diapers. Eager to talk with my baby, I called Michelle on Sunday. When she didn't answer, worry wormed its way in. Was something wrong with my baby?

I tried her number again every fifteen minutes. It didn't make sense. She'd confirmed the time for the phone call during our visit. After two hours of anxious dialing, I finally got an answer.

"Is Lil Vinny all right? Why didn't you answer?" My words tumbled over one another.

"Vinny's fine. It's Ryan. . . " Michelle's voice broke.

"What's wrong?"

"He's sick." The tone of her voice gave the impression he was more than just sick. "Oh, Leigh Ann. I don't even know. It happened so fast. Ryan collapsed. The paramedics took him to the hospital."

My mind flipped through the possible causes of collapse. "Is he conscious now? What do they say it is?"

"He's in and out. They ran tests. The doctor said it's his liver." Her quivering voice gave way to sobs. "He's in the ICU. They said if he doesn't have a transplant soon, he'll die."

The ICU? Transplant? Die? "Oh, Michelle, I'm so sorry." My brain searched for words, but the news was impossible to comprehend. I detested the thought of Michelle having to go through this alone. My sister *needed* me.

"I wish I could be with you."

"Me too. Sorry I couldn't pick up Vinny so you could talk to him, but—"

"Don't even think about that."

"With all this. . . Sorry, but Vinny's going to have to stay with Andrew and Katrina longer."

My stomach churned. It made sense. Of course it did. And I certainly didn't blame Michelle. But the thought of my son continuing to stay with them felt like a hand in my throat, strangling me from the inside. "I understand."

"I have to go." Michelle's voice trembled. "Just came home to get some things."

"I did my best to sound reassuring. "Give Ryan my love. And Michelle—I love you."

"Love you too."

I slammed the phone into its cradle, slid down the cement wall, and trembled in a storm of helpless fury. There had to be a way out of jail. I thought of Ryan fighting for his life, my sister alone at his side. My son living with people who, I believed, hated me.

[CHAPTER FIFTY-ONE]

Church

No one could help me, and I couldn't help anyone. Not even myself. Was there ever a bigger failure at being a mother? A sister? A wife?

I paced the tank. Why couldn't people understand that although I'd done things wrong and had made terrible choices, I didn't murder my husband and didn't deserve jail? I only did what had to be done to save my son and myself.

A grim thought crashed over me. What if my son stopped loving me? My sister would have encouraged his love, but Andrew and Katrina? What if they poisoned him against me?

The idea of Vinny being led astray shrouded my heart. I'd die without him. I threw myself on my bunk and wrote bitter words to my mother before curling myself into a ball.

I can't lose my son.

What if they convinced him he was better off without me?

Would my baby ever forgive me?

I convulsed with heavy sobs. Moans escaped of their own free will.

A hand touched my shoulder. Alisha handed me a wad of toilet tissue. "I know it's hard. Nothing compares to the pain of being separated from your child." She sat on my bunk and hugged me. "At least we're not completely alone. We've got each other, and we've got God on our side."

"God?" I scoffed. "God doesn't care about me."

"Of course He does."

"Why would He care about a worthless loser like me?"

"You're not a worthless loser, and God knows that better than anyone." Alisha ran her fingers through my hair. "Leigh Ann, do you know God?"

"Yeah." Skepticism nudged me. "I've been to church."

"Will you come to church with me tonight?"

"We can go to church?" The idea of leaving the tank piqued my interest.

"They come to us. We join them at the bars."

I shrugged. It wasn't like I had anything better to do.

At seven o'clock, Alisha took me by the hand and led me to the bars where two women welcomed us with smiles that reached their eyes. They sang songs I didn't know and said words I'd never heard. One of the women asked about our favorite verse.

An inmate sitting on the floor next to me mentioned John 3:16, saying although it was a verse everyone knew, it was still her favorite.

I had no idea what "John 3:16" meant.

I'd gone to church on occasion while growing up. My mother tried, but getting four unenthusiastic children ready with no help from my non-churchgoing dad was like parting the Red Sea. Twice a year, however, with the added incentive of celebrating Christ's birth or His resurrection, she got us into our proper attire—tights, dresses, gloves, hats, suits, and ties—and into the car. The reward for her efforts was four children in various stages of slumber soon after Mass started.

Then there was my friend Joy's church. But I only went there for the fun and cute boys—and look how that ended. How could a God who cared let those boys rape me? What kind of God would allow so much bad to happen to me?

Sure, I'd heard of this Jesus dude and knew we celebrated Christmas and Easter because of Him, but I'd never read a Bible and had no idea what a verse was.

At the end of church, one of the women handed me a pamphlet. I thanked her and took it to my bunk. Rolling over on my mattress, I peered out the tiny bulletproof window for a glimpse of the free world, where the good people lived. Could Alisha and those women be right?

Could God love someone like me?

My eyes fell to the tract in my hand. The picture of flames on the cover couldn't burn me, but they distressed my soul. Tears blurred the words as I pondered the proposed question: If I died today, would I go to heaven or hell?

I killed my husband and lied to the police. Although I never cheated on Vincent, I had been a "bad girl" before I knew him. I got drunk, used drugs, and slept around. There could be no doubt. Everything in me quaked as I stared at the picture again—it looked hot in those flames. But how could I avoid them?

Opening the tract with cautious hope, I read a simple prayer. It talked about Jesus and how the whole cross thing was Him paying the price for my sins—all the things I did wrong—with His blood, death, and resurrection. It said belief in this sacrifice of Jesus could save me. I could go to heaven.

Since Jesus gave us Christmas and Easter, he must be real. I read the words again, and then repeated the prayer.

Something stirred inside my heart. An unfamiliar comfort settled deep within. But still, it felt unreal. How could a few words really make a difference?

Later that night, I told Alisha what I'd done.

Smiling, she hugged me tight. "Now you're my sister—my sister in Christ."

Not sure what she meant, I asked, "Am I supposed to feel different?"

She handed me her Bible. "Since you're a Christian now, you need to read God's word. Start with John."

I thought I already was *a Christian.* "What's John?"

Her mouth fell open a bit. "A book in the Bible. Just read all the pages with *John* at the top."

I tried but couldn't make sense of the words. Frustrated, I complained to Alisha.

In response, she chose a Christian book off the library cart and made me promise to set aside a "quiet time" each day to read it.

It's never quiet in here.

Each morning after breakfast, however, the women settled in their bunks. I took advantage of the lack of yelling, singing, and general cavorting. My "somewhat quiet time." The more I read the book, the more I began to believe in the idea that God could forgive me and love me unconditionally. I was filled with a desire to please Him. To know more.

Could God really work all things out for good? Even something as horrible as what led me to this place? How could God use my time here, my separation from my son, for *good*?

One answer came when Alisha approached me for help with her GED homework. After explaining long division in a way she understood, her expression of gratitude gave me the same sense of satisfaction I'd felt when helping Vincent reconnect with his father.

A thought struck me. "Do you think the teacher needs help in the class? I'd love to be a tutor."

"Can't hurt to ask."

I wrote a note to the teacher, which Alisha promised to deliver along with kind words about how much I'd helped her.

After class, excitement danced in her eyes. "Mr. Hardy's gonna see what he can do."

When the guard came to collect the students two nights later, she called my name along with Alisha's.

Mr. Hardy asked my intentions straight-up.

"I love helping people. I'd be honored to help these girls achieve something as important as a GED."

He smiled. "Sounds great to me. Welcome aboard."

From then on, Alisha and I went to class every Monday and Wednesday—she to learn, I to teach—and I had another something special to look forward to each week.

[C H A P T E R   F I F T Y - T W O]

Everyone sat at attention, eyes glued to the television.

"We the jury"—the female foreman's voice began as the camera focused on the defendant—"in the above entitled action, find the defendant, Orenthal James Simpson, not guilty of the crime of murder—."

Cheers, whoops, and hollers broke out, and a banging noise like thunder threatening to break down the walls drowned out the televised voice. The women in the tank danced with glee. The entire jail seemed to celebrate the jury's verdict.

More than ever, I knew I needed a great attorney. I didn't expect to get a "dream team" like OJ had, but inmates' horror stories of long prison sentences and bad plea bargains filled me with dread. Even though the truth should be enough to set me free, innocence wasn't enough in a murder trial. A great attorney was essential.

"Doug Mulder's office, this is Carol. How may I help you?"

I leaned against the wall and took a steadying breath. Would he take my call? "Um, yes, I was given Mr. Mulder's name. Was told he's a good attorney."

"Mr. Mulder's the best. If you'll call at four, he can talk with you then."

Smiling, I thanked her and hung up. The best. That's who I needed.

Five hours later, I called back. My leg bounced as I waited on hold.

"Doug Mulder here." His voice came across strong and confident.

"Yes, Mr. Mulder. A friend gave me your number. Said you could help me."

"What are you charged with?"

Still unable to fathom the word, I swallowed hard and cleared my throat. "Murder."

"Who do they say you killed?"

Fresh tears burned my eyes. "My husband."

After getting more details, he offered to visit.

My old attorney, who'd been paid, never did that, and neither had Peter, my new court-appointed one. "Really? You'd visit me?"

"Is there another place you'd prefer to meet?"

His words caught me off guard. "It's just. . . I'm surprised you'd visit me here."

"Well, that's where you are. How about Thursday afternoon?"

Thinking of him as my attorney gave me hope—something I hadn't felt for a long time. "That would be awesome."

Nervous excitement permeated me as I awaited Thursday's visit. At two o'clock, an officer called me to the bars.

"It's him." I jumped off my bunk and ran to Alisha. "Pray this goes well."

She hugged me tight. "Good luck."

The gate inched open, and the guard took me to a private visitor's booth. An impressive, elegant man stood on the other side of the bullet-proof glass, looking so out of place yet completely at ease in the dreary jail. Sunshine to my thundercloud life.

We picked up our phones. His gold cufflinks glimmered under the harsh lights.

"I'd shake your hand, but. . ." He winked and spread his arms. His dazzling blue eyes penetrated me, as if reading my thoughts and determining my character.

Something about him made the air easier to breath. Salt-and-pepper hair spoke of experience. His expensive suit and tie, looking more like shining armor, told me people paid him well. He exuded a unique mixture of confidence and assurance. Even while he scrutinized me, I sensed compassion.

For the first time ever, I told an alive and awake human being the truth of what happened the night my husband died. As I poured out my soul, he leaned forward, listening intently. At the conclusion, he sat back and rubbed his finger, as though twirling a non-existent wedding ring.

"That's a sad story. But it doesn't have to have a sad ending. The first order of business would be filing a request for a bond hearing. We need you free to prepare for your trial."

Freedom. "Really?"

He nodded. "I don't like preparing for a trial with my client incarcerated."

With no idea how much a top-notch attorney charged for murder, I hoped he was as compassionate as he appeared. "How much?" I held my breath, dreading his answer.

"Your case interests me. I like you and think we'll work well together. I'm going to give you a break. One of the hardest decisions a defense attorney has to make is whether to have the defendant testify in trial. In your case, there's no question. You'll have to take the stand."

My hand pushed on my bouncing leg in an effort to still it. "You expect a trial?"

"Unless the prosecution's willing to offer probation in a plea bargain."

Although I dreaded the idea of a trial, the prospect of no prison excited me.

"If I'm paid $150,000 for murder, it's $50,000 to try the case and $100,000 to decide whether my client will testify. With you, there's no decision. I'll take your case for just $50,000."

I pressed both hands over my mouth. *$50,000?* Was this really how he established fees, or was he joking?

Still unable to speak, I nodded. Nothing would please me more than having Doug on my side. But could I get $50,000 worth of help from my parents? Maybe I could convince them what a bargain it was. A fresh breeze of hope tickled my skin, as if a window had been opened.

"You have my number. Think about it."

"Oh, I'm sold. The problem is, your fee's about $49,999 more than I have."

Although Mom now lived in Vienna, Austria, she visited me every time she made one of her frequent trips to the States and did special things for my son to make up for my absence. When she found out how much getting mail meant to me, she wrote every day.

Dad had also been consistently supportive. He came to court for every hearing and visited me almost every week, even bringing my son with him once.

Both my parents proved their love repeatedly, standing by me with every inch of their beings, even with all I'd done wrong. They also helped me financially, including bond, attorney's fees, and putting money on my books.

But $50,000? Surely that kind of support would be too much.

The next time Mom was in town, I brought up Doug and how confident he sounded. Then I told her the bottom line.

Her silence spoke volumes.

"Mom? Did you hear me?"

"That's a lot of money."

"I know. But he's worth it."

She sighed. "I don't understand. Don't you already have an attorney for free?"

I closed my eyes and rubbed my face. Peter hadn't exactly been the attorney of my dreams. "One who doesn't seem to care or want to fight for me."

"Of course Peter will fight for you."

Her words, like the crash of the stock market that brought on the Great Depression, deflated my hope. "Not like Doug would."

After our conversation, I slumped to my bunk and cried. Was there any way to avoid life in prison now? Caressing a photo of my innocent son, I pulled him close and kissed his sweet face "Oh, Boo. How will I make it without you?"

[CHAPTER FIFTY-THREE]

Gratitude

Desperate to hear from God, I picked up the book Alisha had given me. As promised, I'd been reading it each morning after breakfast. Gathering the mattress cover into a ball for use as a pillow, I reclined and read.

The book was an autobiography about a man who trusted God in everything. He spoke of being filled with the Holy Spirit. I had no idea what he meant, but it intrigued me. I tried to imagine feeling completely loved and accepted. Worthy. Forgiven for everything I'd done wrong. Assured of going to heaven.

But that couldn't be for someone like me.

The preacher at Vincent's funeral believed my husband went to heaven and that I could see him again. Surely in a place like heaven, Vincent wouldn't be able to retaliate or stalk me. Maybe he'd even treat me as wonderfully as he once did.

But why would God want me with Him? All I'd ever done was screw up and disappoint everyone. No, God wouldn't appreciate my presence.

Then again, if He'd accept Vincent, why not me?

I tried to focus on the book. What I read made me laugh out loud. The author said if I could thank God in all situations, no matter how burdensome, and put my trust in Him, He would bring me peace.

This guy obviously didn't know how crushing life could be. How could anyone expect me to thank God for all the crap in my life?

Counting on my fingers, I listed the things I'd lost: my son, husband, freedom, family, job, house, nursing license, money, and, most likely, my future.

Out of nowhere, a voice spoke, as real as if someone whispered into my ear.

"Thank Me, not for the things you've lost, which are nothing compared to what I have in store for you, but for what you can gain. Accept your situation and thank Me, and I will restore you and give you peace."

Restoration? Peace?

Something niggled inside my heart. "Do you really want me, God?"

Warmth flooded me, like sinking into a hot bath. My knees were drawn like magnets to the floor.

"Thank You." Instantly, I somehow knew that no matter what, I could trust Him. Goosebumps popped up everywhere. Tears filled my eyes. "Thank You."

At last, I understood. The prayer from the pamphlet wasn't meant to be fire insurance set to words, but a reflection of a change of heart. A relinquishing of my whole self to God. While kneeling there on the hard jail floor, sobs came out in gulps as I gave myself to Him.

An indescribable warmth engulfed my body, washing me with joy. Joy that doused the fear and depression and unworthiness. His unconditional love filled the hollow center of emptiness that lived inside me for twenty-seven years. Consumed with peace, I was no longer chained. It didn't matter that I stood behind bars. I was released from the bondage of my past, unburdened of my sins, and I wholly accepted the hope of happiness I found by turning my life over to the Lord. Even if I received the earthly consequence of life in prison, my eternity would be with God.

Even though locked up, his truth had set me free.

[C H A P T E R   F I F T Y - F O U R]
Lice

The iron gate opened and four officers stepped in.
"Shake down."

My fellow cellmates groaned in unison, lining up at the bars.

An uneasiness overshadowed me. "What's going on?" I asked Alisha.

"They're gonna go through our stuff."

The guards patted us down, then moved us to a different cell while they spent hours going through our belongings, taking everything they considered contraband.

When we returned, my mouth fell open. I took in the wreckage. Mattresses, blankets, and papers littered the floor, with the contents of each crate strewn about the bare metal bunks. Everything pawed over. Feeling violated, I sorted through my measly possessions.

I frantically searched for the rest of my pictures, pushing my things around with the desperation of a cat missing her kittens.

Alisha came near. "You know, you're only allowed five."

"They can't just take them. Can they?"

She stared at me as though I was a teenager expecting Santa Claus to come down the chimney. "They can do anything they want."

I fanned out the five remaining photos. My jaw clenched thinking of the stolen twenty-five. I slumped in resignation. "They took my favorite picture of Vinny."

Alisha tried to comfort me, but her feverish scratching set off my internal alarm. A check of her head validated my concern. Lice.

That brought the guards back with de-lousing spray, garbage bags for our uniforms and bedding, and bleach for us to wash everything—including tables, bars, and clothes. The guards attacked Alisha first, dousing her like a huge cockroach refusing to die. One by one, we stripped down for the humiliating five-minute bug spray shower. After that, we spent hours cleaning the tank wrapped only in tiny towels that barely covered the bottoms of us skinny girls and left the larger ladies hanging out everywhere.

With everything scrubbed clean, the guards issued new bedding and uniforms. My panties, bras, socks, and gowns, however, all remained hanging to dry. Bone-weary and freezing, I went to bed with naked, numb toes, wondering if jail could get any worse.

[C H A P T E R   F I F T Y - F I V E]

Justice

I glanced at the new girl undressing in front of the shower. "Hey, Shanise, don't forget to wear your shoes in there."

She turned to me and glared. "And why is that? You don't want my bare black feet in your shower? You that racist?"

"No. Trying to be helpful. I'd hate for you to get athlete's foot or something. They're called shower shoes for a reason."

"Just for that, I'm gonna make sure I smear my black ass all over the place."

I rubbed my forehead and went back to my newspaper. "Whatever. It's your body."

Shanise persisted in accusing me of being racist, ignoring the obvious fact that several of my closest friends were black. Every comment, each laugh, even the tone of my voice somehow screamed racist to her.

One Sunday, while watching a Dallas Cowboys football game, I commented how silly one of the players acted with each touchdown he scored.

The next thing I knew, her fist met my face.

"How dare you make fun of him just because he's black."

My heart hammered. Unable to run, I cowered on the floor, covering my head and face as she hit me. Battles with Vincent had taught me how to protect myself against such rage.

Curse words spewed into the air as her fists pounded me again and again. I shrank as small as possible, covering vital organs and forcing my mind into the "numb zone."

Finally, the gate opened and five guards pulled her off me. They dragged us out and threw us into separate isolation cells.

Trembling, I sat on the floor, lay my swollen face on the metal bench, and cried. Although I'd done nothing wrong, justice rarely prevailed in jail. Would they separate me from my friends? Put me in the dreaded H tank, where the problem inmates go? Give me a new charge for assault?

The corporal finally approached. "Bayshore, get over here."

I moved to the bars, creaking and stiff like an arthritic old lady. "Yes, boss?"

"This isn't like you. Wanna tell me what happened?"

As my words spilled out, compassion shone in his eyes.

He took my hands in his and studied them. "Unlike Shanise, you have no wounds on your knuckles. And the girls in the tank confirm your story."

He photographed my face, arms, and knuckles before handing me a bag of ice.

Before long, he returned me to E-tank. My home. "Since the evidence is clear, you can stay here. Shanise has been moved to H tank."

Tears welled in my eyes. "Thank you."

He patted my shoulder. "You're one of the good ones. That's obvious to everyone here."

I soon received a notice in the mail informing me of a new inmate status. "Victim." Shanise had received a new charge, assault with bodily injury, for her actions against me.

Maybe justice could still be found, even in jail.

CHAPTER FIFTY-SIX

Christmas

I wanted to rip the pages out of the case law book and throw them away, as if that would abolish the statute.

This couldn't be true.

But the words made it clear. If someone has control and care of a child for 180 days, they can petition for custody. I slammed the book shut.

How long had my son been with Andrew and Katrina?

My hands shook as I counted the days. 123. What if they found out about the statute? Would they sue for custody? No way could I chance it. Something had to be done.

My weekly hour-long visit to the law library—which I usually enjoyed—couldn't end fast enough. I needed to pace. To pray. To beg Mom to get my son out of my sister-in-law's house.

The days crept by until I finally sat across from my mother. Even with the thick glass separating us, her presence comforted me. With only twenty minutes for a visit, we got right to business.

"Please, Mom..." my voice broke. "You have to get my son out of that house."

Sadness filled her eyes. "And where do you suppose he'll live? Michelle's in Colorado with Ryan while he waits for a liver transplant. She spends every day at the hospital."

My stomach churned with anger and guilt. I should be there for my sister. No way would I ask anything of her.

Mom furrowed her brow and moved the jail phone to her other ear. "You know how demanding my job is. If he lived with me in Austria, he'd be separated from everyone he knows. A nanny would have to take care of him while I traveled and worked. And you'd never get to talk to him on the phone. Is that what's best for him?"

Growing up with his mother was best for him. But that wasn't an option right now, and my son's needs took priority over my fears. "No. Of course not."

With sympathy in her voice, she completed the list of family members, each with valid reasons why they couldn't take my baby.

I wanted to beat my head on the glass. "What can we do?" I'd always been the fixer, but now I couldn't fix anything.

"I'll talk with an attorney about Vinny. And about your financial situation, too. Has the bank foreclosed on your house?"

"Not yet."

"While I'm here, we'll get your stuff packed up and moved into storage."

Images of my neglected house filled my mind. That cluttered mess would take days of nonstop labor. "I hate everyone having to do so much for me. Please let them know how much I appreciate it."

She smiled. "We're family. We stick together."

She was right. I treasured the visit with my dad, when his sadness and tears reached my soul. While the glass between us was impenetrable, his heart wasn't. And Michelle did more than could be expected from any sister, even with her husband gravely ill. They all supported me in countless ways. My throat tightened. My family really did love me.

"Christmas won't be the same without you. But at least we'll have Vin—"

"Time's up." A voice broke into our conversation.

Grief crushed me. "Tell everyone I love them." I stood, kissed my hand, and pressed it to the glass. I felt an overpowering need for my mother's touch. "Give my baby a big hug from his momma."

Her effort at smiling failed. "Have as merry a Christmas as you can."

Christmas came and went with little fanfare, bearing one special gift— talking with my family on the phone. I wanted nothing more than to hold and kiss my baby, but at least I got to hear his joy over all the stuff Santa brought him.

The next Saturday, however, Mom's somber expression when I entered the visitation booth drained my hope.

"The attorney said you're right. If someone cares for a child for six months, they can sue for custody."

Another shovel of dirt deepened the hole I couldn't seem to climb out of. "So what can we do?"

"Aside from taking him out of their house, there's only one option." She hesitated before speaking, like someone about to give shattering news. "If they sue you for custody, given your current circumstances, they'll most likely win. But they probably wouldn't be successful in a battle against me."

Her words sucked the oxygen out of the room. I bit my lip and swallowed hard. *Please God, don't let me lose my son.*

"Wait. He said although they could win custody from me, he doesn't believe they would be successful in a battle against you?"

My mom nodded as my mind tried to register her words. Why—and how—would they fight her?

"He suggested you sign custody of Vinny over to me."

I blinked. What kind of solution was that? To keep from losing custody, I sign my rights away? Questions formed in my mind, but the words wouldn't come.

"It's a formality." She waited, expecting an answer. "It's only to preserve your rights as Vinny's mother."

I won't give up my son.

"You asked me to do something, and this is what the lawyer came up with."

"No," I said. "There's no way."

"As soon as you're able to care for him, I'll give custody back to you. In the meantime, you'll still have partial custody."

My heart dissolved into a black hole of emptiness. "I can't."

Mom leaned forward. "You asked for my help and this"—she held up the papers—"is what the attorney suggested. I don't know what else to do."

"But it's—"

"It's simple, that's what it is. You don't have many options. Either sign custody over to me, or lose it to them."

The black hole in my chest expanded. I lose either way. But I didn't want to lose my mother too.

Tears fell down my face as I nodded.

"Good. I already talked to them about a notary. As soon as you're back in your tank, you can sign the papers. I'll wait for them."

I now understood how it must feel to have to saw off your arm to save your life.

[C H A P T E R   F I F T Y - S E V E N]

Offer

"There's no way around it. You're going to prison." My court-appointed attorney, Peter, dished out the news as if explaining four comes after three. "Hope I can do a little better than the thirty-five year offer from the prosecutor, but you're looking at a long sentence."

Thirty-five years. My eyes widened with fear, then narrowed in disbelief. This man was supposed to do battle for me, but he showed no evidence of a combat gene. Instead, he appeared fine with the idea of me being separated from my son, razor wires and high walls between us until he was old enough to vote. "Don't you want to even *try* to fight for me?"

"Leigh Ann, you shot your husband. Twice. One in the back."

"So, that's it? Because of where he was shot, you think I deserve to go to prison?"

"Never mind me. Think about a jury. How do you explain shooting your husband in the back?"

"I told you. I don't know. It happened so fast. We were fighting over the gun. I closed my eyes. It went off. Twice. Then he ran out the front door. I didn't even realize he'd been shot."

"Surely you can see how that would be a hard sell to a jury."

How could I explain something I didn't remember or understand? "I talked with another attorney, and he said that kind of thing happens. He said Vincent must have spun around with the power of the first shot, so his back was toward me when the gun went off again."

"Another attorney?" His expression turned suspicious. "Who?"

Did I break some kind of rule by talking with Doug? "Is that not allowed?"

"Hey, if someone else thinks he can do better, maybe you should hire him."

If only that were possible. "But *you're* my attorney"—I banged my fist on the metal shelf in front of me, a scream clenched in my teeth—"and I expect you to do your best to keep me out of prison."

"You're going to have to get used to the idea, said Peter. "There's no reason to take this to trial. We'll just have to see what kind of offer we can get from the prosecutor."

I cupped my head in my hands, afraid if I didn't hold it tight, it might explode. "No reason? This is my life we're talking about."

"Right. Your life. I do understand." His face grew cold. "Do you understand another life is over because of your actions?"

I wanted to scream. "Of course I know my husband is dead. But it was self-defense."

He leaned back and folded his arms over his chest. "You have to be able to convince a jury of that. My suggestion is you do the best you can on a plea bargain."

Didn't he care? "He tied me up and tortured me. I had knife wounds all over, including my neck. And one on my leg that needed twenty staples."

His hand worked at the unruly mustache covering his upper lip. "The prosecutor will say your wounds were self-inflicted."

"Self-inflicted?" Incredulous, I slapped my hands on my bouncing legs, trying to keep them still. "That's insane!"

"True or not, they can say whatever they want. And with creativity, they can convince a jury of all sorts of things."

"Where's your creativity? Don't you know how to convince a jury?"

"It's not a chance I think you should take."

"What if I want to?"

"It would be suicide." He put the plea bargain offer into his briefcase, then snapped it shut. "I think I can get them down to twenty-five. That would be a good plea agreement. You'd only serve half before being eligible for parole."

❖ ❖ ❖

I lay on my bunk and cried—again. I could manage little else since Vincent's death.

How could two attorneys be so different? Doug understood and expressed confidence in his ability to win my freedom, while Peter seemed like he wanted me locked up. He certainly didn't seem to care about defending me.

But what could I do?

Nothing.

Feeling weak and helpless, I meditated on the words of Nehemiah 8:10. "The joy of the Lord is my strength."

The joy of the Lord. . . I needed to find that joy again. I opened my Bible, a gift from the chaplain, and found one of my favorite verses in a letter to the Thessalonians. The apostle Paul encouraged them to be joyful always, pray continually, and give thanks in all things. I got on my knees and prayed, asking God to give me His peace, His hope, and to make things work out for good. Then I thanked Him for whatever His will for me turned out to be.

I took out my pen and paper and wrote to my mother, a letter filled with words of peace and trust in God, even though it also included the devastating news from my attorney.

She wrote back. "I'm coming to town and have an appointment with Peter on the fourteenth. We'll get this straightened out."

I called her after her meeting with Peter. Barely taking time to say hello, she started in with questions about Doug.

A tinge of hope sparkled inside. "Why do you want to know so much about Doug?"

"Do you really trust him?" My mother sighed. "Because I just can't get over that man who calls himself a defense attorney. He's not interested in defending you. He actually asked me to convince you to take the plea deal. We need a different attorney."

Thank you, God. "Doug's perfect, Mom. He's who I want."

"Do you still have his number?"

Mom sounded cheerful when I called the next day. "Happy birthday, sweetheart. It must be tough to spend your birthday in jail, but maybe I can brighten your day."

I held my breath.

"Your dad and I figured it out. Doug's your new attorney."

My heart soared. "That's the most amazing birthday gift ever. Thank you."

"There are a few details to work out first, but as soon as we get the money to him, Doug will meet with the judge and make sure you get bond."

A great attorney, and freedom too? *Thank you, Jesus.*

"Although it won't happen before I have to leave for Poland for my meeting with the Ambassador, if everything happens the way Doug expects it to, you'll be free in two or three days."

A burst of hope exploded within. Would I really be free so soon?

[CHAPTER FIFTY-EIGHT]

Judge

My body trembled as I faced the black-robed man. The man who held the power to release me or keep me locked up. I willed my saliva glands to produce enough moisture for speech. "Yes, Your Honor, I understand the importance of adhering to any stipulations you choose."

Judge Harris furrowed his brow and leaned forward, studying me as if to gauge my level of compliance and sincerity.

I felt like an ant with a car-sized magnifying glass hovering above.

The judge sat back and spoke to my father. "And her family supports her release?"

My dad stood. "Yes, Your Honor. Her entire family supports her in every way possible."

The prosecutor fought to keep me locked up, citing everything from concern over disrupting my son's preschool schedule to worries I'd take him and flee the country, especially since my mother lived overseas.

Doug made a face at the prosecutor. "It's absurd to suggest Ms. Bayshore stay incarcerated because of her son's preschool. The child needs to be with his mother. And the idea that Ms. Bayshore's mother, who is a federal law enforcement officer, would have anything to do with her daughter becoming a fugitive is outrageous. Leigh Ann eagerly awaits her chance to gain freedom through a fair trial of her peers, and she will happily surrender her passport."

Judge Harris agreed, saying he had no intention of denying bail based on a toddler's daycare schedule. He went on to say that in the interest of minimizing concerns, he would add bond stipulations regarding visitation with Vinny.

Visitation?

My heart soared at the prospects of being out of jail and spending time with Vinny.

However, my bond conditions hardly amounted to freedom. I would again wear an ankle monitor, be under strict house arrest, and have to report three times a week. In addition, the judge ordered my son to remain in the care of Andrew and Katrina, with supervised visitation to be decided by Vinny's custodian.

Distressed over the judge's decision, I at least found consolation in Mom being the decision maker. I also appreciated having a place to live. Although Michelle and Ryan remained in Colorado awaiting a new liver, I'd be living in their house with Chris and Haley, who'd just moved from out of town.

When I walked out of the jail, my lungs fluttered with the foreign fresh air. My skin tingled with the alien warmth of the sun. My mind reeled from the sensory overload of hundreds of colors I hadn't seen for eight months.

Chris opened the car door and helped get my belongings into the backseat—two brown grocery sacks containing everything my life had become.

He told me the plan on the way home. "Mike's picking up Vinny, and they should be there around six-thirty. Someone's coming at seven to set up the monitor."

My thoughts turned to holding my son, feeling his skin, kissing the top of his head. The simple pleasures of life infused me with joy.

Finally, Mike arrived with the light of my life. My little boy raced into my arms. I scooped him up, squeezing him until he sputtered for breath.

"Mommy, I love you."

With the sound of his sweet voice, I felt like I could fly. "I love you too, Boo. I missed you so much."

He buried his face in my neck and kissed me.

Although Andrew and Katrina had insisted my son and I share less than two hours together, my mother called from her hotel in Poland and said he should stay with me for two days. When I shared the news with

Andrew, he threatened to have me arrested for kidnapping. I reminded him my mother held Vinny's custodianship and she got to decide how long our visits lasted. Andrew reluctantly relented.

That night, with my son wrapped in my arms, I slept as the angels must while perched on their clouds. Two days with my son felt like two minutes, and too soon our time was over.

At my next report to the probation department, my joy skidded to a halt when an officer slapped handcuffs on my wrists.

"What did I do?"

His only explanation was a warrant for my arrest.

I called Doug. He promised to get a hearing as soon as possible.

After the elation of holding my son and tasting freedom, this arrest was the worst. I cried the entire thirty hours it took to get processed, once again enduring the humiliating bug spray shower and freezing temperatures in a holding tank before being dumped in a permanent tank.

Then back to court.

As I faced Judge Harris again, he informed me of his disappointment that I'd breached my bond conditions so quickly. "It has come to my attention you had unsupervised time with your son and kept him two days longer than allowed."

With help from my family, we opened his eyes to the truth—not only were Chris and his wife, Haley, with me for the entire visit, but my mother—the custodian—approved the two days.

Judge Harris apologized to Doug and ordered my release. Several hours later, I walked out of the jail determined to focus on the joy of being free rather than the lies told to my judge.

A knock on the door interrupted dinner mere hours after my release. The stranger handed me a fat envelope, an attorney's name on the return address. My fingers shook as I tore it open. The legal papers contained words that spiraled my nightmare to depths previously unimaginable.

I threw the papers to the ground and reached for my son's pajamas. My knees gave way and I fell to the floor, curling up in a ball. Hugging the pajamas to my face, drinking in his baby scent, I wept.

[CHAPTER FIFTY-NINE]

Preparation

While I had sat unjustifiably jailed, Andrew and Katrina filed a lawsuit—a motion to modify managing conservatorship of my son from my mother to them. Not only that, they convinced a judge to grant them emergency custody.

How could I fight a custody suit while preparing for a murder trial? A crumpled heap on the floor, I thought of burning the papers, rejecting their existence. But fire and denial wouldn't change a thing. Something inside me had expected this since the day my son moved in with them, but my heart had refused to accept it.

Hopelessness weakened my already frail soul.

Please, God, give me strength.

When my mother called and I explained what they'd done, she was infuriated.

"But they promised. After getting custody, I talked with them. Told them I was prepared to take Vinny to Vienna with me and that my top concern was for him to return to you as soon as possible. I left their house convinced we had nothing to worry about. That they would never do anything to keep your son from you."

"And you believed them?"

"They seemed so sincere."

If only she'd taken him.

"They'll never win," Mom said. "We took care of that by having you sign custody to me."

A sense of foreboding slithered through me. "I hope you're right."

We hired attorneys. My sister, who remained in Colorado with her husband while he awaited a transplant, joined the fight. She and Ryan were, after all, Lil Vinny's godparents. The ones Vincent and I had named to care for our child if anything happened to us.

A court hearing soon spelled out visitation with terms that left everyone unhappy—I wanted more time with my son and they wanted me to have less.

After what seemed an endless string of tragedies, Michelle called one Sunday morning with great news. They'd found a liver for Ryan. I drove to church with an impossible-to-remove smile, praising God and singing songs of worship. My sister and her husband would finally be able to come home.

That afternoon, Dad called. "Ryan"—a sob broke his voice—"he. . ."

A chill raced through me. No. It couldn't be. *Please don't say it.*

"Ryan. . ." My dad cleared his throat and tried again. "Didn't make it."

"No!" I crumpled to the floor, where I remained for hours weeping.

That evening, Mike flew to Denver to help Michelle make arrangements and bring her back home. The sight of my anguished sister overwhelmed me. I held her tightly as we cried.

Why God? Why so much grief for one family?

Three things occupied my time over the next few months—spending every allowed second with my son, being there for my sister as much as possible, and preparing for my trial.

During the many hours I spent with Doug in his office, I learned new and painful details about my husband and the case against me.

The medical records from my emergency room visit the night of Vincent's death said I "disappeared" around 1:00 am after my husband was killed and that I was brought to the hospital "in police custody." That explained why they handled me with such disrespect.[3]

In a signed affidavit, Vincent's "old friend" Roxanne said he complained to her all the time about his sex life. She also claimed Vincent was afraid of me.

Vincent afraid of me? I had to laugh at the incongruity. Certainly he'd become quite paranoid in his last few months—most likely due to his drug use—but the idea he was afraid of me was insane. And the fact that my husband discussed his sexual frustrations with this woman aroused even more suspicions about their "friendship."

My brother Chris had been there the night Roxanne and Vincent "reconnected." According to him, she was a dancer, not a hostess as Vincent had claimed. During the party, Chris had more than once seen her sitting in Vincent's lap.

In a police report signed by my brother-in-law,[4] Matt said Vincent told him he originally started a relationship with me so he could "use" me, but ended up falling in love. He added that Vincent always thought I was "fooling around" on him, but that Matt knew me well enough to know I wasn't. Matt also said Vincent was cheating—with a dancer, a girl "he'd always been in love with."

Matt's words pierced my heart, wounding me to the core of my being. Vincent had done many horrendous things, but I'd somehow convinced myself he loved me enough to remain faithful. Now I knew the truth. My husband's likely betrayal of our marriage vows proved nothing was out of bounds for him.

While the documents, affidavits, and transcripts of grand jury testimony dismayed me, one statement made me smile. When questioned by the police, my ex-husband, Keith, told them I was a good person and he didn't believe I killed Vincent. "But if she did, he must have really deserved it. Must have beaten the crap out of her. After all, I did all sorts of bad stuff to her, and she never even threatened me."[5]

Two weeks before my trial, my attorney received a call from Mr. Rice, the Assistant District Attorney assigned to my case. Mr. Rice wanted to talk plea bargain, and he offered a twenty-year sentence if I'd plead guilty to murder.

I stood and walked to the large picture window overlooking downtown Dallas. "Is he crazy, or does he think I am?"

Doug put his papers down and came to my side. "Okay, so twenty years is out, but let me ask you something. Is there any offer you'd consider?"

The idea of avoiding a trial did appeal to me. I thought first of my son, and then the burdens a trial would place on both my family and Vincent's. It would be wonderful to bypass so much pain for the people I loved. But at what cost? Knowing my sentence and not taking the "life in prison" gamble would be the safest thing, but how could I plead guilty to something I wasn't guilty of? Could I surrender to prison time and leave my son's life without putting up a fight?

"I don't want to plead guilty, but the idea of twelve strangers judging me is terrifying."

Doug pressed his lips together. "Juries can be unpredictable. But hey, better to be judged by twelve than carried by six."

Understanding sank in. I stared past the skyscrapers, wishing life didn't have to be so hard. "Living with Vincent was prison enough. I want to be free with my son, and won't accept an offer which takes me away from him."

Doug smiled. "All right, then. That's what I'll tell Mr. Rice."

"One other thing. What happened wasn't murder, and I refuse to plead guilty to that. He'd have to reduce the charge."

Doug clapped his hands together. "I'll let him know."

The following visit, Doug informed me Mr. Rice called with another offer—twelve years. "I told him we wouldn't plead to penitentiary time, but Rice said the victim's family would never let him agree to probation."

"Lovely." I sighed. "Guess that means the fight is on."

I went to Doug's office once more, this time to wrap up some last-minute pre-trial details. As soon as I walked in, he pointed to a chair. "Have a seat."

An icy grip tightened around me.

"Mr. Rice is doing his best to coerce you into prison. He went to a new grand jury and presented your case. Said you were already indicted for murder, then showed them the life insurance policy on Vincent and told them you killed your husband for the money. Convinced them to re-indict you." Doug folded his hands. "Capital murder. Said if we insist on going to trial, he's going for capital life."

Numbness seized me. Capital life? A lump grew in my throat and I swallowed hard.

"Apparently, he's already waived the death penalty. But if you don't take the twelve and end up convicted of capital murder, you won't be eligible for parole for forty years."[6]

I blinked. The *death penalty*? My brain swam, making it difficult to find words. "What do you think?"

"I think it was a smart, intimidating move. Makes a twelve-year sentence look like a walk in the park." He softened his voice. "You'd be eligible for parole in six."

"It wasn't murder. I didn't want him to die. I just wanted him to stop. To leave us alone. How can I face my son someday and get him to believe the truth if I plead guilty to murder?"

"In that case"—Doug reached for the file and opened it—"we'll just kick their ass."

[CHAPTER SIXTY]
Voir Dire

I stared in the mirror.

What will the jury think? Will they see a murderer?

My mother's reflection appeared behind me. New lines creased her face. "You okay?"

Unable to find my voice, I attempted to smile. It fell flat.

She wrapped me in her arms. "I'm here for you every step of the way, sweetheart."

How wrong I'd been to have ever doubted her love. Emotion broke my voice. "Wish I could be somewhere else." *The sufferings of the present trials are not worthy to be considered.* My mantra from the Bible ran through my mind, bringing assurance like it always did. "One way or another, it'll be okay."

She kissed my forehead. "Come on, breakfast is on the table."

Waves of nausea surged. "I'm not hungry."

"You need your strength." Taking my hand, she led me to the kitchen.

I sat with her and pushed food, but ate very little. My stomach protested each bite. Excusing myself, I gathered my purse and keys and drove to meet Doug.

He opened the door before I finished knocking. A grin crossed his face, making his eyes sparkle. "Well, if it isn't the woman of honor. Come on in."

Two men rose from their chairs. Doug introduced the blond man first. "This is Curtis Glover. He's our creative strategist. His specialty is smoke and mirrors." He glanced at the dark-haired man. "And this is John Hagler. He's our law man. What he doesn't know about the law isn't worth knowing."

I shook their hands and thanked them for joining my team.

"These are questionnaires the jury pool filled out." Doug shoved a pile of paperwork into my arms. "The more we know about these people, the better jury we can pick."

Four cups of coffee later, I checked my watch and bolted out of the chair. "We're going to be late for jury selection."

"No worries." Doug smiled. "Can't have rabbit stew without the rabbit."

Rabbit stew? I opened my mouth, but nothing came out.

Walking through the ten-foot tall double doors into the atrium of the courtroom felt like entering a portal into an unstable world with hidden traps in the floor. Dizzy, I sat on the first available bench and prayed for strength. "I'm not ready for this."

"Ready or not, it's happening. Focus on the positive"—Doug winked—"you've got the best attorneys around."

The judge's bench stood tall and ominous, imposing itself over the doleful witness stand. My eyes swept to the left and locked on the jury box. I suppressed an urge to run.

Doug guided me through the bar to the main court area, where the chairs had been moved to face the gallery. I joined John and Curtis at the defense table and stared at the rows of benches, soon to be filled with potential jurors. My family sat in a back corner so they could watch the proceedings while staying out of the way of the jury pool.

Doug placed his leather briefcase on the table and opened it, revealing Butter Rum Life Savers among files and papers.

A bailiff entered from the back of the room. "All rise for the Honorable Judge Jacob Harris."

The judge sat on his perch. "Be seated."

Another bailiff entered from the front. "All rise for the jury." While being seated, some gazed at me with apprehension. Several appeared suspicious. A few gave me unblinking stares of revulsion. Not a friendly face to be found. Cold sweat broke out on my forehead as I did my best to look innocent.

Judge Harris swore in the potential jurors. "It's a privilege and honor to be called as a juror, and I'd like to personally thank each of you for being here. Believe me—we appreciate you a lot more than you'll be paid."

Hesitant laughter filled the room.

Judge Harris continued. "Now, this isn't so much a jury selection as a process of elimination. After strikes and exclusions, the first twelve left are the jury."

He introduced the two prosecutors and three defense attorneys. "*Voir dire* is your chance to ask questions and voice opinions. If you're selected, it's too late. At that point, you become a silent participant. So, take advantage of this." A grin crossed his face. "It's probably the only time in your life you'll get to ask attorneys questions for free."

Chuckles filled the courtroom.

Assistant District Attorney Robert Rice began the jury selection by telling the jury pool he would show, beyond any reasonable doubt, that I shot and killed my husband for life insurance money. He predicted my trial would end with a verdict of guilty of capital murder.

Tears stung my eyes. I pushed down the urge to stand and profess my innocence.

Mr. Rice explained how the evidence would show I lied to the police right after the shooting and continued lying for two years. He begrudgingly revealed Vincent's criminal record. Per the judge's ruling, information regarding final convictions was admissible. The prosecutor stated Vincent had been convicted of robbery and assault by threat, but that the victim served his time and his criminal record shouldn't be held against him.

Then Doug stood for his turn. He smiled and buttoned his tailored suit jacket as he strode toward the bar dividing us from the gallery. Completely at ease, he faced the men and women, walking purposefully a few more paces until all eyes settled on him. "Ladies and gentlemen, thank you in advance for your time and attention." He gave a slight bow. "I hope to get to know you better, as you would if you were interviewing someone for a very important job."

He spoke in a soothing tone, making eye contact with each person. After describing the one-sided process of a grand jury investigation, he held up a legal paper for all to see. "This is the indictment. As the judge will tell you, this is no evidence of guilt. It does two things, and only two things." He held up his index finger. "First, it informs Leigh Ann of the accusation against her so she can prepare her defense. Second,"—he held up another finger—"it advises you of what the prosecution must prove beyond a reasonable doubt."

He placed the paper on the defense table with a flourish, playing to the jury pool as if they were his audience in a Broadway play. "The law says the burden of proof is on the state. In other words, whoever does the accusin' has to do the provin'." He walked behind me and placed his hand on my arm in a fatherly fashion. "The law says Leigh Ann doesn't have to do anything except be here. She doesn't have to prove her innocence or bring evidence. She *can* bring evidence, and she will, but she doesn't have to. The burden of proof"—he gestured toward the prosecutor—"never shifts."

Some of the potential jurors sat on the edge of their seats. None appeared to be snoozing.

Moving with grace from one side of the courtroom to the other, extending his right hand as if leading the way, Doug outlined the order of the trial. "The state goes first." He held up his left hand. "And last." He held up his right hand. "With us sandwiched in between." He brought his hands together. "If I had my druthers, I'd prefer to go first. First impressions are mighty important. Is there anyone here who can't hold off on making a decision until we get a chance at bat?"

No hands. Doug smiled and paced in front of the jury, stopping to study each of their faces. "The law gives the defendant in a criminal case a head start. That head start is called the presumption of innocence. When you came into the courtroom this morning, you probably figured out who the various players were—the prosecutors, the judge, the defense attorneys." He moved to stand behind me and placed his hands on my shoulders, giving me a touch of stability. "The first time you saw the defendant, you probably asked, 'I wonder what she did?' If you did, you didn't give her the presumption of innocence."

Doug removed his hands, crossed his arms, and headed back to the jury. "I don't care whether you presume Leigh Ann innocent or not, I just don't want you to presume she's guilty simply because she's here. I don't need a head start. I just want to start even. Anyone have a problem with that? Anyone who can't let me start out even?"

A man on the second row rolled his eyes. I found his name on the seating chart and gripped my pencil, jotting it down. He didn't need to be on my jury.

Doug walked to the defense table and picked up his notes. He slipped on his glasses and scanned the papers, then looked up, as if waiting for angels to guide him. "Now, I want to get something straight." His voice rose for maximum impact. "This is not a whodunit." He again stood behind me and placed his hands on my shoulders. "Leigh Ann shot and killed her husband, and if you'd been there in her place, you'd have done the same thing."

Shocked faces filled the courtroom.

"Does everyone understand a person has the right to protect herself and her loved ones?"

A woman raised her hand and Doug acknowledged her. "Yes, ma'am?"

The woman stood, put her hands on her hips, and glared at me. "I don't care what the circumstances are. No one has the right to take a life." Pointing emphatically toward the ceiling, she said, "Only God has that right."

Heat rose in my cheeks. I shrank into my chair, praying for invisibility.

"Really?" Doug stroked his chin and considered her. "So, if a bad man broke into your house and threatened to harm or kill someone you love, you'd sit back and allow him to do whatever he wanted?"

She continued her glare. "Only God has the right to take a life."

I blinked and swallowed hard.

Doug put his hands behind his back and paced. "Does anyone else feel that a person doesn't have the right to protect himself against an unprovoked attack?"

No one raised a hand.

Doug took a confident stance. "Ladies and gentlemen, Leigh Ann is the real victim here. She saved her son's life and survived the violence of that night. She's again fighting for her life, but this time, she's doing it with words. Today, the truth is her weapon."

At the conclusion of the *voir dire*, Doug, Curtis, John, and I discussed our observations. In the end, after strikes and exclusions, Judge Harris called the names of the twelve charged with the duty of deciding my fate—eleven men and one woman.

I bowed my head and prayed softly, "Please, God, let them hear and believe the truth."

[CHAPTER SIXTY-ONE]

Opening

Mr. Rice opened the trial by again pointing at me and saying I murdered my husband for money. He insisted forensic evidence would prove I lied over and over about what happened that night when I aimed a gun at my husband, shot him, and left him in the front yard for hours to die.

What??? Left him for hours to die?

I sat there, twisting my hands in my lap, and listened to the prosecutor weave a mortifying tale of how Vincent was afraid of me. How I took out a secret life insurance policy on him in order to pay off my large debts upon his death.

Secret policy? My debts? And he calls me a liar.

I wanted to stand up. I wanted to scream the truth. I wanted to go home. Instead, I clenched my teeth and swallowed my voice, wringing my hands harder.

Doug leaned into me. "Relax. We'll show the truth."

I took a calming breath and willed myself to be still. My silent prayers began in earnest, and I knew they wouldn't stop until the trial was over.

When the prosecutor finished, Doug stood and gave a slight bow. "May it please the court, Your Honor? I'd like to reserve my opening statement at this time."

For the prosecution's first witness, second seat prosecutor Assistant District Attorney Dean called Mr. Turner, a representative from the insurance company. Mr. Turner told the jury I took out a $30,000 policy on Vincent, and that I tried to collect it after his death.

On cross-examination, Doug showed not only did I not seek out the company looking for life insurance, but that the second time they called me, I told them I'd have to discuss it with my husband.[7, 8]

With further questions, Mr. Turner admitted that $30,000 was the smallest policy they offered.

"I see." Doug leaned forward and steepled his hands. "So, if you were planning to kill someone for money, would you go for a measly $30,000, or would you—"

"Objection, Your Honor." Ms. Dean interrupted Doug yet again, having already done so at least a couple dozen times in the short testimony.

"Your Honor, I'm trying to show—"

"That's an inappropriate and irrelevant question," Ms. Dean said.

Doug shrugged. "I don't see how it's irrel—"

"Your Honor." She turned to the judge. "He can't ask—"

Doug turned to her. "You know, I treat you like a lady. Why can't you act like one?"

Ms. Dean's face flushed. Her mouth opened and closed, like a fish gasping for water.

The judge almost disappeared beneath his desk, only his shaking shoulders visible.

Doug flashed a smile at the jury. "I'm just pointing out that a person planning to kill her spouse for money would take out a much larger policy." He turned to the witness. "Mr. Turner, how often do you have someone decide not to collect when a loved one dies?"

Mr. Turner's face scrunched up. "I've... never known that to happen."

"So, you agree there's nothing conspicuous about Mr. Bayshore having a minimum life insurance policy." Doug raised his voice. "Nothing sinister about Ms. Bayshore filing a claim."

Mr. Turner seemed to be working out a math problem in his head. "Right. Nothing conspicuous or sinister."

Doug leaned back in his seat. "No further questions."

For their next witness, Mr. Rice called Detective Dutch. The prosecutor spent an hour asking the detective about my statement and having him read from it. When finished, the jury knew the story I'd given—an intruder got into our house, tied me up, and cut me with a knife. When my husband tried to rescue me, the "intruder" shot him.

Mr. Rice leafed through his notes, checked things off, stacked the papers neatly. "Pass the witness."

"Just a thing or two, Detective." Doug ran a finger over his chin. "When was Ms. Bayshore first read her rights?"

The detective shrugged. "I don't know."

"Was she ever read her rights?"

A long pause. "Not that I know of."

Shock appeared on Doug's face. "Really? And why is that?"

"We only read rights to suspects."

"I see." Doug made a mark on his notes. "So, the night you questioned Leigh Ann, you didn't consider her a suspect? You believed her story?"

"Yes, sir. I mean, we all believed her. We only saw her as a victim and a witness."

"So, while you questioned Leigh Ann, others were actively searching for a suspect?"

"Yes. We put out an APB."

"When did you put out the APB?"

"Right away."

"So, you're telling this jury you put out an APB"—Doug made quote marks with his fingers—"right away, even though no one asked Leigh Ann for a description of the intruder for over four hours."

Detective Dutch shifted nervously. "I'm sure we got the description earlier."

"You don't remember asking Leigh Ann for a description after she received treatment in the emergency room? In the parking lot? In front of her brother?" Doug flipped through more papers. "If my notes are correct, she was in the ER until about 5:30 a.m."

The detective frowned. "I'm sure we asked her earlier."

Doug brought him a paper. "Detective, what is this?"

The witness glanced at the paper. "It's the APB."[9]

"And what is the time stamped on it?"

Detective Dutch took a closer look. "It appears to be 12:34."

"Yes." Doug walked back to his seat. "I'm guessing that's p.m., since at 12:34 a.m., Mr. Bayshore was still alive."

The detective wiped his forehead. "I. . . don't know."

"Well, do you know how many times you questioned Leigh Ann?"

"Twice. Right after the incident and again a few hours later."

"Yes. . ." Doug tapped his notes. "You questioned her for several hours, repeatedly refusing to let her go to the emergency room while she bled on your floor—"

"Objection." Mr. Rice half-stood. "Not in evidence."

Doug leaned back and put his hand on his hip. "So, Leigh Ann went to the emergency room around 4:00 a.m., for knife wounds inflicted by her husband. When she finished getting stapled up around 5:30 a.m., you got the description of the intruder in the parking lot in front of her brother. Then her brother took her to his house. Is that correct?"

Detective Dutch began to nod, then stopped. "Yes, her brother took her to his house."

Doug smiled. "And even though you told her brother she could get some rest, since she'd been up all night answering questions, you arrived at his house two hours later and took her back to the station. Is that correct?"

Detective Dutch pressed his lips together before answering. "Something like that."

"And how many times was Leigh Ann questioned after that morning?"

"None that I'm aware of."

"So"—Doug spread his arms—"would it be fair and accurate to say Leigh Ann has not continued to lie since the night in question, but that she gave her statement, which she didn't sign, and never discussed it again?"

"As far as I know."

"Just one more question, Detective. Did you have occasion to review Vincent Bayshore's extensive criminal record?"

"Objection!" Ms. Dean flew from her seat.

A smug expression crossed Doug's face. "No further questions. I'll pass the witness."

The prosecution called their third witness, Vincent's mother. Mara described her son as a caring man who loved his wife and baby and would never do anything to hurt or threaten either of us.

On cross-examination, Doug asked her questions about Vincent's three psychiatric hospitalizations and his diagnosis of anti-social personality disorder. "What is your understanding of a sociopath?"

Mara took a moment to answer. "I'm not sure, other than they don't fit in society."

"Because they pay no attention to the rules society imposes. And Vincent didn't obey the rules, did he?"

Mara looked toward her family. "I don't know that I would put it that way."

"Well, maybe they're just pranks to you, but breaking into people's houses, stealing their cars, things of that nature—"

"Objection," Ms. Dean said in an irritated voice.[10]

Doug turned to Mara. "Did you consider Vincent violent?"

Mara paused and took a deep breath, then responded that Vincent could be loving one minute and the next minute blow up. She added that although Vincent could get angry and lose control, his violence was aimed at objects, not people.[11]

Doug flipped through his notes. "Were you not informed about an altercation he had with a ward assistant where he broke the lady's jaw during one of his psychiatric hospitalizations?"

Mara fidgeted. "I don't know anything about that."

"Do you recall telling Detective Dutch in your statement to him that Vincent had a violent temper?"[12]

"I don't remember. I never saw Vincent violent toward Leigh Ann or Vincent Junior."

Doug leaned forward, elbows on the table. "You probably never saw your son steal a car or burglarize a home or rob a shopkeeper or destroy other people's property, either, did you?"

Mara blinked and pressed her lips together. "True."

"I believe that's all."[13]

Judge Harris spoke. "I think this is a good time to end our first day. It's been long, and I want to thank the jurors for their attention. Please be back in the morning ready to proceed at 9:00 sharp."

Doug packed his things into his briefcase. "First day down. You're doing fine. Tomorrow should be an interesting day."

Interesting? More like terrifying—as if being on a runaway train, each moment racing closer to my fatal end.

CHAPTER SIXTY-TWO

Prosecution

"911. State your emergency."

"Please! Help! Need—" my breaths came out in frantic panting—"police. Ambulance."

"Okay, ma'am, what's the problem?"

"Help. . . shot." My voice sounded frenzied. Punctuated with panting and wails.[14]

Reminded of the horror of the night my husband died, tears fell. My stomach churned like an unbalanced washing machine.

"Ma'am, who has been shot?"

In the background, behind my panicked breathing, Vincent's moans grew louder the closer he got to death. "Husband."

"Calm down, ma'am. How did he get shot? Who shot him?"[15]

I was even crazier that night than I remembered.

With the end of the recording, Ms. Dean asked the 911 dispatcher several questions about the call. During her testimony, the dispatcher admitted to hearing moans and groans coming through the call.

The state called Officer Stiles, the first officer on the scene, as their next witness.

The officer told the jury he assisted with compressions while I did mouth-to-mouth until the paramedics arrived. He added his belief that I didn't want the CPR to be successful, because he had to talk me through parts of it.

I did my best, but was freaking out like... well, like a wife having to do CPR on her husband she'd just shot.

On cross-examination, Officer Stiles described me as hysterical, panic stricken, and extremely distraught. He also admitted to feeling a faint pulse and hearing the victim burp.[16]

Next, the prosecution called the first paramedic on the scene. He stated the victim had been dead several hours before 911 was called, basing his belief on the fact that lividity—a discoloration of the skin of a cadaver—had set in and that decomposition had begun.

Decomposition? Seriously?

The prosecution brought on two more paramedics, both of whom gave the exact same testimony, word for word, as the first. It appeared one person wrote a report and they all used it as their testimony.[17]

When the third paramedic finished, Judge Harris called lunch. While at the restaurant with my family, two of the jurors entered. Awkward? Yes. But it was good for them to see me as a free person.

We reconvened to the state calling Vincent's friend Kyle to the stand. He said Vincent's biological sister introduced them about a month before Vincent's death, and that he'd hung out with Vincent eight to twelve times in that month. Kyle went on to describe both Vincent's fear of me and his suspicions of my unfaithfulness.

Doug twirled his pen. "Mr. Ford, you gave a statement to the police in which you discussed helping Vincent record some telephone conversations surreptitiously, did you not?"

"Surrep..." Kyle made a face. "I don't believe I understand what you're asking."

"Secretly. His wife wouldn't know about the tap on the phone."

Kyle nodded. "Yes. While talking about our domestic problems, I mentioned tapping my phone, which led to me discovering the truth. Vincent decided to do the same, wanting to find out if Leigh Ann was cheating."

A broad smile crossed Doug's face. "Mr. Ford, do you feel like you need a lawyer here?"

Kyle sat up straight. "What for?"

"You just admitted to committing a federal offense. A felony, in fact."

"But..." Kyle's eyes darted around the room. "I didn't know that when I did it."

Doug laughed. "It doesn't make any difference whether you knew it or not. You can't rob a bank and then say, 'I didn't know it was against the law.' If you did it, you're guilty."

Mr. Rice stood. "Objection, Your Honor. This is just harassment."

Doug turned to the prosecutor. "It's impeachment. If it's harassment, I'm harassing him with the truth." He turned back to Kyle. "So, do you feel like you need a lawyer?"

Kyle's face drained of color. "Uh, yeah."

Mr. Rice stood. "Mr. Ford has requested an attorney. Can the court appoint him one to advise him as to his rights and legal situation?"

Judge Harris pressed his lips together in an obvious attempt at not smiling. "Mr. Ford, how much money do you make?"

I wanted to laugh at the expression of fear and confusion on Kyle's face, but bit my cheeks and held it in.

"Uh, maybe $1200 a month."

"All right," the judge said. "Let's take a recess and get this witness an attorney."[18]

After a short recess, the state called Vincent's brother to the stand. Matt told the jury Vincent was afraid of me because he found out about a life insurance policy on him.

How could anyone believe he was afraid of me? I was the one consumed with fear.

For his turn, Doug asked Matt about the discussion of life insurance.

"He said there was a policy on him he didn't recall having anything to do with."

Doug tapped his lip. "So, in other words, he didn't know one way or the other, he simply didn't recall it?"

"Right. He said Leigh Ann had a letter, and he asked her what it was and she said it was a life insurance policy. She asked him if he remembered it, and he said no."

Doug leaned back in his seat. "And that was the extent of the discussion of life insurance? He didn't say how much it was for or who the beneficiary was?"

Matt shook his head. "That's all he said."

"All right. Were y'all on drugs at the time of this discussion?"

"No, we were not."

"Your brother was known for fabricating stories, a notorious liar—"

Mr. Rice stood. "I'm going to have to object to the attempted smearing of the deceased."

Judge Harris smiled before covering his mouth. "Sustained."

Doug massaged the bridge of his nose. "Let's talk about the frightened demeanor you said Vincent had. Why was he frightened of Leigh Ann?"

"He thought she was going to kill him."

"And with that fright in mind, he went back home?" Doug leaned forward and put his hands on his hips. "Does that make sense to you?"

Matt shifted in his seat. "I tried to persuade him otherwise."

"So, he's afraid his wife is going to kill him, yet he goes back to the home he shares with her." Doug made a show of his incredulity. "Does that make sense?"

"I don't know."

"Your brother robbed with guns, didn't he?"

Matt's head drooped. "He'd been known to."

Mr. Rice stood. "I'm going to have to object to anything about robbing with guns. He was convicted of robbery by *threats*."

Doug turned toward the prosecutor. "He *threatened* them with a gun." He turned back toward Matt. "Vincent had quite a flare for knives, didn't he?"

Matt's eyes moved from Doug to the judge to Mr. Rice and back to Doug, as if trying to catch up with all the back and forth. "Yes. He collected them."

Doug switched gears again, this time going into Matt's criminal history. Next, he had Matt clarify that although he lived with me while Vincent was in prison, he'd had his own bedroom and there was never anything romantic between us. He ended by asking Matt if he came to any conclusions after listening to the recording of the 911 call.

"Yes," Matt said. "It was my brother moaning and groaning in the background."

"Very well, then. No further questions."[19]

Kyle was brought back to the stand with his appointed attorney in tow. After pleading the fifth to anything related to the tapping of the phone, Doug had him verify Defendant's Exhibit Six as his sworn statement to the police.

"So, Mr. Ford, the detective asked you to tell him everything you knew about Vincent, and then reduced to writing what he considered critical to the investigation, is that right?"

"Yes."

"In the two-page affidavit, you don't say anything about Vincent being frightened, do you?"

Kyle shook his head. "I haven't read it lately."

"Nothing in here about Vincent being scared to death or fearful for his life?"

"I'd say something should be in there, but—"

"In fact, you go into great detail about health care, but nothing about him being concerned for his health. Although you do mention his jealousy."

Kyle hesitated, then looked at his attorney. "Yeah, he wanted to know if she was cheating on him."

Doug leaned back and crossed his legs. "Nothing further."[20]

Day Three

Mr. Rice placed his pen on his notepad. "The state calls Dr. Ian Sadler, Medical Examiner."

My heart pounded. The man who took my husband's body apart and put it back together mounted the stand.

"Dr. Sadler, please tell the jury what you found during the autopsy of Mr. Bayshore."

"Mr. Bayshore had a non-fatal entry gunshot wound of the left abdomen, which caused hemorrhage and laceration of the left abdominal wall muscle and left psoas muscle. His death occurred by gunshot to the left back, which ricocheted off a rib and lacerated his heart."[21]

Doug began his cross-examination by replaying the 911 tape. "Dr. Sadler, were you able to listen past the panicked pleadings of Leigh Ann and hear the moans and groans in the background?"

The doctor held his tie to his chest and leaned into the microphone. "Yes."

"In your experience, do dead people make sounds like that?"

"No, sir. It would be impossible for a dead man to moan and groan. Even with CPR, once someone is dead, all of their air is expired out. With no air in the lungs, noises like that wouldn't happen."

"Thank you." Doug sorted through a pile of photographs, pulled one out, and brought it to the witness. "Doctor Sadler, can you please tell the jury what this photograph portrays?"

He studied the photo. "It is the victim."

"Can you tell when and where the photo was taken?"

"Before the victim was moved. In his front yard. I believe around five in the morning."

"Very good. Now, do you see any evidence of lividity or decomposition?"

"No. The only thing going on there is insect activity. The victim fell onto an ant mound."

Upon further questioning, Dr. Sadler said the type of injury Vincent sustained would bring unconsciousness within one minute, and death within ten.

"Doctor, taking the autopsy and all the evidence into consideration, can you determine what time Mr. Bayshore died?"

"Although I can't come up with an exact time, everything considered, the victim couldn't have expired before 1:00 a.m."

"Thank you." Doug returned to stand by his chair. "So, what you're telling this jury, Doctor, with all your years of experience as a medical examiner, is that there's no way the victim lay dead in the front yard for hours, or even minutes, given the moans and groans heard on the 911 call at 12:56 a.m."

"Correct."

"Thank you." Doug smiled at the prosecutor. "Oh, one more question, Doctor. Did the drug screen on Mr. Bayshore come back negative, or positive?"

"Positive."

"Thank you. No further questions."[22]

The state called the first paramedic back to the stand in an apparent effort at salvaging their contention I'd waited several hours to call 911 while my husband lay dead in the front yard.

When the prosecutor finished, Doug clasped his fingers together. "Just one question. Isn't it a fact that if somebody is moaning and groaning, they aren't dead?"

The paramedic stared, his mouth wide open.

Doug leaned forward. "It's not a trick question. I'm not asking you to explain Einstein's Theory of Relativity. When someone's dead, they don't moan and groan, do they?"

The paramedic visibly gulped. "Um, no."

Doug smiled. "Now, that wasn't so hard, was it?"[23]

As if all this testimony wasn't difficult enough, the state called my husband's alleged lover to the stand. Roxanne told the jurors Vincent talked to her often about his awful marriage and what a terrible wife I was. She said Vincent was afraid of me, adding that he rigged his bedroom door in order to feel safe enough to sleep.

Heat rose up my neck as I considered her knowledge of anything in his bedroom.

"Just a thing or two, Ms. Ross." Doug ran a finger over his jaw. "Where do you work?

"I'm a hostess at Lace."

"A strip club. You ever dance there?"

Her hands made a "no way" signal. "It's a gentlemen's club. And no, sir. Only a hostess."

I wanted to shake the truth out of her.

"Ms. Ross, how often did you and Vincent have these talks?"

"All the time. We talked on the phone a lot and sometimes he came to my place."

Folding his arms across his chest, Doug said, "And you expect the jury to believe a man comes to your house, calls you at all hours, and discusses his sex life, all with someone he's not intimate with? Isn't it true you and Vincent were having an affair?"

Her eyes darted to the prosecutor, then moved to the jury. "Yes. I mean, no. I mean, yes he talked with me and no, we weren't having an affair."[24]

Now I wanted to do more than just shake her.

CHAPTER SIXTY-FOUR

In My Defense

Doug stood and gave a slight bow to the jury, then turned to the judge. "Your Honor, the defense calls Leigh Ann Bayshore to the stand."

Murmurs rippled through the courtroom. As I walked to the stand, my body threatened to collapse. I sat, took a deep breath, and surveyed the jury.

They already think I'm guilty.

My stomach twisted, turned, shrank into a hard knot.

The twelve strangers stared at me from behind the waist-high wall. Strangers who hadn't lived my hell, been terrorized with abuse, or killed to save their child's life. Eleven men and one woman who would decide my fate.

I scanned their faces, searching for compassion, finding none. The blond in the blue shirt leaned back, scrutinizing the ceiling. The man in the green shirt smiled at the prosecutor. The lone woman studied me with an impossible to interpret expression.

How could I convince strangers to believe me when Vincent never did?

My ears tuned in to each small noise—the ticking of a clock, the tapping of a pencil, a man clearing his throat, even the crossing and uncrossing of legs. My body sensed every breath the people around me took, every eye focused on me.

Like a small, scared child, my mind replayed over and over the memory of my baby's panicked cries from that night.

"State your name for the record." The judge's voice boomed.

My tongue stuck to the roof of my mouth. I reached for the small paper cup, my quaking hands causing water to dribble onto my skirt. Steadying it with both hands, I took a drink. The tepid liquid did nothing to quench my thirst.

The rails of the tiny witness box pressed in on me like bars in a jail. An invisible vice grip made it impossible to fill my lungs with enough air. Perspiration formed on my upper lip. A cold sweat saturated my neck. *Please God, help me.*

"Ma'am." The judge leaned toward me. "State your name for the record."

My voice came out as a whisper. "Leigh Ann Bayshore."

"Raise your right hand."

I dropped my wadded-up tissue into my lap and obeyed, swallowing hard in preparation for what came next. I'd seen it on TV—they'd put a Bible under my left hand and ask me to swear to tell the truth. Did I even know the truth anymore? How many times had I lied for Vincent? Would God smite me if I got confused after swearing on a Bible?

Judge Harris spoke. "Do you swear to tell the truth, the whole truth, and nothing but the truth, so help you God?"

Where was the Bible? Did they forget? Should I ask? It didn't matter—I'd tell the truth, Bible or no Bible.

"Do you swear?"

My mouth was a desert, my palms a wellspring, my mind the morning fog. I looked to my parents for courage. "I do."

Reality came back and slapped me in the face—my future could be life in prison, without the possibility of parole for forty years.

I tried to focus on the positive—the prosecutor waived the death penalty. Thoughts of my son safe and alive were worth life in prison, but I didn't want him to grow up without his mother. He needed me. I needed him.

Pushing aside my panic, I faced Doug. With confidence in his bright blue eyes and a tender smile meant for me, he approached. Close enough to touch, he gave me one quick nod, magically transferring courage to my trembling body.

Doug strode around the courtroom with the proud gait of a confident man. He was substantial—not in the sense of being large, but in the sense of being significant. While he had torn others to shreds on the witness stand, he handled me with consideration and care.

"Leigh Ann, did you love your husband?"

Tears brimmed my eyes. "Yes. Probably too much."

With his questions, Doug guided me through my life with Vincent. The ups and downs, the love and fear, the terror that ruled me during his last few months. Vincent's kidnapping plan notes. The night he died. Alternating between panicked tones, exasperation, and humiliation, I poured out truths with a quaking voice. Truths I'd kept locked inside, hidden from everyone, even myself. My parents' tears crushed me. Looking at Vincent's family filled me with grief. So I turned away, eyes aimed at my trembling fingers wadding and smoothing a tissue over and over.

When Doug finished, leaving me as emotionally drained and numb as the night my husband died, everyone knew how I'd killed my husband.

After lunch, Mr. Rice attacked me about my statement to the police. With each question, he asked if what I'd told them was the truth or a lie. For two hours, I admitted to being a liar.

"And why," Mr. Rice asked, "should anyone believe you about the so-called abuse? Your history of lying, and lack of telling anyone about abuse prior to Vincent's death, proves it didn't exist."

His claim validated my lies and secrecy. No one would have believed me if I'd told.

The prosecutor continued his barrage. "Ms. Bayshore, isn't it true it was actually your husband who was afraid of you?"

The seriousness of my situation kept the reflex to laugh locked inside. "Absolutely not. Aside from the paranoia Vincent experienced in the last couple months of his life, he wasn't afraid of anything but going back to prison. He thrived on the adrenaline rushes he got from things that would scare normal people into paralysis."

"So, why did witnesses testify he told them he was afraid of you?"

I shrugged. "He liked to tell stories. And he was paranoid. Wouldn't eat out because he thought strangers wanted to poison him. He even believed his brother was plotting to kill him."

"So you want this jury to believe he lied about his fear of you?"

"Maybe he figured it would help him get out of trouble when he finally went through with his threats and killed me. He lied all the time."

"Isn't that what you're doing, Ms. Bayshore? Trying to get out of trouble by lying?"

I leaned toward the microphone, pausing to gather my thoughts. "We all know I lied to the police. Partly out of wanting to protect my husband from going back to prison. But I'm telling the truth now, and the only person in that house consumed with fear was me."

Next, Mr. Rice began hammering me with questions regarding the details of the night my husband died. In thirty different ways, he asked about the timeline. He asked which knife wound was first, last, third, or second, as well as exactly how and where I sat for each wound, doing his best to trip me up or get me to change my story.

An hour into the prosecutor's attempts at tricking me, Judge Harris ordered a sidebar. After a brief discussion with the attorneys, the judge called a recess.[25]

Doug walked me outside. "You're doing fine. And this is good news. The judge said the jury needs a break. Apparently, the prosecutor's putting them to sleep."

The air was lighter. My lungs expanded.

"Keep up the good work. Seems Mr. Rice has a lot of questions left in him."

When recess was over and I was back on the stand, the prosecutor walked to the front of the jury box and motioned to me. "Ms. Bayshore, please come here."

I turned to Doug for guidance. With his nod of approval, I joined the prosecutor.

"Now, I want you"—Mr. Rice moved to his table and picked up a bag containing the gun—"to hold this."

The gun that killed my husband. My stomach clenched. Turmoil raced through me, a tsunami that threatened to take me down. I slowly shook my head.

Mr. Rice took the weapon out of the bag and held it toward me. "Your Honor . . ."

Judge Harris looked at me, compassion in his eyes. "Ms. Bayshore, take it."

My hand refused to move. *No, no, no. I can't do this.*

The prosecutor took my hand and put the gun in it. The frigid steel, the weight, the memories collapsed my soul. Tears burned my unblinking eyes as I stared at the weapon.

"Ms. Bayshore, please show the jury how you held the gun as you shot your husband."

The pistol fell from my quaking hand. "I can't. I don't remember." My eyes moved to the prosecutor's. "How am I supposed to know that?"

He picked it up and put it back in my hand, again beseeching Judge Harris for help in making me do what he asked. With much prodding and assistance from the judge, he forced me to recreate my posture, how I held the gun, the angles, the bend of my knees. Even though I had no remembrance of any such things, I received strength from the presence of my family and tried to do my best.

When he finished with the spectacle, Mr. Rice had me return to the stand for more questions. On and on they went, ending only after I'd spent over seven hours testifying.

Doug winked at me, letting me know I did a good job. "Just a couple other things, Leigh Ann." He brought a stack of papers to me. "Can you please look these over and tell the jury what kinds of insurance you had in place?"

Flipping through the pile, I read them off. "Homeowner's insurance, health insurance, supplemental health insurance, accidental insurance, car insurance, medical malpractice, renter's insurance, disability insurance, life insurance—"[26]

"Let's talk about the life insurance. Do you remember receiving the phone call?"

"Yes. The guy told me it was free for three months. Cheap after that. Easy, because it would be billed to my credit card. I told him I needed to talk to my husband about it."

Doug gave me a reassuring smile. "And did you talk to Vincent?"

"Yes. We agreed it would be a good idea."

"So, you never kept it a secret from him? Never hid anything that came in the mail?"

A tear escaped and rolled down my cheek. "I could never keep a secret from Vincent. He knew everything. Had ways of finding things out. And he wouldn't allow me to check the mail."

"Was there life insurance besides the JC Penney policy?"

"Yes. There was a policy with American Express Life Insurance that insured both of us, but it had lapsed for non-payment."[27]

Doug's eyes and mouth went wide as he scanned the jury. "You had a life insurance policy on your husband that lapsed for non-payment? Interesting."

[CHAPTER SIXTY-FIVE]

Day Five

Two of my neighbors testified, both saying when they saw me in the car alone, I waved, but when with Vincent, I appeared frightened. They said they believed Vincent was abusive, as they frequently heard fights, which consisted of him yelling and me crying. One neighbor said our fights came through her baby monitor, and she admitted to moving it so she could hear us better.[28]

What good are nosy neighbors who know so much and never do anything to help?

With the completion of their testimony, Doug stood. "The defense rests, Your Honor."

As their first rebuttal witness, the state recalled their forensics expert. Mr. Darrell said he listened to my testimony and watched me reenact where I stood and how I held the gun, and it didn't match the cartridges found on the scene or his reconstruction of the trajectory of the warning shot. He also indicated concern over finding very little blood on the carpet where I said I sat when Vincent cut me.[29]

Doug marked his notepad, and slowly looked up. "Mr. Darrell, do you find it curious none of the shell casings are in the beaten path of a normal walkway, as numerous people contaminated the scene walking from one room to another and back again, kicking them around?"

"They don't normally get kicked around."

"I wonder how a casing got under a chair, then, without being kicked there. Did you realize at least twelve officers were present, contaminating the scene?"

Mr. Darrell shook his head. "I didn't find out how many people had been in there."[30]

"Didn't find out?" Doug raised his eyebrows. "Okay. Well, you seem so concerned with the lack of blood on the carpet, yet you aren't concerned with the lack of blood where Ms. Bayshore knelt while performing CPR in the presence of police officers. Can you explain that?"

Mr. Darrell hesitated. "I can't, but it should have been on the carpet."[31]

"What about the black overnight bag you found? The one with Vincent's clothing and boots. Can you explain Vincent's need for a bag with dark clothing, flashlights, and knives, two of which had blood on them?"[32]

"No."

Doug sat forward. "Any explanation for Vincent's positive gunshot residue test?"[33]

"He'd obviously fired a gun recently."

"Or maybe he was fighting Leigh Ann for a gun and it went off?"

"That's possible."

"What about the three walls of the garage covered with numerous knife penetrations and the several knife holes noted on Vincent's bedroom wall, including one that extended all the way to the handle, greatly enlarged by the handle? Any explanation there?"[34]

With no good response, Mr. Darrell was excused.

The prosecution next called Dr. Tanaka, the physician who stapled my thigh in the emergency room. Dr. Tanaka gave the opinion my wounds could have been self-inflicted.

On cross-examination, Doug asked him if he'd ever seen self-inflicted wounds.

"Yes," the doctor answered. "Not a lot, but yes."

"So, Doctor, are you familiar with the term 'hesitational cut'?"

"Yes."

Doug brought a picture of my thigh wound to him. "That's when someone decides they're going to cut themselves, but it hurts more than they expected, so they stop and start again. There'll be a cut, then kind of a jerk, and then more cut. You see any of that here?"

Dr. Tanaka studied the picture of my wound. "No. It's a clean cut."

"Very good." Doug tapped the picture. "And is it a deep wound?"

"It's a deep wound. Yes."[35]

Next, the prosecution called a blood spatter expert who testified he believed there wasn't enough blood on the carpet from my leg wound to support my story. When Doug had him examine the shorts I wore that night, however, he agreed the "large contact stain" of blood on my shorts could account for the lack of blood elsewhere. He also admitted that some large wounds bleed very little, while small ones can bleed a lot.[36]

With the conclusion of his testimony, the state rested—and with that, Judge Harris dismissed us for the weekend.

At a restaurant that evening, Doug, Curtis, John, and I discussed our strategy for the remainder of the trial.

"First week's behind us." Doug winked at me. "It's not looking bad, and we have a couple of experts in our wing who'll really help."

"It's not feeling so great to me." I gave a weak smile, feeling numb. "This could be my last weekend of freedom."

[C H A P T E R   S I X T Y - S I X]

Experts

My weekend had been unbearable. It might have been my last as a free woman, and the visitation schedule with my son was such that I wasn't allowed to see him.

I sat in my seat at the defense table and stared at the witness box in a trance. Would Dr. Grigson's testimony help the jury understand my actions?

Doug started with preliminaries, qualifying Dr. Grigson as an expert witness who specialized in forensic psychiatry. In thirty years of private practice, Dr. Grigson examined 14,000 individuals with charges pending, 1,400 of them charged with murder and 400 charged with capital murder. In addition, he'd testified 660 times in murder and capital murder cases, the overwhelming majority being requested by prosecutors and judges as an expert for the state.

"Dr. Grigson." Doug sat back and crossed his left leg over his right. "What was your purpose in examining Ms. Bayshore?"

"To do a complete psychiatric examination and determine what her state of mind was at the time of the alleged offense."

"Doctor, are there psychiatric techniques that you, as a psychiatrist, employ to determine whether or not someone is being candid with you or whether that individual is trying to fudge or, perhaps, influence the outcome of your evaluation?"

Dr. Grigson slowly nodded. "Yes. Several, in fact. One has to do not only with the words the person is saying, but also the emotion they're expressing."

Mr. Rice tried to object in every way possible, but he couldn't stop the train that was coming.

"Okay, Doctor, based on your psychiatric evaluation of Leigh Ann Bayshore, can you, within reasonable medical certainty, describe for the jury the condition of her mind during the altercation with Vincent that resulted in him getting shot?"

"She was absolutely terrified for her life and the life of her son. Her actions were based on self-preservation, not aggression."

Mr. Rice stood. "May we approach the bench, Your Honor?"

Five attorneys huddled around the judge, returning to their seats a moment later.

Doug leaned forward. "Doctor, let me give you a hypothetical situation. Assume a young man is institutionalized on three separate occasions for drug use and failure to obey the rules of society." He continued, giving a twenty-minute monologue in which he described my husband, my marriage, the abuse, and the night of Vincent's death down to the greatest detail, all the while using the word "assume."

Doug's description of what my marriage had become, Vincent's extreme violence and abuse, how messed up my mind was, echoed in my head like the tick-tock of a grandfather clock. Something about hearing someone else describe my tumultuous life made my stomach churn.

"Now, Doctor," Doug continued, "can you, as a psychiatrist, based on that hypothetical situation, make a diagnosis of the man in that hypothetical situation?"

The judge overruled yet another objection by the prosecutor.

"Yes, sir, I can. He would have a severe antisocial personality disorder, commonly called psychopath or sociopath. Those are individuals who don't have a conscience. They repeatedly break the rules. Only interested in their own self-gratification and pleasure. Extreme manipulators, they have intense disregard for others' property and, at the very severe end, disregard for other people's lives."

"And Doctor, does the man in this hypothetical sound like someone at the severe end?"

Dr. Grigson leaned in to the microphone. "Most definitely."

"Could this just be a stage an individual is going through? Something to grow out of?"

"No. The majority of sociopaths never become severe, but when they get to the severe stage, whenever they're involved in acts of violence, they continue to do that the rest of their lives."

Through more questions, the doctor told the jury it would be extremely unusual for an individual going through what I went through that night to have any recollection about how I held a weapon or where I stood when it was in my hands. He also added that most battered women don't tell anyone about the abuse out of shame and embarrassment.

Dr. Grigson summed up his testimony. "With everything Ms. Bayshore went through that night, with everything she knew about the deceased, with what he had done before and he had done to her, it is most definitely my opinion she truly felt and believed he could carry out whatever he said and that he was going to kill her and possibly the baby at that time."[37]

Doug sat back. "Thank you, Doctor. That's all."

As our last defense witness, Doug called a criminologist. "Mr. Parker, what experience have you had in the investigation of shooting crime scenes?"

Mr. Rice addressed the court, requesting an opportunity to question the witness outside the jury's presence.

Upon direct examination, Mr. Parker revealed twenty years of experience as a police officer for the city of Dallas, eleven in the Crimes Against Persons section of the Dallas PD homicide unit. During that time, he personally investigated several thousand shooting scenes and reviewed eight to ten thousand more. In addition, he described testifying as an expert on reconstructing a shooting scene both in Dallas and several other counties, as well as working with various police departments and government agencies across the country in the investigation of shootings and homicides, almost always working for the police and prosecutors.

After qualifying him as an expert, the judge recalled the jury.

Doug had Mr. Parker recount his experience to the jury, as well as his education and training. "Now, Mr. Parker, will you tell the jury what you, as an investigator, do when you first arrive at a shooting scene you're going to investigate?"

"First order of business is to protect the scene and determine contamination."

"What is contamination?"

"There are a lot of people there who move about. Police, paramedics, firefighters, investigators. They go to the bathroom, use the phone, get a drink in the kitchen, move things. So, I find out who's been at the scene and make a list of those people."

"Mr. Parker, with the thousands of homicides you have personally investigated, can you, or anyone for that matter, look at a crime scene where the bullets and shell casings are lying around and tell what position the shooter was in at the time those shots were fired?"

"No. I don't know how that could be done. There are too many variables involved in possible positions and posture of the shooter, the way they hold the gun—the slightest angle changes the trajectory. Also, the evidence gets moved, kicked about, stepped on. It's just not reliable."

"So, shell casings can be kicked around?"

"Oh, yes, and they come out spinning, tumbling. If they strike an object, they bounce. I've seen them get caught in clothes."

"Have you, Mr. Parker, ever seen a crime scene that wasn't contaminated?"

"No, sir, I have not."

"Very good. Now let me ask you this. Does the absence of blood in a crime scene mean a person wasn't cut or shot in a particular place?"

"No, sir. You can't say someone wasn't cut or shot there. It just means someone's blood didn't get left there."

"Is it unusual for a witness to not recall exactly where they were and what their position was in any given moment in a shooting?"

Although the prosecutor had several objections, the judge allowed the question.

Mr. Parker continued. "It's not uncommon at all for a witness to not remember. Adrenaline pumps. Whether you're a civilian, inexperienced, or a trained police officer, it's common to be very excited and not remember."[38]

Doug scanned his notes. "Thank you, Mr. Parker. I believe that's all. The defense rests, Your Honor."

Judge Harris recessed us for lunch.

Curtis put a hand on my shoulder. "Things are looking good."

I wanted to smile, to feel optimistic, but Doug's monologue summarizing my life with Vincent played over and over in my head. Questions relentlessly tormented. How could I let it get so bad? Why couldn't things have been different?

While Doug, Curtis, and John gathered their things to work on the charge for the jury, I ran to the bathroom and vomited.

[C H A P T E R   S I X T Y · S E V E N]

Closing

"All rise for the jury."

I watched the deciders of my fate enter the jury box. Most of them kept their heads down, but two contemplated me, questions in their eyes.

"Be seated," Judge Harris said. "The state may continue."

Mr. Rice cleared his throat. "The state rests, Your Honor."

Doug lifted his hand. "The defense rests."

"Very well, then." The judge turned to the jury and explained that their duty for the day was done. "Be back at nine in the morning for closing arguments."

The bailiff escorted the jury out of the courtroom. As soon as the door closed, Judge Harris asked the attorneys for their thoughts regarding the charge.

Doug took a wide stance, hands on hips. "Your Honor, my advising you how to charge a jury would be like me advising Jesse James how to rob a train."

When the judge stopped chuckling, Doug held up his hand. "Actually, Your Honor, there is one thing. Although Leigh Ann admitted to pointing a gun at Vincent, she made it clear she never intended to shoot him, only to scare him. That opens the door for aggravated assault as a lesser offense."

The judge and the prosecutor both agreed to accept the lesser charge.

When my trial reconvened the next morning, Judge Harris read the charge to the jury. *Capital murder.* The words ricocheted in my head. I could spend the rest of my life in prison.

Assistant prosecutor Dean began, rehashing the laundry list of evidence against me. Like a voodoo doll on the receiving end of someone's pointed vengeance, each accusation stabbed me anew. Her final insinuation—no proof of Vincent's abuse—deflated me.

Next, Curtis stood, walked toward the jury, and thanked them for their service. He explained the court's charge, reminded them the burden of proof lay with the prosecution, dismissed the life insurance as meaningless, and beseeched them to read the parts in the charge about self-defense. "Let's go back and look at Leigh Ann's state of mind and what contributed to her fear that sinister, awful night. She finds kidnapping notes in his handwriting—"

"Objection." Mr. Rice stood. "There's no evidence they were his handwriting."

Yet another outrageous ploy from the prosecution sent tongues of fire through my veins.

"Well, she said it was his handwriting, and the burden of proof is on them—" Curtis pointed at the prosecutors. "If it wasn't his handwriting, you should have been told. A handwriting expert should have taken the stand and told you."

Curtis read each entry of the six pages of notes. "Can you imagine what she thought? 'Bomb, fire, dark clothes, flashlights, knives, guns. Should they be *killed*?'" Raising his voice for emphasis and shaking his head, he moved on to the inventory list. "Scanner, tight black gloves, black pantyhose, wire cutters, flashlights. . . "

The numbness, the nausea, the internal earthquake from the night I found the notes slammed against my mind, choking the breath from me.

Curtis again raised his voice. "Killed! Can you imagine? He even mentions his buddy Kyle. Take these notes to the jury room. Read them and see whether or not they contributed to her state of mind that horrific, sinister night."

Walking back and forth in front of the jury, Curtis described Vincent's bizarre, drug-induced behavior the night of the offense. "Knife holes in walls everywhere. No respect for anything. Treats Leigh Ann like a dog. Cuts and nicks to her neck, face, arms, and then"—he held up a picture of my thigh wound—"look at this, folks. It's an awful wound. Take it to the jury room and look at it. See for yourself the doctor was right—deep and no hesitation."

My fingers massaged the scar on my thigh, the pain now far deeper than physical.

"She knows with this wound, it's over. Something's got to be done. So she talks doll to him, convinces him to let her check on the baby. You may ask why she didn't just leave when he cut her loose." Curtis slammed his hand on the wall of the jury box, causing several jurors to jump. "And leave her baby alone with this crazy man? No! She goes back and gives him the opportunity to leave. But instead, he laughs at her. She didn't want to shoot him, but he came toward her, tried to get the gun."

With the jury's full attention, Curtis explained my deceit that night, saying the officer put the idea in my head. "Look at her state of mind, think of the adjectives the officers used to describe her—extremely distraught, hysterical." He leaned toward the jurors as if sharing a secret. "That was real, folks. Her deceit wasn't decided upon until the officer asked if the guy who shot her husband was the same guy who cut her. It was self-preservation, plain and simple. But she leveled with you and with her conscience about what happened.

"This was a level of passion and terror very few people experience." He pointed at me. "She did. She resorted to the means at hand to resolve it. She had to fire the gun to get him to leave. To save herself and her child. To find her guilty of anything is a travesty of justice. The terror, the sinnisterism, the horror of that evening, it reeks in this courtroom. To say it was contrived is a disaster. It is wrong. There's only one proper verdict here—not guilty." He gave a slight bow. "Thank you, folks. Thank you, Judge."[39]

Curtis returned to the defense table and Doug took his place in front of the jury, buttoning his jacket and smiling as he thanked them for their time and attention.

"It's important for you to analyze the parties involved." Doug pointed at me. "This lady, in all her years on this earth, has not demonstrated one single act of aggression. But we've heard great details about the violence Vincent displayed. We heard about him kicking their dog to the extent she thought it was dead, and we know about him killing a neighbor's dog because the neighbor reported him to the school administration. We know about him throwing his wife down when she was pregnant, causing bleeding and complications. We know he hit her in the jaw to the extent she thought it was broken. We know all sorts of things about Vincent, and they have all been unchallenged. We also know it was Vincent who had that bag with the tools of trade for a hijacker. He—"[40]

"Your Honor!" Mr. Rice shot from his seat. "Demeanor of this courtroom. I mean, really. The hijacker?"

Doug folded his arms across his chest and asked the prosecutor, "What do you call him? Armed robber?"

Mr. Rice narrowed his eyes. "I call him dead."

"Well, the dead armed robber." Doug faced the jury again. "The former armed robber tied his door shut to keep Leigh Ann out, not from fear of her"—Doug raised his voice—"but so he could sneak out and prowl around using his black bag with flashlights, dark clothing, and knives—two of which had blood on them. He was on probation for robbery and theft when he committed armed robbery and aggravated assault with a deadly—"

"Objection." Mr. Rice again stood. "His conviction is for robbery by threats."

Doug turned to the judge with a smirk. "I didn't say he was convicted of armed robbery. I said he committed it. I don't care what they pled him down to. Now, look at how Dr. Grigson described a sociopath. 'Going to do and take what they want—to hell with anybody else. Pleasure oriented with no thoughts of tomorrow.' Compare that to the notes Leigh Ann found in Vincent's handwriting. And it's absurd to suggest this is anybody but Vincent Bayshore's handwriting. They've had the originals since right after the night in question. His mother and brother both took the stand, and neither of them denied it. Listen and see if this doesn't sound like the Vincent you've come to know."

Doug put on his glasses and read from the notes, once again filling the courtroom with Vincent's disturbing plan. Each ominous word blended with vivid details of my husband's sociopathic behavior, constricting my chest and depriving me of air.

"Let's talk about evidence." Doug pointed toward the prosecutors. "Their forensics guy, Mr. Darrell, said Leigh Ann's testimony didn't match. 'If she fired like this, she would've had to have been closer. If she'd fired like that, it would've been fine." Doug used his fingers as a gun and maneuvered around the room in a mini-reenactment as he spoke. "With the trauma of the night, who would remember that stuff? If I'd been through what she went through, you could've water boarded me and I wouldn't have been able to remember how I stood or held a gun."

Giggles moved through the courtroom, some coming from the jury box. Judge Harris covered his mouth, but couldn't hide his amusement.

"Mr. Darrell also worried about the lack of blood." Doug picked up my bloody shorts. "Remember these? They solved the lack-of-blood mystery. Cleared up by the prosecution's expert. If I'd known about him, I'd have called him myself."

The sight of my shorts from that night, the left leg covered in dried blood, revived memories of the slashing knife. Vincent's frenzied eyes. Doing CPR on my husband.

"Mr. Darrell was also troubled about the shell casings. But what did Mr. Parker tell you? Contamination is always there. Stuff gets kicked around. You can't determine where someone stood based on shell casing locations.

"Another expert of theirs helped us as well." Doug picked up a Marks-A-Lot and wrote 12:54 on a large tablet. "This is when Leigh Ann says the shooting occurred. Vincent's minutes were numbered. The fuse had been lit. According to Dr. Sadler, dead within ten minutes." He wrote 1:04 on the tablet. "We hear him moaning and groaning at 12:56." He put that number between the other two. "Dr. Sadler testified the time of death couldn't have been before 1:00 a.m. You remember him saying that? Perfectly consistent."

Doug gestured toward the prosecutor. "They know a scene like this needs time to set up, so they make up this story and have a paramedic tell you he was dead for hours before she called 911. Absurd. Who you going to believe? A paramedic, or the medical examiner and what your own ears heard on the recording of the 911 call? His own brother identified the moans as belonging to Vincent. On top of all that, the police officer who helped with CPR said he felt a pulse and heard a burp."

The jury kept their eyes on Doug as he fought for my freedom. "Unlike the prosecution, I don't believe in trying to hide the ball from the jury. The truth is, although they could punch holes in Leigh Ann's intruder story, they couldn't have proved her guilty of murder beyond reasonable doubt. But I made it easy for them." He patted his chest. "I told you during *voir dire* this wasn't a whodunit. She killed him. And if I'd been her lawyer from the beginning, I'd have had her 'fess up much sooner, but she 'fessed up for y'all."

Regret over my lies plagued my soul. *Please God, forgive me.*

Putting his hand to his chest again, Doug stood poised in front of the jury. "Lady and gentlemen, this wasn't murder. I submit to you"—he pointed to the ceiling—"this was divine intervention. That bullet ricocheted off a rib and went right through Vincent's wicked heart."

The jurors sat riveted, three leaning forward as if trying to receive the full impact of Doug's words.

"Think of the contrast here." Doug extended his hand toward me. "For eight years, she dedicated her life to helping people. Saving people. Contrast that with Vincent. The longest job he ever had was in the penitentiary. I could understand a big question if Vincent killed her and claimed self-defense, but this fits like the paper on the wall. And let's think about her being a nurse. If, in fact, you wanted to kill your husband and you were a nurse and he were a doper, don't you think it would have been much cleaner and easier to give him an overdose?"

Doug walked toward the jury. "Now, let's talk about insurance. You remember what Leigh Ann said about the kinds of insurance she paid for? Even disability insurance for Vincent." He shook his head and laughed. "Talk about a waste of money. As useful as a bag of hammers. But what about the life insurance with American Express that lapsed? Don't you think anyone who possessed a lick of sense and wanted to kill their spouse for money would be sure the policy hadn't lapsed before they pulled the trigger?"

Several jurors smiled in my direction. Their attention and the metallic taste of blood made me stop chewing on my lip.

Next, Doug introduced the concept of self-defense, describing it as the perfect offense. "The law says you have the absolute right to meet deadly force with deadly force and take a life if that's what it demands."

Pointing at the witness chair, Doug said, "You remember what Dr. Grigson said when he sat right there? He said there are ways to determine someone's state of mind during an event. Techniques to assess for deception. Now, if this doctor couldn't do that, they'd have a witness up here saying so." Doug leaned on the wall of the jury box, as if sharing a secret. "You know, it's awesome to go up against the resources of the State of Texas. It really is. If Bill Parker or Dr. Grigson weren't exactly right in what they told you, they'd have somebody here quick as instant coffee to tell you. But Dr. Grigson said Leigh Ann was being truthful and she acted out of self-preservation, not aggression."

Doug clasped his hands together and looked full-force at the jury. "Self-preservation, not aggression. There can be no question in this case. Leigh Ann is not guilty."[41]

[C H A P T E R   S I X T Y - E I G H T]

Waiting

"Did we do enough?" I asked Doug, hoping for reassurance.

He gave my arm a quick squeeze. "Too late to do any more. It's up to the jury now."

Wishing to be anywhere else—well, except locked up again—I sank onto a bench. Down the hall of the courthouse, at least a dozen benches lined the walls, many filled with attorneys and their clients huddled in deep conversations. Some appeared happy, others cried.

Should I have taken the offer? What if they come back with a guilty verdict for capital murder? Or even murder? My leg bounced furiously as I contemplated life in prison. Could I accept life, knowing I could have agreed to twelve?

After spending a few minutes in prayer, peace took over once again, assuring me I did the right thing not pleading guilty to something I wasn't guilty of.

My mother sat next to me and took my hand. "Doug, Curtis, and John did great. There's no way the jury thinks it was murder."

Over the next six hours, my family rallied around me, holding me, sitting with me, giving me words of support as I paced, cried, prayed, and waited. Then the bailiff announced the jury had questions. We reconvened in the courtroom.

Standing for the jury as they returned to their seats, I tried to read their expressions. Most of them stared at the floor.

"Be seated," Judge Harris said. "The jury is requesting testimony regarding the knife wounds the defendant received."

I contemplated what this could mean as the court reporter read to the jury.

If they bought the prosecution's lies about my wounds being self-inflicted, they'd convict me of murder for sure. But if they believed the truth, they'd have to see it was self-defense.

After the read-back, the jury filed out of the courtroom to continue deliberations.

More praying, pacing, and waiting with my family.

A couple of hours later, the bailiff appeared announcing a verdict.

Doug checked his watch. "Eight hours and ten minutes."

I swallowed hard. "Is that good, or bad?"

He winked. "Let's go find out."

CHAPTER SIXTY-NINE

Verdict

"Will the defendant please rise?"

I grabbed hold of the table for balance. My blood drained to my feet as I stood. The courtroom grew shadowy. My heart hammered at the speed of a hummingbird's wings. Crushing pain rose in my chest, taking my breath away. *Am I having a heart attack?* Doug's arm circled my waist and steadied me.

Time slowed as I searched each juror's face for any hint of my future. The young man in the green shirt turned away when we made eye contact. The man with white hair gave a slight smile. The lone woman appeared as though she'd been crying. My heart crashed into my stomach.

Trust in the Lord. He makes everything right. My eyes swept the courtroom. The prosecutor tapped his pencil. The judge adjusted his robe. My mother-in-law drummed her fingers on her leg.

Breathe. Just breathe. Whatever it is, at least my baby is alive.

"Has the jury reached a verdict?" Judge Harris asked.

The answer came from the foreman. "Yes, Your Honor, we have."

The world stood still as the bailiff took the paper from the foreman. Walked to the judge. Handed it to him. Judge Harris unfolded the paper. Stared at it. His face gave nothing away.

Seconds ticked off like hours as the tension escalated. Couldn't he just read it?

"We the jury find the defendant, Leigh Ann Bayshore, guilty. . ."

Guilty? Frigid fingers pulled at me, doing their best to collapse my legs. Doug's grip tightened as he held me up.

"... of the offense of aggravated assault."

Relief flooded my body. I looked toward heaven. "Thank you, God." Doug hugged me. I glanced at the jurors. Five of them smiled. I gave a slight nod and tried to return the smiles. A tear escaped and ran down my cheek.

My mother gave me two thumbs-up and mouthed, "I love you."

Aggravated assault. My mind worked to calculate the possibilities. Being acquitted of murder and capital murder, I no longer faced life in prison. Instead, I was looking at two to twenty.

"I'd like the jurors polled." The prosecutor's voice sounded deep and mournful.

Doug leaned over and whispered. "He's not happy with the verdict."

The judge asked each juror if the verdict given was theirs, and each answered in the affirmative. He thanked them for their service and excused them for the day. "Please be back at nine in the morning for sentencing."

It wasn't over. Not yet. I could be incarcerated tomorrow. The terror of receiving the maximum penalty was eased by knowing it couldn't be life. The thought of twenty years without my son smashed the short-lived relief to shards of worry. Even a day without him was too much. My thoughts raced, changing second by second.

It could have been worse. It should have been better.

After the jurors cleared out, my family rushed to me. Mom wrapped me in her arms. "Sweetheart, I'm so happy. I knew they'd see it wasn't murder. We can deal with this."

My sister hugged me, squeezing tears from my eyes. "You okay?"

I bit my lip and sniffed. "I could still go to prison." A new reality punched me in the gut, making me stagger. "I'm a convicted felon."

My dad touched my shoulder. "Hey, you're alive and your son is alive."

My mother took my hand. "You're not going to prison. The jury knows it wasn't murder. They'll give you probation. You just wait and see."

I tried my best to believe her.

Mom turned to Doug and smiled. "Thank you for everything you've done."

"I don't think they'll send her to prison." Doug handed me his handkerchief. "You ready to strategize your sentencing defense?"

"Yeah." I wiped my face. "Let's do it."

Doug ushered me out of the courthouse for a strategy dinner with my legal team, during which we discussed who would or wouldn't make good witnesses for my defense.

Back at home, fear and hope warred within. Confidence in Doug and belief in the possibility of probation gave way to practicality. I stuffed my duffle bag with every item I'd be allowed to bring into the jail: my Bible, all the cash I had, a carton of cigarettes, pictures of loved ones, a regulation nightgown, and three sets of panties, socks, and bras. I zipped the bag shut and put it by the door.

That night, I dreamed of being locked up. Sadness and despair overwhelmed me as I sat alone on my bunk, staring at the bars. Out of nowhere, a comforting feeling warmed me. A voice instructed me to have faith—it wouldn't be long. The bars opened, and I was free.

[CHAPTER SEVENTY]

Sentencing

I loaded my bag into the car and brought it with me to the courtroom, leaving it with my mother.

The state had no new evidence or witnesses. They simply reminded the jury to consider testimony raised during the guilt phase of the trial.

Doug called my sister, brother, mother, and my sister-in-law's mom as character witnesses. He guided each of them through his questions, establishing me as an extremely remorseful, victimized person with strong family ties who deserved a chance to better myself through counseling—not a career criminal deserving prison.

My mother told the jury about my positive attitude while incarcerated and how I did what I could to improve myself, including tutoring GED classes and teaching first aid to inmates.

After a break for lunch, Doug called Officer Walker, the deputy who worked in the GED classroom. Mr. Walker characterized me as a positive role model who never caused problems and went above and beyond to help other inmates, giving me an A-plus on my chance to succeed. "If she's not a candidate for probation, there probably never was one."

Since the prosecution waived giving a statement until after the defense finished, Doug stood and addressed the judge. "May it please the court?" He turned to the jury and spoke with a grave voice. "Lady and gentlemen, I would be less than candid if I didn't tell you it's difficult to get up here and talk to you at this time. I felt very strongly about our position, and I'd not be fair if I didn't tell you how terribly disappointed I am in your verdict. But you've—"

Mr. Rice looked stunned. "I'm going to have to object as being totally improper."

Judge Harris hesitated, appearing equally stunned. "Overruled."

Doug continued. "You've done everything expected as a jury. You listened intently and worked hard on your verdict. You're to be commended for that. You did what you thought was right, and I want to make it abundantly clear, you're not here to make me happy. Only twelve people need to be satisfied with your verdict, and that's you, so we're ready to move forward."

Curtis leaned to me. "Now that's a great strategy."

"A lot of things have been disputed in this case, but one thing can't be quarreled with." Doug extended his hand to me. "When Vincent Bayshore walked into her life, Leigh Ann was an honor student at a university. On the Dean's List. Never been in trouble with the law. She had a beautiful future awaiting her as a nurse. The skies were blue, the birds were singing, the flowers were blooming. Then Vincent came along and played her like a bass fiddle, subjected her to abuse and misuse. You know the kind of guy. Her family was about as happy with him as a brother-in-law and son-in-law as I suspect you'd be if he married your sister or daughter. They knew from the beginning this was a recipe for disaster, and their predictions came true."[42]

Why couldn't I have listened to my family?

"Since he came into her life, Leigh Ann's had to take a life to save a life. Surrendered her RN license. Spent some nine months in jail. But you've heard how she handled that time in jail—with grace and a positive attitude. This is indicative of what you can expect from her in the future. And now she's been convicted of a felony and her fate lies in your hands." Doug turned to me. "She may well have lost custody of her son, and I don't know how much more a mother can be punished than that."

Several jurors gazed at me with compassion in their eyes, bringing tears to mine.

"Do you really think the citizens of our county will be safer with her locked up in an iron cage? It's true—if she isn't a candidate for probation, there just isn't one. And it's a can't-lose situation. If she messes up on probation"—Doug pointed at Judge Harris—"that man right there can rectify it. He can revoke her and send her to Huntsville."

Doug moved behind me and put his hands on my shoulders. "This woman has been punished enough, and I beseech you to give her probation." He turned to the jury and dipped his head. "Thank you again for your service." Taking a seat next to me, he leaned to my ear. "Think we got 'em."[43]

Curtis picked up a copy of the charge and walked toward the jury. "Thank you again for your courteous service." He smiled. "The judge has read you the charge, and I want you to read through the conditions of probation. They're pretty stringent, folks. But the fact is, there are some twenty other conditions the judge can impose, and he's an experienced criminologist in his own right. If you give probation and it's an error, the judge can rectify that. He has power over her, but if you send her down to the penitentiary, he loses all power."

I shivered at the idea that this one man had such power over me. However, it was certainly better than being under the submission of a warden, guards, and the Board of Pardons and Parole.

"Now, lady and gentlemen, think on what you heard about Leigh Ann's positive attitude. You heard everyone talk about it—and you may think her family is biased, and they are, but realize the amount of support they will give her. And then consider the testimony of Mr. Walker. A deputy sheriff, a responsible father of eight who's obviously concerned about his fellow man. And he described her as enthusiastic. Positive. Helpful. Concerned for others. Gave her an A-plus in regard to being able to make it on probation.

"Folks, you couldn't get a less biased and more genuine recommendation. And he has thirty-five years of experience judging these folks," Curtis said. "I submit to you, you can give his testimony a great deal of credence and let it guide you in your decision. I beseech you, give Leigh Ann probation and let her get back out in the world and follow the positive track everyone has 100% said she's on. Let her pursue her freedom and her son."

Curtis gave a slight bow. "Thank you."[44]

When Curtis returned to his seat, Mr. Rice gave his close, telling the jury they should assess prison time to show the victim's family his life was worth something. He also pointed out that since the judge had to revoke my bond, it showed I couldn't succeed with probation.

The jury filed out to commence deliberations.

[CHAPTER SEVENTY-ONE]
Deliberations

My future was in their hands. Would they be harsh and go for the maximum, or have mercy and recommend probation?

After nervously pacing the halls of the courthouse, I returned to the courtroom for one of Doug's Life Savers. When I entered the now quiet room, a lone figure sitting on one of the benches caught my attention. Matt motioned for me to join him.

Afraid of what he might say, I cautiously approached my brother-in-law. Would he yell obscenities at me? Tell me what a horrible person I am? Say he hopes I get twenty years?

He smiled—the same crooked smile my husband used to give me. We sat side by side, silently staring toward the empty jury box. After several minutes, he said, "You know, the jury should give you probation."

His words brought instant relief. "You think?"

Nodding, he turned to me. "You don't deserve prison. If anyone knows how crazy Vincent got, it's me. I know what he was capable of."

Even if the jury came back with prison time, having Vincent's brother believe in me brought unspeakable comfort. After all, he was the only person other than me who truly knew my husband.

"He was so obsessed with you." Matt looked toward the jury box again, as if not wanting to face his words. "He never would have left you alone. Even if you'd been able to divorce him, he never would have stopped tormenting you."

He was right.

"And Vincent Junior, he belongs with you." Picking at his nails, just like his brother used to do, Matt confided that he disagreed with the family's desire to keep my son from me. "But I have to go along with it if I want to stay part of Vinny's life. He's all I have left of my brother."

I cried on his shoulder as he held me.

Mom entered the courtroom. "Everything all right?"

Matt hugged me one last time and whispered, "I hope you get probation, and I hope you get Vinny back real soon." Then he stood and left.

Wiping tears from my face, I looked at Mom and smiled. "It hasn't been this good for a long, long time."

Just shy of two hours after beginning deliberations, the jury returned with their verdict.

"Will the defendant please rise?"

Standing with Doug's assistance, I gripped the table and took deep, cleansing breaths. Was I about to lose the deliciousness of free air?

"We the jury assess punishment as confinement in the Institutional Division of the Texas Department of Criminal Justice for a period of seven years."

Prison. I'm going to prison. For seven years. A vacuum sucked all the air out of the room, leaving me dizzy. *At least it wasn't twenty.*

"And we the jury further recommend that the imposition of her sentence be suspended, and that she be placed on community supervision."

Probation? Air rushed into my lungs, filling them, making me gasp. Not prison. *Thank you, Jesus.* My chin quivered and tears filled my eyes.

Doug winked and smiled. "We did it."

Judge Harris thanked the jury for their service and dismissed them.

I'm going home. Today. Free to fight for my son. Unable to stop smiling, I did my best to keep my joy aimed toward my family and not Vincent's.

"Just a few more matters, Ms. Bayshore." The judge spread several sheets of paper on his desk, checking off items as he listed my probation conditions. Most were the usual, such as reporting, drug screens, paying court costs, and not committing any new offenses. He also ordered counseling and four hundred hours of community service.

Four hundred hours? That could take years to complete. But at least I'd be free to do it.

"In addition. . ." Judge Harris folded his arms on his desk. "You will serve 180 days in the Tarrant County Jail as a probation condition."

"What?" My voice came out a whisper. "I have to go back to jail?"

Doug looked kindly at me. "Looks that way."

Six more months in jail. Another six months of not being able to fight for my son. Of being away from my family. Another Thanksgiving, Christmas, and New Year's Eve locked up.

My mother held me tight. "You can do this. This is nothing compared to what you've already been through." She put her hand to my chin and lifted it, looking into my eyes. "I'll write to you every day. We're all here for you and love you."

I gave her a quick smile and straightened my shoulders, wiping the tears from my face. "I'll be fine." After receiving hugs from my loved ones, I gathered my prepared bag and presented my wrists to the bailiff.

[CHAPTER SEVENTY-TWO]

Felon

Now a convicted felon, I no longer qualified for the first offenders tank. Twenty-eight hours after the bailiff handcuffed me, a sheriff's deputy took me to the area fondly known as "the old, old jail." Dark, dank, and saturated with a haze of smoke, it felt more like a dungeon.

Prickles covered my body as the officer walked me through unfamiliar territory. My new home for six months held one tiny window, but instead of letting sunlight in, it faced the hall. The phone receiver next to it confirmed what I'd heard—visitation would be at the tank in this part of the jail.

Seven sets of bunks lined the walls, allowing for a population of fourteen inmates. Aside from me, everyone in the tank was a veteran—either headed back to prison for a new crime or being held on a parole violation.

Finding the last unoccupied bunk, I hoisted my mattress high.

"Lookie here, ladies. I found me a new wife." The voice sounded more like a man's, but I knew better now.

Ignoring the laughter, I turned. A large black woman took a drag on her cigarette and smiled broadly, blowing smoke through three gold teeth. A shiver raced through me. No fleeing in here; I'd have to be clever. "That's really sweet of you," I said, "but I have a boyfriend on the outside, and he wouldn't like me hooking up with someone else."

Sometimes a lie was still a good thing.

She chewed her lip. "Too bad. Let me know if you change your mind. Name's Precious."

As soon as an officer brought my belongings, I handed out free-world cigarettes to everyone, making new friends. Once settled in my bunk, I took care of my first order of business, sending a kite—a request note within the jail—to the teacher, Mr. Hardy, requesting reinstatement as a GED tutor. A guard called me out to class with the students two days later, and I gratefully resumed my old job.

I utilized skills learned during my previous incarceration, finding ways to both fit in and isolate myself at the same time.

In time, Precious became my protector. I helped her write letters to her parole officer and lawyer, and she made everyone believe I was her wife and off-limits. With inmates catching the chain to prison each week, her claim on me was particularly helpful when new inmates were brought in to fill the empty bunks.

My days consisted of socializing and tutoring the other inmates with their GED math or helping with spelling and vocabulary. One woman was illiterate and I read her letters to her and wrote responses as she dictated. I learned from the others, as well. They taught me words to gospel songs and how to do the popular Tootsie Roll dance, performing it well enough to be told I was "black on the inside." We played games such as "bones," cards, and "truth or dare." The things people admitted to during truth or dare could educate a fleet of sailors.

I spent my alone time on my bunk, writing letters, reading, and doing Bible studies and crossword puzzles.

One weekend, Chris and Haley brought my son for a visit. My brother had to pick Vinny up so he could see my face through the window and talk to me on the phone. After ten minutes of holding him, Chris set him down.

Haley's muffled voice came through the phone. "No, Vinny. Don't go in there. Come back!"

"What's going on?" I wished I could see.

"Vinny ran off and Haley's chasing him."

Goodness. A toddler running around in a jail. No telling what he could get into. Haley returned and got on the phone. "He ran down the hall and wouldn't come back. When I told him not to do that again or he'd get into trouble, he said he wanted to be in trouble."

"Wanted to?"

She frowned. "Said he wants to be in timeout with his mommy, because he misses you."

A tempest of anguish burdened my heart. "My poor baby."

That night, haunted by my son's desperation to be with me, shame and guilt held my mind captive, thwarting any chance of sleep. How would he ever forgive me?

[CHAPTER SEVENTY-THREE]

Battle

"**Bayshore, roll it up** all the way," a voice crackled over the intercom.

The words I'd been waiting to hear for 180 days.

I jumped off my bunk and packed six months' worth of letters, pictures, and Bible studies into bags, then doled out my no-longer-needed items to the other women in the tank.

Six hours later, I devoured crisp, clean, free-world air. The first day of the rest of my life. Thanks to my sister's generosity, I had a place to live. And thanks to my judge's mercy, I didn't have to worry about the 400 hours of community service—he agreed with Doug that my hours volunteering in the GED class covered it.

With my trial and jail-time behind me, I longed for two things—winning my son back and getting professional help to deal with the trauma and grief of shooting my husband.

My new psychologist, Dr. Hardin, peeled away the blinders of denial, opening my eyes to the severity of my husband's abuse and how the detrimental effects of battered women's syndrome had influenced me. He showed me how my co-dependent personality and hunger for love and acceptance shaped me into a prime target for such a passionate, manipulative, needy man. Thanks to my unrestricted ability to be honest and Dr. Hardin's guidance and wisdom, I moved from victim to survivor.

No longer able to work as a nurse, I got a job as a waitress in a steakhouse. Although my earnings were only half of what I made as a nurse, my biggest job stresses involved getting orders right and keeping drinks filled.

I spent every second allowed with my son, making sure each moment revolved around us doing something together, even if it was just reading or watching a movie. During the many hours we couldn't be together, I searched for ways to keep myself busy. Not having to answer to an overly possessive husband, shades of normalcy entered my life, including hanging out with coworkers after shifts and on days off.

The battle to win my son back included home studies, court dates, mediation, and psychological testing and evaluation. Dr. Cantrell, the court-ordered psychologist, gave the opinion I was well on my way to being a stable and reliable parent, but did recommend I find a job better suited to my experience and education. In her conclusion, she stated Vinny should be returned to me with a transition period to help him adjust to the change.

Dr. Cantrell's report seemed to be the key to bringing an end to the stalemate in mediation. With the psychologist's recommendations, the mediator said she would push Andrew and Katrina to give up custody and settle for visitation.

With Doug's help, Judge Harris granted me permission to leave the country for ten days to visit my mother in Vienna, Austria. The wonderful news could only have been better if Vinny had been allowed to join my sister and me, but Andrew and Katrina denied our request. Michelle and I packed our bags and headed off to some much-needed sister-mother time in Eastern Europe.

Rejuvenated by my vacation, I returned home optimistic about life. Surely at the next mediation, Andrew and Katrina would relent and allow me managing conservatorship. So close to getting my son back, my taste buds danced with anticipation.

Then, a message on the answering machine blew my world inside out.

"Leigh Ann," my probation officer's voice sounded stern. "You need to call me immediately. Your last urine drug screen tested positive for cocaine."

The edges of my vision faded as the room spun. Impossible.

I called Doug and, at his suggestion, set an appointment with the man known by prosecutors and judges as the most reliable polygraph examiner. If I passed the polygraph, Doug could use that to try to convince the judge of my innocence.

Then I called my probation officer. There was nothing she could do. She said my urine test results had already been turned into the court. "Since you have an attorney on record, the court will notify him when they set a probation revocation hearing."

My stomach clenched. Probation revocation? I could go to prison. "They can't revoke me. I didn't do anything. This has to be a mistake."

As I drove to Dallas for my polygraph the next day, my hands shook and sweat dripped down the back of my neck. What if he read my nervousness as lying?

The examiner assured me the machine would accurately determine the truth regardless of my sweaty palms and dilated pupils. "As long as you tell the truth, nothing else matters."

My breathing slowed enough to stop the tingling in my fingers. After an hour-long interview, he put a blood pressure cuff on my arm, a sensor on my finger, and wrapped straps around my chest and abdomen. I begged God to let the truth shine through.

The man switched between relevant and control questions. When he finished, he unhooked me and took the printouts to another room. He returned smiling.

"You passed with flying colors."

I blew out a deep sigh. "Now what?"

"We'll send a report to your attorney. It'll be ready before you go in front of the judge."

Buoyed by his news, I went home with renewed hope.

Three days later, I opened my door to two men in blue with a warrant for my arrest. After fifty-two hours in lock-up that felt more like fifty-two days, I again faced Judge Harris with Doug at my side. Fortunately, the judge agreed to bond and set my probation revocation hearing for two weeks later.

I set an appointment with Dr. Cantrell regarding my false-positive drug screen. The only possibility outside a lab mistake was that as a waitress, I handled money all the time, sometimes licking my fingers to count bills. "Maybe someone used a bill to snort the drug and then gave it to me as a tip?"

Dr. Cantrell agreed with the results of the polygraph. She still planned to testify my son should be returned to me.

Two days later, I landed an interview regarding a resume I'd submitted for a job as a quality analyst with a medical evaluation company. When the manager offered me the job, I figured being up front about the pending charge was only fair. Surprisingly, he was impressed enough with me to wait and see what happened.

At my probation revocation hearing, Doug called a witness from the lab where the drug screen was performed. His account of chain of custody showed areas of possible fallibility. Judge Harris told Doug he wanted to drop the charge, but the prosecutor insisted on revocation.

To placate the prosecutor, the judge ordered thirty days in the county jail—to be served on work-release so I could continue to pay child support. I'd report to the jail each Friday evening no later than eight, and be released at six on Monday morning. Each weekend would constitute four days of my sentence.

Both thrilled and devastated by his ruling, I resigned to spending eight weekends behind bars. Although I hated the idea of going back to jail, at least it wasn't prison. And I could start my new job.

At my next counseling session with Dr. Hardin, I discussed my mixed feelings about the judge's ruling. I also vented about my anger toward David, a man I'd started dating not long after being released from jail. Kind and gentle to a fault, he treated me right and never got angry, but a month after my urine test came back positive for cocaine, he confessed he'd used the drug.

Dr. Hardin leaned forward. "Did you use it with him?"

"Absolutely not. And I can't imagine he'd. . . he knew I was being tested."

After a long beat, Dr. Hardin said, "Are you still seeing him?"

"No. As soon as he told me about his drug use, I broke things off."

At the next mediation, Andrew and Katrina refused to negotiate due to my positive drug screen, meaning I once again had to face a jury trial. After months of preparation, a new job using my experience and education, and getting help through counseling, I headed to court with positive thoughts. After all, Dr. Cantrell was on my side.

On the second day of trial, Dr. Hardin approached me, his face like death on ice. "Leigh Ann, I'm so sorry. I had no idea Dr. Cantrell didn't know. I told her how proud I was of you for breaking up with David.

When she asked about it, I said you were devastated when you learned about his drug use. She's hopping mad you didn't tell her."

"But I didn't know about his using cocaine when I saw her."

"She said it was the last straw. She's going to testify Vinny should stay where he is."

Numbness shrouded my heart. Wrapped around my insides. Made my feet not work. I stumbled to a nearby seat. Would I lose my son?

During the trial, a future with my son became less and less likely with each of the judge's rulings, including her refusal to allow me to testify about the facts surrounding my husband's death. The only thing the jury knew was that I killed him and spent time in jail for doing so.

I begged my attorney for reassurances. "They can't prove me unfit, right? Since I'm his mother, they have to give me custody."

My attorney sighed heavily. "The judge ruled to remove your parental presumption."

"What does that mean?"

"Normally, the judge tells a jury it's in the best interest of a child to be with a natural parent—however, their attorney argued you don't have that presumption because you already gave up custody."

My heart hitched. "But. I didn't want to. It was to keep me from losing him."

"Now it just makes things worse. In fact, the judge agreed with their argument that in order to keep the jury from going along with the innate nature of believing a child should be with a parent, she's going to specifi- cally tell them *not* to consider it in his best interest to be with you because you're his mother."

Desolation pushed up my throat and extinguished any remnants of hope.

At the end of the trial, the jury retired for deliberations armed with the charge that it wasn't in Vinny's best interest to be with me. They be- lieved I murdered my son's father in cold blood and signed away custody because I didn't want my child. Add Dr. Cantrell's testimony that Vincent should stay with Andrew and Katrina, and what had originally seemed like an impossible-to-lose trial disintegrated into wondering how I could overcome this fiasco. Tears of grief dimmed my eyes as we awaited the jury. The only solace was found in my family. As with my murder trial, they supported and encouraged me through every minute of testimony.

The jury finally filed in. Two of the jurors watched me with tears in their eyes.

That couldn't be good. My insides trembled, my heart tripping over itself.

Just like that, the judge awarded Managing Conservatorship to Andrew and Katrina, ripping my soul in half.

I sunk to a weeping heap on the floor. "No. Please God, this can't be."

Hands pulled me up, dragged me from the courtroom. Somehow I ended up at home, alone in my room, wondering how other mothers dealt with losing their children. Did they smash things? Break down? Or did they accept the injustice?

I'd rather be dead without my baby.

The next day, the judge offered horrendous visitation. Instead of the usual month each summer, I'd only get one week the first year and two the second. In addition, she ordered a judgment against me for attorney's fees.

Devastated, I tried to convince myself that even a little time with my son was better than none. I had to be strong for him. He needed me.

The visitation schedule included first, third, and fifth weekends, as well as a two-and-a-half hour visit for dinner each Wednesday night. Vinny's Saturday games of t-ball or soccer gave me another opportunity to see him.

After getting only thirty hours with my son over Christmas, resentment set in. I again accepted financial help from my mother and hired attorney John Nation to appeal the unjust custody verdict. He drafted and filed a brief with the appellate court, arguing the trial court erred on four points.

In a counseling session with Dr. Hardin, I circled the drain of depression. Always fighting the loss of my son and the impossible road to appeal.

He listened while I spilled my grief and despair, then leaned forward and rubbed his chin. "You've talked often about God. How's your relationship with Him now?"

How did I feel? Angry? Disappointed? Abandoned? Yes. Abandoned. "Like He left me to deal with this alone. How could He let this happen?"

"Do you still read your Bible?"

I gave a slow nod. "Most days."

"Go to church?"

Guilt poked my heart. "Haven't found the right one."

"Do you think God abandoned you, or could you be the one who walked away?"

Ouch. It was true. With weekend visits, Wednesday dinners, and Saturday games, I spent at least twenty-five hours driving over 700 miles each week, just to be with Vinny. Add to that a full-time job, chores around the house, and spending time with my family, and I'd squeezed God out of my busy life. With no one to hold me accountable, it had been too easy.

"You should check out Fellowship Church," Dr. Hardin encouraged. "I've heard great things about their singles ministry. It's time you not only get involved in church, but meet some nice Christian men."

The following Sunday, I headed to Fellowship, where the music and presentation of the message left me awestruck. In the New Member Class, the pastor recommended Connect Groups. Being twenty-nine, I chose the class for "Twenties and Thirties." Anxiety bubbled in my stomach the next Sunday as I tried to find a seat in the room crowded with at least two hundred people. Several guys looked me up and down, creepy smiles on their faces. Was this a bar, or Sunday school? By the end of the hour, three guys had asked me out.

I resolved to make church about God. I'd stick with dating Jesus.

I found a new class—the "Forty and Ups." In this smaller, more inviting group, the women were the ones who welcomed me and showed interest in getting to know me. Just what I needed. Friendship with genuine Christian ladies.

Church and reading my Bible became my new priorities. I arrived early every Sunday to volunteer as a greeter before Connect Group, then attended second service. Once a month, I worked in the nursery. Tuesday night was Bible Study. The first Wednesday of each month, I picked up my son and we attended a special worship service. Sunday evenings was Home Team.

Four months after joining my new church home, Vinny and I were baptized together. Michelle joined us, taking pictures of the momentous occasion.

The more involved in church I became, the more God's presence completed me. When my attorney called with news the appellate court would hear arguments, I handed my anxieties to God, deciding to trust in Him no matter how it turned out.

[CHAPTER SEVENTY-FOUR]

1999

The last year of the twentieth century would begin in five hours. Over four years since Vincent's death. Fifty one months of struggle, sorrow, and walking on the road toward healing. Would 1999 bring suffering or joy? Would it be the year I won my son back?

My friends and I strode into the decorated ballroom. This was exactly what I needed—a church-sponsored New Year's Eve party with my four best friends—Toni, Deb, and the two Kathys. "The Fab Five." A gift straight from God. Each week we met for food, fun, and friendship, as well as accountability.

Several guys from our Connect group joined us at our table, but one man's sincere smile lit up the room, igniting a deep joy within me. After showing off his fancy footwork swing dancing with my friends, he introduced himself to me.

"Hi. I'm Lonnie." Even through his glasses, his eyes shone. He put his hand out in invitation. "Wanna dance?"

Part of me wanted to. The other part worried about making a fool of myself. The only dancing I'd done since Vincent was the Tootsie Roll in jail. "I don't know that dance."

He leaned forward and took my hand, gently pulling me to the parquet floor, his smile bigger than ever. "I'd love to show you."

The fast-paced music and upbeat moves were invigorating. Energizing. Innocent. So different from Vincent's erotic gyrations.

After six songs of twirling, stepping, and rocking, Lonnie suggested we take a break. He drained a glass of water and turned to me. "How long have you been going to Fellowship?"

"Almost a year. How about you?"

"Since July."

How had we been in the same class for six months and not met? Yes, my focus had been Jesus, but I should have at least noticed his presence.

Conversation with Lonnie flowed naturally. Pleasant. He intrigued me. His eternal smile calmed me. He felt comfortable. Genuine. Safe, even. I sensed no expectations. No demands. No agenda.

After several more dances and ringing in the New Year as a group, we decided to go to IHOP. Lonnie sat next to me at the restaurant, showing interest in everything I said, asking questions and listening to the answers. The conversation didn't continually flip back to him. *Different.* Although eight others were in our group, it felt like sitting at a table for two.

Our class soon had another social. Once again, Lonnie and I danced and talked all night.

When he told me about his education and work experience—which included a doctorate from seminary, working as a youth minister, and opening a counseling center—his ability to put me at ease made sense.

He'd gone through a failed marriage, and business problems had led to selling his counseling practice.

Empathy stirred within. I knew what it was like to be married to a controlling spouse and have to start over with a new career. My heart told me to trust him with the words of my life, but my head worried the truth would send him running far and fast.

Could he accept that I killed my husband? Was it too soon to share? We barely knew each other, but I couldn't keep something so huge from him. I thought it best to tell him right away.

Lonnie's compassionate response melted my heart. My story hadn't scared him off. In fact, the next day he invited me to dinner. Alone. He was gentle. Caring. Stable. So unlike anyone I'd ever dated.

How could such an incredible guy be interested in someone like me?

One night we leaned against my car gazing at the stars and Lonnie asked if he could kiss me.

Asked. No one had ever asked before. They'd just taken.

I nodded and his lips met mine as if they belonged there. That kiss was the beginning of something new, something cleansing, something amazing. And after two months of dates and hours of talking on the phone, I felt secure enough in our blossoming relationship to include Vinny in our plans.

Lonnie's affectionate interactions with my son encouraged seeds of love to grow roots. His prayers and reassurances gave me strength as I faced both the appellate court to win back my son, and the Board of Nursing to regain my RN license.

I finally understood what it felt like to date someone who cared about my feelings and put me first. Someone I didn't have to work at keeping happy—because he was in charge of his own happiness. A man of God who wanted to be a better person. Who could see his flaws and improve himself without blaming someone else or expecting me to fix him. And who, like me, was committed to sexual purity until married.

Five months after we began dating, Lonnie introduced me to his fourteen-year-old son, Bailey. Meeting him solidified the seriousness of our relationship.

But that didn't stop my mind from doubting. All my life, whenever things were going well, something bad happened. Could such a good thing really last?

[C H A P T E R   S E V E N T Y - F I V E]

Court

Finally, a legal situation to rejoice over—which I did to everyone who would listen, and even those who wouldn't. The appellate court overturned the jury's verdict in my custody case, stating the parental presumption should have applied in my trial. In addition, they said the trial court abused its discretion when it gave the jury the no-parental-presumption instruction.

Just like that, everything in my world was right. Not only would I get my son back, but the judgment against me was reversed.

Vindicated, I approached Andrew and Katrina about working out a custody agreement without having to go through another trial—instead, they appealed to the Supreme Court of Texas.

Would this roller coaster ever end? Desperate to spend more time with my son, I extended my work hours every Thursday to allow a three-hour lunch, giving me time to eat with him, read to his class, and watch him play at recess, as well as drive the sixty miles.

Three visits to the Nursing Board, extensive psychological testing and evaluation, and a pile of positive reference letters convinced the board to reinstate my license. Exuberant, I began the required nursing refresher course right away.

In April, 2000, my mother accompanied me to the Supreme Court. Two months later, they published their crushing opinion. Based on a technicality, they reversed the court of appeals' decision.

With that, my roller coaster life crashed again into a mountain of despair.

A technicality? I lost my son over a stupid technicality?

Even worse, the Supreme Court refused to remand the case back to the appellate court for the previously unconsidered points. How was that even legal? How could they refuse?

My heart imploded. *Please, God. I can't keep going like this. It's too hard.*

Lonnie held me, loving me with his presence. "Don't give up. You've got me and we've got God. Keep faith."

Then he dropped to one knee, presented a ring, and asked me to marry him.

[C H A P T E R S E V E N T Y - S I X]
How Great Thou Art

Perfect.

I admired my reflection, amazed by the gown. Elegant. Beautiful. Designed and tailor-made just for me. Shoes and veil to match, nails and makeup done, and three hours in the salon, styling my long hair into a romantic up-do.

Seven-year-old Vinny bounded into the room. "Mommy! You look so pretty."

I handed him the pillow with four rings secured to ribbons and reminded him again of his important job. "You're not giving me away, but presenting me to your new daddy, so you'll stay up there with us and give us the rings when we're ready for them."

He beamed an eye-brightening smile. "I remember, Mommy."

After our vows, but before Lonnie's best friend Ron pronounced us husband and wife, I presented a ring to my new son Bailey and Lonnie gave one to Vinny.

An elegant yet simple reception followed the ceremony. Then Lonnie and I slipped away for a real wedding night—the night we'd waited for in purity for almost two years.

Home from our blissful honeymoon in Santa Fe, I moved in with Lonnie and began the process of becoming Mrs. Leigh Ann Bryant. With my official name change, I sent in the paperwork to the Nursing Board for my new RN license.

Soon I was both working as an RN and pregnant with Lonnie's child. Only one void remained in my heart.

Vinny had lived with Andrew and Katrina almost six years. Now that he was eight, he was old enough for the judge to hear what he'd told anyone and everyone all the years he lived there—he wanted to live with me. The judge would listen, but didn't have to agree.

Lonnie and I considered the pros and cons. Suing for custody could be another massive let down. Or it could be a win. There'd been so many positive changes in my life, how could I not try to get Vinny back?

"He's your son," Lonnie said. "We want him to live with us, and he wants it, too. We should do everything we can to make that happen."

Before filing the lawsuit, we asked Andrew and Katrina to negotiate. They agreed, but things dragged on too long.

Ten days after our first wedding anniversary, I gave birth to Joseph. Vinny still hadn't been able to come home. His anger and frustration over not being able to live with us shredded my heart.

To strengthen our position, Doug filed a motion for my early release from probation. Given how well I was doing, Judge Harris agreed and set me free.

After much back and forth, we finally signed papers awarding me custody just before Vinny turned nine. My son came home to live where he belonged, bringing on a celebration as though it was the Year of Jubilee.

Two Sundays later, our family went to church together. Vinny ran to his Sunday school class and I dropped Joseph off at the nursery before meeting Lonnie in the worship center. We stood side-by-side as the choir began singing, "How Great Thou Art."

Tears flooded my eyes and poured down my cheeks. Pure joy warmed my heart.

Now I get it. Now I understand how a father could sing this at his son's funeral.

God had faithfully fulfilled the promises He made in the early morning hours of that October day in 1995 when I gave my life to Him. He restored me to my family and to Vinny. He gave me freedom and returned my nursing license. And then He went above and beyond anything I ever could have imagined by giving me a godly husband and two new sons— one by marriage and one by birth.

Truly, Lord, how great Thou art.

Epilogue

I often wonder at the unfairness of life. Of course, I understand there are no promises life will be fair. But Vincent's life seemed doomed before he could even walk, and sometimes that unfairness seems too great. His life was so full of pain—I wanted so much to give him joy and for us to be a normal, happy couple. I wanted us to raise three kids together and grow old and gray still delighted with each other. It seems so wrong that we never had a chance for any of that. As hard as I tried, as much as we both wanted these things, knowing they were an impossibility breaks my heart. We didn't stand a chance, and that, too, just seems too unfair.

My husband wasn't a horrible monster. He had a variety of mental illnesses that were no fault of his own. He wanted to be good, but one bad choice after another sucked him into a deep, dark hole ruled by the demons of his past.

Vincent's life was too short. Too tragic. At least I can look back on memories and pictures and know I gave him the happiest times of his life. We shared a son, took trips to Hawaii, New York, and Washington D.C., and enjoyed mundane things, such as fishing, kite-flying, and watching movies.

Vincent gave me so much no one else ever had. Yes, he brought terror and pain and fear, but he also brought more love, passion, and pleasure than I'd ever known before meeting him. His love consumed me. Saturated me. Satiated me. He was so good at loving. Unfortunately, he was equally good at tormenting.

Many of my memories with Vincent are vivid. The most painful are buried deep. I didn't write much about the escalation of the terror and abuse because I wanted to remember the good things about him. The love. The charm. The really bad stuff scarred me and left deep, painful memories for which I received a lot of counseling.

Near the end of his life, he stepped into severe psychopathic/sociopathic behavior, which is tough to come out of—most likely impossible while off his bipolar meds. I believe it was the combination of taking drugs he shouldn't have while discontinuing the ones he needed that sent him over the edge.

September 16th will never pass without me feeling profound guilt over what happened during those early morning hours in 1994. Some people don't understand how I can still feel so decimated when I only did what had to be done to save myself and my son. Perhaps it is true I only did what I had to do that night—but what about the many other opportunities before then? Surely I could have made different decisions along the way. Maybe his tragic death wouldn't have been the outcome. What if I'd run with my baby? What if I hadn't gotten the gun? What if I'd called the police when he first hurt me? Vincent may have found me, punished me. His friends may have come after me, made me pay. Maybe our situation would have ended worse, but maybe not. If not, then at least my son could be visiting his dad in prison instead of at his grave.

Since Vincent's death, a few people have alleged that Vincent told them he knew about my gun, and that I had pulled it on him a couple of times before his death. Whether or not Vincent knew about the gun, I am not certain. He did spend countless hours going thruough my things. But in terms of me pulling a gun on him prior to September 16? This is not true. During the trial, the prosecution tried in vain to make this seem like truth, but the statements about it were discredited.

Also, for the sake of full disclosure, I'm ashamed to admit I did relapse in my abuse of pain medications in 2007, but I am happy to say that I have been clean and sober since then. I have been active in SMART (Self Management and Recovery Training) and Celebrate Recovery (a Christ-centered program which adds biblical principles to the 12 steps of AA). After completing the intensive Step Study, I am now a leader in Celebrate Recovery, and I recently received my chip for six years clean time.

Finally, I understand that because of my husband's increasingly violent behavior toward others, it is quite possible he still would have died young. But his death wouldn't have been by my hand.

And justified or not—accident, self-defense, whatever you call it—the fact is, I took a life. All life is sacred, and one was lost because of me. And not just any life, but the life of a man I loved wholeheartedly. The man who meant everything to me. The life of my son's father. For that, I continue to struggle for self-forgiveness.

ENDNOTES

1. Transcript and recording of 911 call

2. Tape recording of the funeral

3. Emergency Room Note from Dr. Roy Yamada, dated September 16, 1994, transcribed September 18, 1994.

4. Sworn affidavit to police detective dated September 20, 1994

5. While I do not have a copy of this statement, it is corroborated by Keith.

6. State's Written Notice of Waiver of Death Penalty, dated July 29, 1996

7. Testimony recreated from transcript of closing argument of Curtis Glover, Reporter's Record Volume 6 pages 6 and 7, as well as from extensive handwritten trial notes from Doug Mulder and myself.

8. State's exhibit 2A, JC Penney Life Insurance solicitation record.

9. Copy of the APB, SVC MSG TX2200900, released on September 16, 1994, time stamped 12:34.

10. Cross examination, taken from Reporter's Record Volume 2, pages 7, 14, 15, 16

11. Police department Offense/Incident Narrative, dated September 20, 1994.

12. Cross examination from Reporter's Record, Volume 2, page 19.

13. Second cross examination of this witness, Reporter's Record Volume 2 page 20.

14. Transcript, dated January 18, 1995, and tape-recording of actual 911 call on September 16, 1994.

15. Transcript and tape-recording of actual 911 call on September 16, 1994.

16. Recreated testimony using Police report of said officer, extensive notes taken by Doug Mulder during the trial, and closing arguments, Reporter's Record Volume 6, page 29.

17. Sworn affidavits for Firefighter/Paramedics of the City of Euless which are dated September 21, 1994 and are, aside from the names and employment histories of the men, word for word the exact same statement through the entire two pages.

18. Defendant's Exhibit 6, sworn affidavit to the police dated October 11, 1994, as well as Reporter's Record Volume 2 pages 20-24.

19. Reporter's Record, Volume 2, pages 25-36, 49, and Volume 3, pages 4-5.

20. Defendant's Exhibit 6 and Reporter's Record Volume 2, pages 44-47.

21. Autopsy report, Office of Chief Medical Examiner, Tarrant County, Texas, dated September 16, 1994.

22. Testimony recreated from Autopsy Report, dated September 16, 1994, extensive notes taken by Doug Mulder during the trial, and closing arguments, Reporter's Record Volume 6, pages 27-30.

23. Recreated testimony from Doug Mulder's closing argument, Reporter's Record Volume 6 page 31.

24. Testimony recreated using notes taken by Doug Mulder during trial.

25. Read back to the jury, Court Reporter's Record pages 79-80,82. 85-88, 151-153, 155, 158, 164-170, 199-201, 235.

26. Recreated from transcript of Doug Mulder's closing argument, Reporter's Record Volume 6 pages 40 and 41, as well as Defendant's Exhibits 16, 17, 18, 19, and 20.

27. Defendant's Exhibit 16.

28. Police reports from neighbors, Doug's notes from the trial, and closing arguments from Report's Record Volume 6, pages 32-34.

29. Reporter's Record Volume 6 pages 24-25.

30. Recreated from Reporter's Record Volume 6 pages 35-37.

31. Recreated from Reporter's Record Volume 6 page 26.

32. Recreated from closing arguments of Doug Mulder, Reporter's Record Volume 6, pages 19-20, as well as Forensic Consultant Services Field Investigation Report page 6.

33. Certificate of Analyses, Forensic Chemistry Laboratory, dated October 13, 1994.

34. Forensic Consultant Services Field Investigation Report, pages 4 and 8.

35. Testimony of ER doctor from Reporter's Record, Volume 4, pages 4-7.

36. Reporter's Record Volume 6 page 25.

37. Transcript of Dr. Grigson's testimony, Reporter's Record Volume 5, pages 5-29.

38. Transcript of Mr. Parker's testimony, Reporter's Record Volume 5, pages 30-55.

39. Curtis Glover's closing arguments on merit, Reporter's Record, Volume 6 pages 4-18

40. Defendant's Exhibits 14 and 15, Hospital x-ray and bill.

41. Doug Mulder's closing arguments on merit, Reporter's Record Volume 6, pages 18-43.

42. Doug Mulder's closing arguments on punishment. Court Reporter's Record, Volume 7, pages 4-8.

43. Doug Mulder's closing arguments on punishment. Court Reporter's Record, Volume 7, pages 4-8.

44. Curtis Glover's closing arguments on punishment. Court Reporter's Record, Volume 7, pages 8-12

Go to www.leighannbryant.com

- For missing chapters from the book

- For speaking engagements or book signings

- If you think you or someone you love
  may be a victim of abuse

- To learn more about domestic violence

- To sign up for Leigh Ann's blogs

- To learn more about Leigh Ann or her ministry

- To contact Leigh Ann

- For information about future books

- To buy books or donate books to domestic
  abuse survivors or inmates